INDIAN NATIONAL ARMY

A Documentary Study

INDIAN NATIONAL ARMY

A Documentary Study

(In 5 Volumes)

Volume-II

(1943-1944)

T. R. SAREEN

GYAN PUBLISHING HOUSE
NEW DELHI - 110002

INDIAN NATIONAL ARMY—A DOCUMENTARY STUDY

Rs. 4,500/-

ISBN : 81-212-0833-5 (Set)
ISBN : 81-212-0845-9 (Vol-2)

Published in 2004 in India by
Gyan Publishing House
5, Ansari Road, Daryaganj
New Delhi-110 002
Phones-23282060, 23261060, Fax-23285914
Email : gyanbook@vsnl.com
Visit our Website at : http//www.gyanbooks.com

Lasertype Setting by: Tact Computer Graphics, Delhi
Printed at: Chawla Offset Press, Delhi

To
Manu and Kayako

List of Documents

Introduction

This is the Second Volume of the series "Indian National Army—A Documentary Study". The documents presented here cover the period from January to December 1943 and deal with events after the crisis which resulted in the arrest of General Mohan Singh. His order for the dissolution of Indian National Army was not accepted by the Japanese authorities. The President of Council of Action Rash Behari Bose took upon himself the entire responsibility of keeping the movement alive. Though no formal reply had been received, but the reply by Japanese premier to an interpellation in the House of Representatives of Japan on 4 Feb, 1943, reiterated that Japan had no territorial ambitions in India and on the contrary she would give all out assistance to see India free. Inspired by this statement the President, Rash Behari Bose placed before Iwakuro Kikan a scheme for reorganising the Indian National Army (Document-I). A Military Bureau was created under the Indian Independence League to look after the "Military administration and operations".

The scheme of Rash Behari Bose got the approval of Iwakuro Kikan (Doc-2) and the statement was issued by Col. Iwakuro clarifying the Japanese attitude towards I.N.A. and the Indian Independance Movement.

However, these developments did not satisfy certain members of the Indian Independence League in Malaya and they broke away from the Council of Action. They even submitted a memorandum voicing their concern for delay in getting a formal declaration clarifying in full the policy of Japan towards India.

Having set the army in order, Rash Behari Bose reorganised the Indian Independence League. The draft constitution was submitted to the Joint Conference of the representatives of the Indian communities in East Asia which was held at Singapore between 27 and 30 April 1943. The documents pertaining to this Conference (No. 12-15) gave a new working basis to the Indian Independence Movement. During the Conference it became fairly certain that Subhas Chandra Bose would soon be in East Asia to take charge of the movement. At the close of the Conference even Rash Behari Bose announced that Subhas Chandra Bose would be here very soon.

The entry of Bose in East Asia was announced in the Japanese press. The documents included here throw light on the significance which was attached by the Asia Press to his arrival in East Asia. There is no doubt that the presence of Bose reinvigorated the movement in South East Asia for Indian Independence. During three weeks following his arrival in Tokyo he made number of speeches, broadcast over Radio and held press conferences in which he outlined the plan which was to bring Indian freedom to fruition. Some of these documents are reproduced here as reported in the *Nippon Times*. Rash Behari Bose very graciously handed over the charge of the movement to S.C. Bose on 4 July, 1943 at a ceremony in Singapore (Dec. 25). Bose was moved by this gesture and while thanking the people expressed his views about the Indian Army of liberation. Bose said "Throughout my public career, I have always felt that though India is otherwise ripe for independence in every way she has lacked one thing, namely, an army of liberation. It is your privilege and honour to be the first to come forward and organise Indian National Army. By doing so you have removed the last obstacle in our path of freedom" (Doc. 23-24), I.N.A. was renamed as *Azad Hind Fauj*.

Bose was keen to set up a Provisional Government of free India to mobilize effectively the forces of nationalism in East Asia. The document shows as to how the task was acccomplished and how in its proclamation. Bose presented to the Indians a complete manifesto of national movement, which he was determined to pursue (Doc. 28-32).

It is interesting to note that the British Government in India did not underestimate the impact which Bose's activities in East Asia was having on Indians inside the country. The counter measures which they undertook to defuse his influence, their overall assessment of Bose's activities are reflected in the document included here (Doc. 29, 37, 43)

No doubt, the Indian National Army had been solely organised by Indians and it was meant to play a dominant role in the battle for India's freedom, still its standing with the Japanese Army was not clear.

Bose met Field Marshal Count Terauchi, the C-in-C of the Southern Expeditionary Forces and discussed with him the role of the I.N.A. in the forthcoming Japanese campaign in Imphal. Through his persistant efforts and arguments, the role of the I.N.A was clarified and an order was issued by the Hikari Kikan outlining its position (Doc. 49). The Documents also show the reorganisation and expansion of the I.N.A. under Bose's leadership. In the process of reorganisation, Bose even raised a regiment, named after the Rani of Jhansi. Although the regiment's primary duty was to nurse the wounded I.N.A. troops, still the picture of women carrying arms had immense propaganda impact. On 22 Oct. Bose formally opened the training camp for the regiment (Doc. 39).

The documents also throw light on Japanese policy towards India's Independence, Bose's participation in the Greater East Asian Nations Conference, and his assessment of it (Doc. 42). The Japanese permission to visit Andaman and Nicobar Islands, which had been placed at the disposal of the Provisional Government, British drive for anti-Japanese propaganda, the precautions taken by British authorities to safeguard the Indian Army from the propaganda of Bose are also reflected in the documents.

Not only the British, even the Americans were interested in the activities of Bose who was considered as a traitor by them. The office of the Strategic Services of the U.S. Government carried out studies on his collaboration with the Axis Power, one such report on the activities of Hikari Kikan is reproduced here (Doc. 48). It is a comprehensive report and throws light on how the U.S. Government viewed the collaboration of Bose with the Japanese. Though it covers the details about the Imphal Campaign, it has been included since a major part deals with the activities of Subhas Chandra Bose after his arrival in South-East Asia.

The documents presented here are by no means exhaustive, they merely indicate to the research students the nature of material's available and may generate some interest in I.N.A. who are more familiar with the Indian National Congress, activities of Gandhiji and Jawahar lal Nehru. The contribution of Subhas Chandra Bose and other patriots who mobilised support from abroad for weakening British hold over India cannot be minimised. The documents strongly hint at the impact which Bose's collaboration with Japan had on the British.

The documents have been arranged in the chronological order and as far as possible no changes have been made in the text. The documents have been selected from archival repositories both in India and abroad. The extracts from the *Nippon Times* were selected, when I visited that country as a fellow of Japan Foundation. The University of Tokyo gave me all the facilities to consult microfilm of the newspapers and to prepare photocopies gratis. I am very grateful to them for allowing me these facilities.

I am equally obliged to the Diet Library, Tokyo for permitting me to prepare Xerox copy of the O.S.S. Reports on Indian Collaboration with Japan.

Besides Japan, documents were also collected from the India Office Library and Records and Public Record Office. Explanatory notes have been added while the reference to the source is given on the first page of each document.

T.R. Sareen

1

Rash Behari Bose to Iwakuro Requesting Permission for Re-Organising the Indian National Army (INA) After the Dismissal of General Mohan Singh[1]

6 February, 1943

Sir,

I have the honour to state that, as the President of the Council of Action of the Indian Independence League, I have decided to reform the Indian National Army which was originally organised with your recognition and has been receiving your support and to clarify the real significance of organising this army and to promote friendly relationship between the Japanese and Indian Armies, I beg to submit herewith the following articles for your approval and consent:[2]

1. The Indian National Army is an army of the Indian Independence League and is under the direct control of the Council of Action of the Indian Independence League.

   The Indian Indepedence league will assume the responsibility of safeguarding the best interests of the Indian National Army and will request the Indian National Government when the Independence is achieved to keep this Indian National Army to form as nucleus of the future army of India.

2. The Indian Independence League is the only Political Organisation in East Asia and is organised and managed by Indians for the purpose of attaining the complete independence and establishing the full sovereignty of India free from any foreign influence, control or domination.

1. Indian Independence League Paper F. No. 45/3. History of Freedom Movement Unit. National Archives of India. (Inf future referred to as I.I.L paper F. No. 45 3).
2. Colonel Iwakuro Hideo belonged to the Imperial Guard Division. Succeded Fujiwara in February 1942 as head of the Japanese liaison agency (Iwakuro Kikan) to help the Indian Nationalists in South East Asia. But unlike Fujiwara, his relations with them were never cordial. Due to his helplessness, he could neither give permission to General Mohan Singh to expand Indian Natioal Army nor even to get clarification about the Japanese policy towards India.

The League's programme and its execution will be so guided, controlled and directed as to bring them in line with the aims and intentions of the Indian National Congress.

3. All officers and men of the Indian National Army shall be members of the Indian Independence League and shall owe allegiance to the League.

4. The Indian National Army should be made use of only:

   (i) For operations against British or other Foreign powers in India;

   (ii) For the purpose of securing and safeguarding Indian National Independence;

   (iii) For the defence of the areas where the Indian National Army is stationed in the course of advance to India.

5. The Indian National Army shall be organised on a voluntary basis. Once enlisted, each member of the Indian National Army shall be governed by the Indian National Army Act to be framed by the Council of Action.

6. The table showing the different ranks of the Indian National Army is as in the Appendix[3].

7. The Indian National Army consists of the following units:

   (i) Headquarters, Indian National Army.

   (ii) Field Force Group.

   (iii) Guerilla Regiment.

   (iv) Special Service Group.

   (v) Intelligence Group.

   (vi) Reinforcement Group.

   Further expansion to the maximum extent of the Indian National Army depending on the Indian Manpower available shall be carried out as facilities are offered by the Japanese side.

8. The organisation of each unit will be provided separately.

9. For the purpose of dealing with matters concerning the military administration and operations, a military department will be established by the Council of Action of the Indian Independence League. The staff of this department will consist of officers and men of the Indian National Army.

---

3 Not Included.

10. The status of the Indian National Army shall be deemed to be the same as that of armies of allied nations of Japan. Salutes and courtesies should be exchanged on a reciprocal basis to foster and strengthen good relationship between the two armies.

11. The Japanese side will give all possible assistance to the Indian National Army when requested by the Indian Independence League.

Awaiting myself of this opportunity, I beg to express my highest respect to your good-self.

2

Iwakuro to Rash Behari Bose Approving the Scheme for Re-Organising the Indian National Army and the Objective of the Indian Independence League (I.I.L.)[1]

6 February, 1943

Sir,

I have the honour to acknowledge the receipt of your esteemed letter dated February 6th, 1943, and to note that you have decided to reform the Indian National Army which was originally organised with our recognition and has been receiving our support and to clarify the real significance of organising this army and to promote friendly relationship between the Japanese and Indian armies. You request me to give approval and consent to the articles enumerated therein.

I hereby approve and consent to the understanding with the condition that "the Indian Independence League will be so guided and directed as to keep in line with the guiding of the Indian National Congress as long as it contrives to fight against the British and aims at the attainment of the complete Independence of India."

I confirm here under the articles as enumerated in your letter. (Articles I to II as in President's letter to Colonel Iwakuro.)

I have the pleasure to take this opportunity to express my high esteem to you.

1. Ibid, For further clarification of Japanese policy see the statement issued by Iwakuro in Sopan Netaji Subhash Chandra Bose, His Life and Work (Bombay 1946) /p. 240.

3

A Yellape[1] to N. Raghavan[2] Informs About the Developments in Singapore Regarding the Re-Organisation of the I.NA. and I.I.L. Under the Leadership of Rash Behari Bose; Refers to the Questionnaire Handed Over to the Officers for Their Consent to Join the I.N.A.

12 February, 1943

I hope to be excused for the delay in sending a report of the events that have happened here since Dalal left for Penang.

I.N.A.

Since I returned from Penang, we had discussions regarding the draft on the "Understanding regarding the Indian National Army" The alterations suggested by you were all accepted except as to Clause (4) sub-clause (3) where I found out that the Army people wanted the words "For the defence of the areas where the I.N.A. is stationed in the course of its advance into India." I believe I gave this information to you some days ago on the phone.

The "understanding regarding the I.N.A." was confirmed by Colonel Iwakuro by exchange of letters. The only condition imposed by the Japanese side is contained in Para two of Colonel Iwakuro's letter.

---

1. *Ibid*, N. Raghavan, born in Cochin, was educated at Christian College after studying law in U.K., became a prominent lawyer in Penang, joined Indian Independence League and was member Coucil of Action : Was President Malaya Branch of Indian Independence League (I.I.L.) took part in Tokyo and Bangkok Conferences, but due to differences with Rash Behari Bose, he quit Council of Action; he was not convinced about Japanese sincerety. He was, however, persuaded by Subhas Chandra Bose to join the Provisional Government of India. After Independence he served as India's Ambassador in China and Switzerland.
2. A. Yellappa, a prominent lawyer from Singapore who had come from Coorg to Malaya before the war; was adviser to the Provisional Government of India; was responsible for organising the Azad Hind Bank in Burma; died in 1945 in the bombing raid of north-east Burma.

With regard to the organisation and running of the Military Department and your suggestion of creating the post of a Deputy Director and the substitution of an Army Council in place of the War Council, I regret to say that Mr. Bose did not discuss this matter, so far as I am aware, either with the Japanese side with the army people. I believe the scheme regarding the actual organisation and running of the Military Department is as set out in the original draft shown to you at Penang.

Since my return from Penang there has been a lot of discussion with the Japanese side and the Indian Army people with a view to expedite the reorganisation of the Indian National Army. On 11th February a set of questionnaire was handed over to over 200 officers of the I.N.A. Almost 50 per cent of them have agreed to remain in the I.N.A. unconditionally. 25 per cent more will, I suppose, come in immediately reorganisation starts. As to the rest it is very doubtful and my own view is that for the time being at least, it is better that officer like Bhagat and Parkash Chand, who are unwilling to come in, are kept out of the Movement.

I understand Bhonsle will be appointed Director of the Military Bureau and Kiani, Chief of the General Staff (That is to say in charge of the Operations Department and second to Bhonsle) and acting army commander. Kiani does not, at least to the present, want to accept the substantive appointment of Army commander, perhaps because, if he does so, it may give rise to a feeling that he manouvred to get Mohan Singh out to make a place for himself. It looks that there is nobody else who can be entrusted with the post of the Army Commander—not, at any rate, at the present moment. I gather that this arrangement Bhonsle and Kiani will not give rise to any mutual jealously. What the reactions of some of the other senior officers would be, I am not quite sure. But I feel that this is perhaps the best arrangement under present circumstances.[3]

Dil Sukh Man apparently is keeping out of the Movement because he wants the highest post. If he does keep out, a large number of Jats may, for the present at least, be out of the Movement. Parkash Chand's case appears to be similar and this will affect the Dogras who number quite a lot. The Sikhs are none too happy in the army and quite a number may keep out. However, on the reorganisation and on the appointment of Bhonsle and Kiani, I expect more than 50 per cent of the officers and men are sure to come into the I.N.A. forthwith. And if matters are properly handled, as many as 75 per cent may remain in the I.N.A.

3. A Military Bureau was set up after the arrest of General Mohan Singh by Rash Behari Bose on 21 Feb, 1943 to look after the Indian National Army. Lt. Col. J.K. Bhonsla was appointed as its Director. The Bureau had five sections dealing with Military administration.

A Pledge has been drawn up and I tried to put into that Pledge as such as I could out of the Pledge drawn up by you for the Volunteer force. Mr. Bose is anxious that immediately on reorganisation the Pledge should be taken by those who remain in the I.N.A. But I doubt whether this can be carried through as there is a feeling in the Army that until the vacancies in the Council of Action are filled up it may not be quite safe for them to take the Pledge.

Council of Action

Coming to the question of filling up the vacancies in the Council of Action I think the need for it is immediate and urgent. I understand Bose wished to leave for Bangkok immediately after reorganisation and will only make arrangements after his return to Syonan. In the meantime, I do not know what arrangements are to be made regarding carrying on of the work. I do not feel quite happy under present circumstances as without your guidence, I sometimes find myself completely at a loss. There are various matters which need tackling as they arise without any delay whatsover and as you will appreciate even if my views are correct they do not carry very much weight. I am rather anxious that matters relating to the I.N.A. as also other matters should be very carefully handled as soon as the reorganisation takes place otherwise we might find ourselves in a worse mess than before. Goho is sometimes very helpful but he also finds it very difficult to pull his weight. Mr. Bose does not take Goho into confidence in all matters.

Office

The sudden appointment of Lingam as Assistant Secretary came to me as a rather unpleasant shock. I cannot yet understand the reasons for this. I showed your telegram to Mr. Bose re P.N. He was rather upset about it and said that you ought to know that there is complete trust between you and him and that P.N. was second in importance to me only in this office. I suggested to Bose that P.N. may be made Assistant Secretary. He did not object to this proposal but whether he will give the appointment letter or not I do not know.

Institute Graduates

Dr. Lukshumeyya wrote to Mr. Bose suggestion that they be granted temporary commissions as Second Lieutenants. Apparently he had discussed this matter with Major Somasundaram also who came here about two days ago to choose another batch of Instructors. I am affraid the position is rather complicated. I gathered from a conversation with

Somasundaram that there is no difficulty regarding Aiyer's position but that with regard to the other graduates he feels that if they are given a temporary commission, the N.C.O.'s may not like it at all. In view of the fact that a larger number of N.C.O.'s are going down to Kuala Lumpur, we will be faced with an unpleasant situation if commission are granted. The position would have been different entirely if commissions were granted before the I.N.A.N.C.O's went over to Kuala Lumpur. Now it might be interpreted as a deliberate attempt to give these Institute Graduates a status which from their point of view, they might not deserve.

With regard to the attitude of the recruits, Somasundaram told me that the matter could be easily settled by his issuing an order as camp commandant that all recruits must salute the Institute Graduates as if they were officers and he thought that he could issue instructions by which all N.C.O's would exchange the courtesies with the Institute Graduates. From Somasundaram I gathered that the problem arose because the Institute Graduates were touchy. They perhaps thought that from the very beginning they would receive officer's treatment from the N.C.O's and the fact that the N.C.O's did not honour them with Military Salutes rather hurt their susceptibilities.

I discussed this matter with Mr. Bose who was rather puzzled about the whole affair. He has not yet made up his mind and I personally would like to know your views on this matter before I breach the subject again to him.

It is of course difficult for me to understand the exact situation without being on the spot but my feeling is that these Institute Graduates should try to fit in the existing camp organisation without loosing their distinctive civilian status. I do not want to blame them at all but perhaps a little more accommodating spirit might have prevented such a situation arising. Somasundaram does not think it is very big problem but Dr. Lukshumeyya seems to be insistent on their having commissioned ranks.

Somasundaram originally suggested that some of the Institute Graduates could be attached as assistants to the Adjutant, Quarter Master and Company Commanders and when they themselves received some military training, ranks of 2/Lieutenant could be conferred on them.

I would like to have your considered views on the matter.

India Swaraj Institutes

I discussed the future of the Institute with Mr. Bose. He intends to make this an Army Officers' Training School, but that cannot start until the reorganisation of the I.N.A. is completed. In the meantime he does not want the buildings to be vacated lest the Navy or Osman should take possession of them.

As to the students who are still in the Institude, Bose requests you to reconsider the question of sending them to infiltrate into India. He suggests that you should take this matter over with Lt. Kanako and find out if infiltration is now possible. He thinks it is better that persons who are reliable should infiltrate rather than people of the type Osman or others have in view. The latter may do a lot of harm to our cause.

Bose himself has no idea of what is to be done until the Officer's Training School is opened. He thinks you are best fitted to devise some scheme by which the buildings will remain in our hands and the students utilised to the best advantage of the Movement.

Information and Publicity

There have been no further development since Dalal left for Penang except that Col. Kagawa has submitted another scheme to Goho, I feel extremely unhappy about the whole situation regarding this Department. Dalal was asked to start on the clear understanding that the Press and the Broadcasting Station were handed over to us and the details were to be adjusted. Now everything seems to be in the melting pot.

4

Rash Behari Bose to the Officers of the I.N.A Informing them about the Re-organisation Despite the fact that there were many who were not Willing to join the I.N.A.

13 February, 1943

I have studied carefully the answers by officers of the I.N.A. to the questionnaire put to them by me on the 10th February. I note that practically all the Officers are prepared to fight and sacrifice for the Freedom of our Motherland but I regret to say that not all of them are willing to remain in the I.N.A.

These Officers fall into the following categories—

1. Those afraid of taking action against the British.
2. Those who do not seem to have full faith in the Indian National Congress.
3. Those who believe in Dominion Status for India, which assumes a British Victory.
4. Those who do not wish to remain in the I.N.A. under the "present circumstances."

Such views if expressed by Prisoners of War may well be understood but coming as they do from Officers of the Indian National Army they naturally give rise to speculations as to the motives which promoted these Officers to join the Movement which was intended solely to fight for the complete Independence of India, and not for the attainment of Dominion Status. Whatever the status of a Dominion, it remains a Dominion of Britain and as such is a watch-dog of Britain.

1. Ibid., Singapore 1943. Even Iwakuro had met the I.N.A. officers at the Bidadari Camp and spoke to them about the advisability of joining the army, but with no effect. Subsequently they agreed to continue in the I.N.A. only under Subhas Chandra Bose.

As for those who wish to remain away from the I.N.A. under the "present circumstances," I can only say that I am hardly to blame for the present state of affairs in the Army. As you know India's fight against Britain has now reached a critical stage. Mahatma Gandhi has undertaken a three-week fast to bring still more pressure on the British to quit India, thus finally disproving any chance of a compromise. Our duty now is clear. Some of you may be anxious to know what will happen to those rejected from I.N.A. Unfortunately, I shall have no control over those who deliberately choose to quit the I.N.A. at the present juncture. I cannot speak for the Japanese, nor say in what manner or at what place they may be employed by the power whose prisoners they choose to be. Those of the Officers who do not wish to reconsider the views will have to appear before me at 11-30 hours to-day and give their reasons before I separate' them from the men. The appointments to the various Officers in the Indian National Army will be made by me as President of the Council of Action very soon. Needless to say no appointment have yet been made, but I can assure you that no Communal, Sectarian or Provincial bias will be shown.

(Sd.) Rash Behari Bose, President, Council of Action,
Indian Independence League.

5

Action Committee of the Youth Movement to Ex-Officers of the I.N.A. Requesting Them to Join the I.N.A. for Achieving India's Freedom[1]

8 March, 1943

We the Indian youths assembled here this evening extended to you a most hearty welcome into our midst. This greeting of ours not only applies to those who are present here but also to all those who are absent from the Indian National Army in this gathering.[2]

Your kind presence here today is an eloquent testimony to show that you are one with us. We duly reciprocate it.

As we see daily with our eyes how rapid strides you are making for the freedom battle of India. We feel extremely proud of you and express our profound thanks to you without any hesitation and also beg to add that your names would go into the history of India as the persons fully responsible for the realisation of Mahatma Gandhi's vision of an Indian National Army.

We make bold to assure you that we are banded together to lay down our lives for the liberation of our sacred motherland. India, from the cruel and inhuman exploitation of the Anglo-American Powers, whose machinations to make India still more a slavish country are gaining momentum daily. Your purpose also being the same as ours, we request you to take us all into your camp as youths who have willingly dedicated their lives for their country. Though we were a neglected flock all the while, we could not afford to remain like this any more.

1. I.I.L. Papper. F. No. 45/3.
2. Youth Movement, it was organised under the patronage of Iwakuro Kikan with the intention of weakening the Indian National Army. This move was never liked by N. Raghavan and other members of the Territorial Committee of Malaya. They represented against this move of the Japanese to the President, Indian Independence League, Rash Behari Bose. For details see S.A. Das and K.B. Subbaiah, *Chalo Delhi*, Kuala Lumpur, 1946. pp. 98-103.

We confess that we have no training or discipline or qualification of any kind to join you; but we boldly claim kindred with you as sons of the same soil with the same blood running in our veins. Whatever failings we have, let our ardent spirit of patriotism compensate them all and we are also confident that under your able leadership, guidence, and instructions we would prove ourselves worthy of your confidence and trust in no time.

In fine, it is our solemn conviction that you would not hesitate to be one with us and mutually pledge for the independence of our Holy Hindustan.

6

Statement of Rash Behari Bose Assuring the Indians in South-East Asia About Japanese Sincerity[1]

9 March, 1943

The Indians in their determination were greatly encouraged by the repeated declarations of Japan's accredited leaders and Statesmen such as the Prime Minister and the Foreign Minister of Japan. As early as the 16th of February 1942, addressing the members of the Imperial Diet on the fall of Singapore, Premier General Tojo referred to India and said:—

"It is a golden opportunity for Indians having, as it does, several thousand years of history and splendid cultural tradition, to rid herself of the ruthless despotism of Britain and participate in the construction of the Greater East Asia Co-prosperity Sphere. Japan expects that India will restore its proper status as India for the Indians and she will not stint herself in extending assistance to the patriotic efforts of the Indians. Should India fail to awaken to her mission, forgetting her history and tradition, and continue as before to be beguiled by the British cajolery and manipulation and act at their beck and call, I cannot but fear that an opportunity for the renaissance of the Indian people would be forever lost."

Again on the 12th of March 1942 in his message to the Imperial Diet, after the fall of Java and Rangoon, Premier General Tojo referred to India and said :—

"As to the Indian people, Japan entertains, of course, not the slightest thought of antagonising them. I desire, however to reiterate clearly that the determination of Japan to crush thoroughly the American and British influences will undergo no change whatever."

"Burma for the Burmese is already on its way to realization. It is my firm belief that now is the time to establish India for the Indians, which has for many years been aspiration of the 400 million people."

1. I.I.L. Papers, F. No. 45/3.

"Great Britain has for long deceived and continued her arbitrary rule over India. What the reality of the British promise made to India in the last Great War must be still fresh, I believe, in the memory of the Indian people. Now Great Britain is trying again to deceive India with all sorts of cajolery. If the leaders of India, misled by such British cajoleries, betray the long cherished aspiration of the Indian people and thus fling away this Heaven-sent opportunity, I believe there will be change for saving India forever and there will be no greater misfortune befalling the 400 million Indian people.

"Will India rise as India for the Indians to have the honour of co-operating for the establishment of the Greater East Asia Co-prosperity Sphere, or will she permanently stoop under the shackles of the Anglo-American Powers to leave her name as a slave to posterity? She is now face to face with the time when she should liquidate her past, see the new situation correctly and make her final decision ."

After the capture of Andamans, Premier General Tojo once again referred to India on the 7th of April 1942 and said:—

"The Imperial Forces which previously occupied Rangoon, an important base in Burma, and then took possession of the major strategic point in the eastern Indian Ocean, the Andaman Islands, which have hitherto been a place of exile for patriots of Indian Independence, have now at last dealt severe blows to the British forces and military establishments in India.

"The grim determination of our Empire to crush the United States and Britain is thus being steadily translated into action. If India should remain as before under the military control of Britain, it would, I am afraid, be unavoidable that, in the course of our subjugation of the British forces there, India will suffer great calamities.

"As it is, of course, fartherst from the thought of Japan to consider the Indian people as an enemy, Japan deeply sympathized with them who are likely to suffer the ravages of war.

"What Japan's intentions are toward the Indian people was made clear in my address delivered before the Imperial Diet on March 12th. In short, I am firmly convinced that now is the golden opportunity for the Indian people to exert their utmost efforts for the establishment of their long-desired "India for the Indians" in order to secure India's status as it ought to be.

"The British influence in India is now about to be exterminated. I wish once again to repeat at this juncture Japan's expectation that not only the leaders in India but the four hundred million people there, while avoiding unnecessary calamities which will result from their being misled by sweet flatteries of Britain, the nation destined to downfall, will take full advantage of this heaven-sent opportunity and break away from the British bonds which have so long shackled them and thus go vigorously forward to realise truly their long-cherished aspiration, of "India for the Indians."

When the mission of the agent of British Imperialism, Sir Stafford Cripps, to India ended in failure, Premier General Tojo addressing the members of the House of Representatives in Tokyo on the 28th of May 1942 again referred to the Indian problem and said—

"The fact that the British-Indian negotiations, with the British Lord Privy Seal, Sir Stafford Cripps[2], acting as the central figure, ended at last in rupture without accomplishing anything whatsoever, demonstrates that India has already become spiritually independent from Britain. Thus, the spiritual basis of British possession of India may be said to have disappeared already, and the first historic step toward Indian independence has just been made. "There still remains in India a framework of British possession with various military establishment, and the military forces are being steadily increased. As long as there remain Anglo-American military forces in India, Japan is determined inflexibly to crush them thoroughly. To our regret, it is, indeed, unavoidable that in the progress of such campaign some misfortunes may befall innocent Indians. What I expect at this juncture, however, is that the Indian people will rise with an intrepid spirit, expel the Anglo-American forces as well as their influence completely from India and thereby realise the Independence of their Fatherland."

These repeated declarations and assurances by the most responsible statesman of Nippon who not only heads the Government of the Empire but also as the Minister of War the whole machinery of war, have not only offered a great hope to the Indians for the future of the Indian nation but have made them greatly interested in our struggle for freedom from without. They have removed the doubts and misgiving regarding Japan's mission and have created confidence in Japan's intentions towards India.

We Indians know that if we wished to take advantage of the present golden opportunity to help our fighting Nationlist forces in India in bringing our long drawn out war of Independence to a successful conclusion, there was one and only one way to do it and that was to seek Japan's help

2. Sir Stafford Cripps (1889-1952) was a Minister in the British Cabinet, was sent to India in 1942 to negotiate with the Congress leaders for cooperation during the war. Cripps proposals for solving the constitutional deadlock were rejected by all the political parties.

and cooperation in this great task. The only thing that hampered the Indians in East Asia in seeking this help was the influence of Anti-Japanese British propaganda which had created some doubts in some minds. The long bitter experience of British Imperalism had made the Indian mind so pliant that they fell easy victims to the shrewd British mischief mongers and they were unable to realise and understand Japan's sincerity in the early stages. These vivid, hopeful declarations have done a lot to remove misunderstanding and create confidence. The successful celebration of the Independence Day throughout East Asia is positive proof of this fact as it is proof of our dauntless patriotism and of our burning desire to be free.

No one after reading the above declarations will question the statement that it has now become a natural thing for Indians in East Asia to associate Japan with India's fight for freedom. The reason is plain. Japan is not only the most dominent Power in Asia but, of more material importance to Asiatics, is the fact that it is Japan who has smashed Britain and America in East Asia and is now busy pulling out the last noxious weeds of Anglo-American Imperialism from the gardens of Asia which she has occupied and is holding in trust for the rightful owners, the people, who will be given control when the Greater East Asia Co-prosperity sphere becomes a living reality. Indians who thus have come into contact with the Japanese find the letter to be human beings, men to whom the doing of a kind deed is an obsession, men who from early childhood have been taught the value of the pledged word, loyalty to a cause and people, and the intrinsic worth of that thing called mercy and compassion. One foreign writer paid this tribute to Japan five years ago: "Wherever one turns one sees a people of heroes, a political constitution of imperturbable strength and authority: an administration working with high ideals; a military power equal to that of the Great Powers of the world an Empire making progress in all directions; a nation which always places in the forefront of its foreign policy "A pledge is a bond which cannot be broken whatever the circumstances." What this writer has had to say has been confirmed in our every day contact with the Japanese and things Japan. When Japan says a thing she means it and does it. It is because of this conviction that the promises of all-out aid to India without any notice of self-interest or designs of conquest has been accepted by Indians with all the sincerity with which it has made by Japan. And the letter realises that it is only a free, Independent India which can make the ideal of "Asia for the Asiatics" come true. Japan, therefore, is ready to help India gain her freedom from British misrule and to help to eradicate the evil influence which has for long and so oppressively been making the lives of Indians a misery and

India an object of world pity.

Great Britain, a past master in the art of wilfully misinterpreting the pure motives of others, has been using the clear, unambiguous and definite declarations of Japan concerning India as a spur to compel Indians to defend themselves under British control against Japan. To do so they have immorally perverted all that has been said by Japanese leaders, Statesman, politicians and Diplomats, and re-manufacturing the statements by the insertion of sentences to suit their own ends, has presented Japan to India as being menace to India. Only poltroons, knaves, rogues and liars are capable of so gross and infamy and the British have voluntarily placed themselves in each of the above classifications through the fabrication of falsehoods which they know to be falsehoods. British propagandists in recent months have been trying to whip Indian public opinion into the belief that a crisis is facing India. That crisis, again according to the British is no other than the possibility of a Japanese offensive into India. But how foolish, how untrue, how unreal such a story sounds. It is fanastic, the creature of Britain's own imagination. It is not a Japanese army which will drive the British out of India lock, stock and barrel. It is an Indian Army, which, like avenging angels, will forcibly eject the British from India at the point of the rifle and the bayonet—that is if Field-Marshal Wavell and his British hordes do not themselves stage another 'glorious retreat" this time from Indian soil.

Japan has never harboured a will to antagonize the Indian people. Far from it, Japan sympathizes with their long cherished desire and have announced their readiness to co-operate, if, mark these words, *the Indians desire it.* If Japan had any desire to harm Indians why should she, whenever she gets ready to destroy the bases of British Imperialism in India, ask the Indian Independence League broadcasting station, to advice Indians to quit such areas? Make no mistake about it, the "Crisis of India" means nothing more than the very patent and obvious fact that Britain still rules India. The prolongation of the crisis depends on how soon Britain quits India.

Japan's relations with India are as clear as crystal. Her intentions have been plainly stated and often reiterated. In the previous pages we have quoted Premier General Tojo at length to show how Japan has assured India that she has no antagonism towards India and how she wants to help us in freeing our country. If there is any doubt left in any mind even after the great Premier and General has committed Japan very definitely in his very recent declarations, then there will be no such thing as sincerity in this world. On February 4th, 1943, replying to an interpollation posed by Mr. Ryo Koyama in a Budgetary Committee meeting of the House of Representatives in Tokyo the Premier, General Tojo, reiterated the statement that the Japanese Government has no territocial ambitions in India, but rather on the contrary desires to see India regain its Independence as soon as possible. He said that whatever propaganda the enemy nations may use to counteract or discredit oft-repeated statement will amount to nothing before the overwhelming realities, indicated in the shining existence of the over-growing Empire of Manchukuo and the up and coming National government of China at Nanking. He continued by saying that the Japanese Government is the staunch unholder of righteousness and shall at all times abide by its promises. He asserted that Japan stood by its assurance given to Thailand to respect the sovereignty of its territorial integrity, as a consequence of which Thailand is now fully collaborating with Japan in the prosecution of Greater East Asia War. Japan's attitude towards Burma has been already clarified, continued Premier Tojo, adding that the Philippines, too has been assured of independence provided it comes to realise its place in Greater East Asia and collaborate fully with the Japanese policy. Asserting that realities speak more eloquently than any malicious propaganda aimed to discredit Japan, Premier Tojo declared that India, at the present juncture needs only to turn a deaf ear to enemy propaganda and to concentrate in the efforts of the immediate task before it. He concluded by saying that Japan has no territorial ambition whatever in India.

This statement by General Tojo is looked upon as being an inspiration to Indians everywhere. The Indian Independence League Headquarters in the course of a statement commenting on General Tojo's declaration said:-

"Premier Tojo's present declaration has completely shattered Anglo American mallicious propaganda to Indian people to the effect that Japan entertains no territorial ambition. The statement that Japan is striving to bring back India to its original status as enunciated by Premier Tojo has given the greatest inspiration to Indians who now realise all the more Japan's lofty spirit for construction of Greater East Asia. Premier Tojo's promise to grant independence to Burma within this year and his present statement to the effect that similar treatment will be accorded to the Philippines has given concrete proof of the ethical basis of Japan's war aims, namely eradication of Anglo-Americans Imperialism from East Asia and the construction of Asia for the Asiatics. Fully comprehending General Tojo's statement the Indian people have come to trust Japan more than ever and their Independence movement in consequence will make a rapid advance hereafter ."

7

General Staff, Headquarters to G.O.C. Indian Army Informing him about the Subversive Activities Directed towards the Indian Army from within and ourside India Specially by those who were Collaborating with Japan[1]

18 March, 1943

In letter No. DMI/4746 of 4th Nov. 1942 tentative information about the Japanese sponsored Indian National Army and views on counter measure were given and it was stated that comments and further suggestions would be appreciated. Since then additional information has been circulated and constant references to the dangers to security which the movement represents have been included in Part III of GHQ (I) Weekly Intelligence Summary. The fact that no comments or suggestions have so far been received, together with some recent events, suggests that the potentialities of the situation have not been fully realised in all quarters. The object of this letter is to outline certain recent developments which have come to light, to describible arrangements made by GHQ Security Staff for watching the situation and to stress the necessity for complementary measure in formations and units without which success in dealing with these problems cannot be achieved.

It is now quite clear that a double attack is being made on the morale and loyality of Indian troops—one directed from without India by the Japanese, assisted by renegade Indians, and the other directed from within India by Congress or Congress inspired organisations. These two compaigns are identical in aim and to some extent in method though no direct connection has yet been established between them as regards coordination or control. That in practics one is complementary to the other as regards the effect which may be produced is shown in an example quoted later in this letter. Both these campaigns are assisted by radio

1. Ministry of Defence. F. No. 601/10569/Historical Section.

propaganda in Hindustani and English from German Radio stations[2] some of which pose as secret stations in India. In the direction of this propogands Subhas Chand Bose has hitherto played a leading part. The tendency is to transfer Indian Prisoners of War captured in the middle East to Germany where it is known efforts are being made to develop "Free India" units, on the I.N.A. model.[3] A letter from an Indian P of W recently referred to the excellent treatment they were receiving and remarked that all arrangements were in the hands of Subhas Chand Bose. The following is a typical extract from German radio propoganda directed to India—

> "Let me remind you once again that the two fold object of the non-violent guerilla warfare that you are now carrying on, should be: Firstly, to paralyse the civil administration in India and secondly to destroy war production in India. I should also like to tell you that the time has come to intensify our propaganda within the Indian Army. This could be done best by sending our Partymen in large numbers into the ranks of the Indian Army. In the last phase of the national struggle, the Indian Army will have to play an important role."

Congress Party manifestos and secret instructions and correspondence which have recently been seized clearly show that the underground leaders have concluded that the main barrier to the success of their movement to obtain power is the staunchness of the Indian Army. The following is an extract from a document captured some time ago. The similarity with the extract quoted in para 2 above is worthy of note.

> "........our objective must be the capture of power from the foreign Government. How is this to be effected? We have seen that it was possible in Bihar and the U.P. to paralyse civil administration and capture power at least for sometime. That is, it was possible to bring to a standstill the machinery of civil administration. You can break the police, but what of the military.....I would press upon the organisers to think out means to meet the menace of the army."[4]

---

2. German Radio. This refers to Azad Hind Radio (Germany) which was started by Subhas Chandra Bose when he went to Germany in 1941. Bose's broadcasts had great impact on public opinion in India and abroad. For details see British Weekly Intelligence Summary F.No. 601/7378/H.S. Ministry of Defence, New Delhi. For Bose's activities in Germany. See also T.R. Sareen, *Subhas Chandra Bose and Nazi Germany*, New Delhi, 1996.
3. This refers to the Free India Centre and Indian Legion formed by Bose from P.O.W. in Germany.
4. This refers to the appeal issued by General Mohan Singh to the soldiers of the Indian Army to desert and join the Indian National Army for the liberation of India. Even after Mohan Singh's arrest by the Japanese in December 1942, the appeal in his name was still utilised for propaganda purposes by the Indian Independence League.

At Appendix 'A' is a copy of a document subsequently captured in which this problem is appreciated and the opening presented especially by expansion of technical recruiting for the Royal Air Force is stressed. At Appendis 'B' are copies of correspondence believed to be addressed to the organiser of the Northern Congress Zone, which indicate attempt to put into practice the scheme of the "League of Armed Forces" referred to in Appendix "A". While it is probable that the claims of progress made in this correspondence are coloured by enthusiasm, it must be accepted that there has been some degree of success at least in making contacts and establishing cells for the distribution of propaganda. No confirmation of such attempts has yet been obtained from local police or military sources in the Punjab but recent events in a battalion in Arakan (referred to below) indicate that a recent draft had been infected by Congress propaganda before leaving their training centre in the Punjab. One of the main immediate dangers of such attempts to win over military personnel is the possiblity of subversive organisations thereby obtaining supplies of explosives, etc. for sabotage purposes. In both Delhi and Bombay the police have received information and recently discovered large quantities of live bombs, revolvers and explosives obtained from friend and sympathisers in....Arsenals and Ordnance Depots. An even greater danger is the ultimate effect on morale and fighting efficiency, which will not become apparent until contact with the enemy is made.

As regards Japanese inspired activities, there seems to be no falling off in the recruitment of agents from among both Indian prisoners of war and Indian civilians in Japanese occupied territory and their despatch from Malaya and Burma, there is good evidence that parties have been sent from Hong Kong. As in the case of Germany, Indians are comparatively well treated and civilians are given the status of third national. Those Indians P of W who accept membership of the INA are freed—those who do not are subjected to harsh treatment and constant propaganda. There is evidence that numbers continue to refuse, that numbers given in and join with no intention of fulfilling the pledges they are called upon to make, but that a relatively large number, the leaders of which include regular Army ICOs, VCOs and NCOs, have become active members of the INA. From these and from civilians, parties of agents are selected for despatch to India.

While the arrangement outlined below have met with some measure of success intercepting and discovering these agents, there is no doubt that considerable numbers have slipped through. In a disquieting number of cases, individuals have managed to conceal from interrogators the fact that they have been Japanese hands, have been coached in espionage and subversive propanganda and sent back with specific instructions. Cases are now coming to light of "stragglers" who rejoined as long ago as August and September and have successfully concealed these facts. In spite of instructions issued under A.G. Branch 30065/AG. 22 of 27/7/42 in some cases such men have been reposted to units in Eastern Army, or having joined them direct have been allowed to remain there. In other cases military personnel have disguised themselves as civilians, returned to their districts and failed to report to their units for some months. These all represent a potential danger to security, however innocent they may appear to be. Such a situation cannot be treated with complacency and it is essential that commanding officers of all Indian units be warned of the necessity for ascertaining whether in fact their units contain stragglers who have not been properly interrogated.

The Japanese are now reinforcing these "deep penetration" agents with leaflet and radio propaganda addressed directly to Indian troops and issued in the name of the Indian National Army. Manuscript letters in vernacular script (translation at Appendix 'C') and emanating from Capt. Mohan Singh have been piched up by our patrols in Arakan, while Punjabi Mussalman and Sikh Personnel were recently observed from a Battery O.P. in Arakan fighting along side Japanese troops. There is no doubt that a detachment of INA is in the Akyab area.

Individual desertions of Indian troops have been reported and in a recent case a platoon sent out on patrol is believed to .....have deserted. The "Security" history of this unit is given in Appendix 'D'. Enquiries now in progress show that the company (Sikhs) to which the platoon belonged had been infected firstly by subversive Congress propaganda circulated by a draft recently joined from the Training Unit, secondly by local contacts with Mugh and INA propagandists and thirdly by INA pamphlets. (It was this company that firstly reported the Mohan Singh leaflets referred to above). This case illustrates the potential and the actual dangers to which this double attack exposes us and also the need at all times for the closest scrutiny and sifting of any reports however far fetches or even ridiculous they may appear at the time. It is essential to avoid the complacency that in so many cases leads to entries in unit intelligence reports suggesting that morale is high and subversive tendencies absent because outward and visible signs are lacking. Nearly all the units in which trouble has occurred have submitted negative security reports for some time before open signs are visible.

It is desirable here to summarise frankly some of the reasons which should dispel any feeling of complacency. The Pre-war Indian Army was in practice still a mercenary army with its morals and loyalty based on four main factors:-

(a) Recruitment from classes with long-standing martial and professional traditions which have for long been centred on loyalty to the "Sarkar" and to the King Emperor and which were still strong enough to withstand the interest of those classes.

(b) Experienced British officers able to command the respect and affection of their men.

(c) Pay and conditions of service sufficiently good to make service in the army attractive in comparison with conditions in civil life.

(d) Establishments low enough to maintain competition for vacancies.

In respect of at least (a) (b) and (d) the situation has radically changed, while it is now questionable whether (c) is still sufficiently potent to counterbalance the loss of stabilising effect of the other three. Changes in the classes from which men and particularly Indian commissioned officers are drawn, shortage of experienced British Officers with knowledge of the country and able to command personal respect and affection, combined with consistent "nationalist" propaganda are sapping the foundations on which the morale and loyalty of the old Indian Army was based. At the same time the concept of "loyalty to India" which in theory should be developed by "nationalistic" propaganda is unable to replace the other loyalties referred to above in the case of newly introduced elements or of the older element's (i.e., the martial classes). The letter are so bewildered and confused by political developments which they do not understand but which they instinctively feel will react to their disadvantage in the long run, that these older loyalties are rapidly losing their potency. It is against this background, which favours both Japanese and Congress inspired activities, that these problems must be viewed and tackled.

If the above analysis is correct, it is obvious that administrative contentment assumes increasing importance in the interregnum between the casting off of the old loyalties and the development of the new. Apart from this, it is essential that Commanding Officers and senior Indian Officers should be made to realise these factors where this realisation is not already the case and that every effort should be made to watch for and counter subversive activities of the type outlined. The basis of action in this connection is knowledge and no neglect of any clue, however trivial it may appear to be initially. It is also essential that efforts should be made continuously to impress on men, especially of the recently introduced classes, that they are fighting in India's interests and that a Japanese Victory would be disastrous to their own future.

This raises the question of publicity and propaganda about the INA and other Japanese activities. Hitherto this has not been attempted because:-

(a) It might engender lack of confidence in their troops among British officers and commanders.

(b) It would give valuable information to the enemy who is at present largely ignorant of the extent of our knowledge of his plans and activities and of the degree of success his scheme for infiltrating agents has achieved in practice.

The disadvantages of silence are that it has encouraged unwarranted complacency in many quarters. It is felt that at present publicity and open propaganda should not be allowed but that measures outlined below should be taken to ensure that the facts are more widely known to formation and unit commanders and to trustworthy Indian commissioned officers and senior VCOs.

Apart from the establishment of—

(a) a screen of Forward Interrogation Centres in Assam and Bengal for the collection, preliminary interrogation and classification of personnel returning from enemy occupied territory, and staffed by combined police and military personnel;

(b) a combined civil and military interrogation centre (C.S.D.I.C.)[5] in Delhi for the further interrogation of suspects and of personnel subsequently apprehended who escape (a),

(c) a combined civil and military staff in GHQ (know as G.S.I. (b) (i)) which sifts reports and initiates counter action against the Japanese IWAKURO organisation (outlined in GHQ (I) Weekly Intelligence Summary, Part III, para 6, dated 5th March 1943) and recommends the disposal of personnel,

It has now been decided to appoint Lt. Col. Himmat Singh (now GS O I in charge of G.S.I.(b) (i)) as GHQ Liaison Officer to visit formations and units in connection with INA and kindred matters and to assist in enquiries and to follow up specific cases such as that referred to in paragraph 8 above. He will also periodically visit security staffs at HQs Armies/ Commands with a view to concerting coordinated action and giving any assistance in his power. He will be available to visit training centres to

5. C.S.D.I.C. Combined Services Detailed Interrogation Centre was established by the Army Headquarters during the war. It had its headquarters at Red-Fort, Delhi. The centre was interested with the task of interrogating all those who were coming from enemy occupied territories especially Burma. Subsequently, it interrogated almost every soldier who was connected with the Indian National Army. They were divided into three categories— Black, Grey and White.

explain the situation and discuss security measures.

In view of the importance of countering both Congress and INA activities, it is requested that in each Army/Command, (and in lower formations at Army Commanders discretion) a member of the Security Staff, or alternatively an experienced and reliable British or Indian Officer be employed as Liaison Officer for INA questions to supplement Lt. Col. Himmat Singhi's work in following up specific cases and in ensuring that a constant watch is maintained in all units, especially training units. These officers should periodically visit G.S.I. (b) at GHQ (I) and C.S.D.I.C. Delhi to obtain the latest information. It is requested that in addition steps be taken to bring the situation and its potential dangers forcibly to the notice of all formation commanders and commanders of Indian units. Enclosures at Appendix 'A' and 'B' to this letter should not however be distributed below Brigade Commanders and burned after perusal. The necessity for making full use of material on INA and Congress, activities directed against the Army which is published periodically is Part III of GHQ (I) Weekly Summary should be impressed on formation commanders. Commanding Officers should now be authorised to put the facts of the situation, as given in these summaries, plainly to selected Indian Commissioned Officers and Viceroys Commissioned Officers where this has not already been done. For this purpose suitable extracts from these summaries may be made by Brigade, etc. Commanders for distribution to Battalion or equivalent commanders.

Finally, attached at Appendix 'E' is an extract from a letter written by a KCIO to the Director of Military Intelligence on the question of the extent to which the Army generally should be taken into our confidence regarding these developments.

The writer is a member of a family with long tradition of service in the Indian Army, but who personally is strongly imbued with nationalistic ideas. He has been in Japanese hands and was fully in the confidence of both the INA leaders and their Japanese sponsors before escaping. His views endorse much of what has been written above. This Appendix should not be distributed below Brigade Commanders and copies should be destroyed after perusal.

His Excellency the Commander-in-Chief wishes Army Commanders to give the contents of this letter their personal consideration and to submit any views or recommendations they may have for dealing with the problem.

Sd/-

Lieut.-General,

CHIEF OF THE GENERAL STAFF.

APPENDIX ' A' TO DM/4746

League of Armed Forces in India Secretary's Review of the Indian Situation

The Congress raised the moral of the nation but failed to contact the powerful machine of the Indian Army. If the British Goverment decided to destroy the Indian Political leaders, nothing could happen in this country to harm the British interests seriously. Again and again we have asked why the British, staunch Imperialists as they are, have not done so. The answer is the same every time, British have lost their old courage and dare-devillery. They have become sedate citizens of a glamorous world ready to guard their hoards but prizing their lives above all.

The Congress who we had always looked so far for leadership failed us when they miserably underrated Britain's strength, resources and diplomacy. We all know the result. But, where the Congress succumed, their teaching survived. Several independent bodies and parties, angry at the impotency of their leaders behind the bars, trumpeted revolution.

Several of these bodies we have helped and in some cases we have even engineered their issues. Our aim in aiding these operations of local sabotage was to help the country to obtain a favourable world opinion. From the informations at our disposal I can safely announce that the American and particularly the Chinese and Russian opinions have distinctly and effectively tilted in India's favour. This would be a help.

But, a settled Government like the British, cannot be over-thrown by world opinions or resolutions. Even sabotage of a vast magnitude would only result in the destruction of our own countrymen (the Police and the Saboteurs), each party pathetically imagining itself to be in the right. The only feasible answer to this fracas, is the active cooperation of the armed forces in this country.

Churchill's extraordinarily provocative declaration and the subsequent attempts at its justification, very nearly tipped us off our balance which would have resulted in enormous bloodshed and eventual, positive, defeat on our part. We thank the Providence for getting us out of that impasse.

Indian Army–Its Psychology

Today our army measures nearly one and half million. Over forty Brigades are serving outside the country. Every day, reports of terrible atrocities committed by the British Officers on the Indian troops pour in to us. Reports of British cowardice on the battlefields have nearly filled our files. Still the Indian Army is apparently intact - loyal to the British. Why? Because, deep down in the heart of every Indian, from rank and file to high above, there is a distinct feeling that the British would win in the end. Since the day of the mutiny, its disastrous effects on the Indian sepoys has always been rubbed into the Indian ranks and hence their sense of awe towards the British power.

In spite of these failings of the Indian Army it still remains an excellent machinery, which alone will be instrumental towards achieving the National Government.

Support the Congress

While we are reviewing Indian aspects in general we must not forget that it is only the issue of National Government that confronts us. It is the Congress that we wish to help. In all our previous meetings we had decided to avoid any contact with the Congress, yet. But now, time has come when we must join resources.

During our eleven months work we have grouped up 32 per cent of Indian Officers in our Army. This is a satisfactory figure considering that we are working under a lamentable stress of lack of funds. The ratio of British to Indian Officers today in our Army is 4.7 to 1, but even this ratio is steadily decreasing. Shortage of man-power in England makes the British Government dependent on Indian manpower not only for the Army but for the technical arms for the Air Force. The Government is evidently willing to /be taken in any Indian with the requisite education into the vital technical arm and perforce has to trust them. By the end of December 1942 a huge programme of Indianising the whole or the technical staff of the Royal Air Force is going to take effect. The replacement will be to the extent of 50,000 men and the recruitment of this staff is entirely in our hands. The whole of this enormous technical man-power will have to be recruited within two months and trained within a year entirely at Government expense. Every man recruited for this job will sign an allegiance to us and not the Government. The only unfortunate tragedy of this affair is that we face great difficulties in finding the right type of men. The Congress call not to enlist in the Army has effectively set back well over 60 per cent of the intelligent students. Although we have put our men at various universities working for the Government under Air Force training scheme, we find considerable difficulty in persuading the correct type of boys that we need for the great work.

If at this stage it could be engineered, such that the Congress could make peace with the Government of India, even under terms that may sound a little trifle and undignified, we could within the space of a year put at the disposal of the Congress vital armed forces strong enough to oust the British Government of power. Besides, a call from the Congress could let loose the intelligentsia, the material which is most suitable to us. Congress, once out of the bars should concentrate to capture power in departments of Home, Finance, Information and Broadcasting Communications, Wireless, and Civil Aviation. With Congress Ministers guiding the policy of these departments and we securing a strong foot-hold in the Armed Forces, the power of the Commander-in-chief would be null and void. It may be of interest to note that the C-in-C should be strictly left alone and even a Defence Minister's issue should not be forced.

Under our scheme of operations C-in-C's position will steadily deteriorate. Considering these factors we feel that it is essential for the Congress to patch up with the Government under whatever guise they consider best, as long as we get our material and formal support from the Congress Ministers.

Lately, reports have come to us stating that there have been considerable infiltration of Congress-minded youths into the Army. / lthough we have been able to suppress this dangerous allegation successfully, it only shows how much easier the whole process of recruitment would be for us under legal guise.

Under the new scheme of expansion of the Indian Air Force we shall have twenty squadrons of fighters and bombers within the space of one and half years. This, again, would be entirely our fabrications and would pay a vital part in our final operations.

Reviewing the world situation I strongly believe that Britain would eventually be victors. But whatever happens Germany's last blow to England would be so staggering that it may not be possible for them to recover for some time. It would be then that we would strike. With the essential services under our control and a majority of the Armed Forces on our side it would not be particularly difficult to overthrow the British Government in India. Once this is done, (which, incidentally would cause plenty of bloodshed throughout the country), we, the armed forces shall stand by the Congress in its efforts to form a National Government, till such time as it needs us, or alternatively, till the whole Indian Army is Nationalised.

APPENDIX 'B' TO DMI/4746

Extracts from Letters Addressed to the Organiser Congress Northern Zone

(A) In my last report I had mentioned that how we have worked our way into various Regiments. I also wrote about the contracts we have established. But for want of money we could not stabilise that work. Except the distribution of one pamphlet we did nothing further:

(ii) Now when we have established contacts 'above' our work is progressed methodically. Reliable contacts have been placed at Rawalpindi, Compbellpur, Jhelum, Sialkot, Lahore, Ferozepur, Ambala, Jullundur and Gurgaon. These persons have in turn developed their own contacts in the Regiments stationed at these places. It is expected that they will be able to distribute literature once a month at least.

(iii) We do have relations with the Regiments in the Frontier but we have no reliable men there. Therefore, there has been no work in that province so far. Contacts are established with soldiers when they proceed on leave to their villages. There is a great difficulty being experienced in the Frontier due to the strict vigilance of the Military Authorities. Often these regiments are in camps where even relatives cannot meet them. Besides there are many Cantonments where entry without permit is prohibited. We have got connections at Nowshera, Peshawar, Quetta and Landikotal. Pamphlets can be distributed to soldiers in the Regiments at these four places only when they proceed on leave.

(iv) Response from Gorkhas and Jats stationed at Abbottabad is very encouraging. Pamphlets in Nepali were distributed amongst the Gorkhas. One copy is sent herewith (no copy was actually received). There is a great enthusiasm amongst the soldiers.

They hate British Officers because of their (British Officers) discriminatory treatment towards them. This hatred is assuming a national character.

(v) It is our intention to extend our work to the Frontier from Abbottabad. How far we will be successful cannot be said.

(vi) In the Punjab, we have developed intimate relations with the Regiments stationed at Ambala, Gurgaon and Lahore. Great enthusiasm prevails here. We are very hopeful of the results. Cells are being established at these places.

(vii) We have trained our workers how to establish cells in the Regiments stationed in the Punjab Province.

(viii) There are aerodromes at Gurgaon, Mandauthi, Ambala, Lahore, Ferozepur and Sialkot. The pilots, who are generally from outside, include many Madrasis and Maharashtrians. We have not so far been able to establish any contact with these Pilots but efforts are being made and we hope to succeed soon.

(ix) We have good relations with M.T. walas. They have British officers but are ignorant of 'Nationalism' and Revolution. They take very long time to understand political matters. Besides, the question of bread always hounts them. But we are trying to make the best out of their hatred towards the British Officers. It has often been noticed that our pamphlets or preachings do not carry much weight with them as the talks of their own fellow soldiers. We have, therefore, tried to win over Jemadar, Havaldars and Naiks in every Regiments. They can easily influence soldiers to their point of view. The Jats are very enthusiastic about our work. The Dogras, Brahmins and the State Regiments easily accept our suggestions. Sepoys are keen to hear sensational news. At several places they have expressed desire to come to us. We have already established groups in villages who distribute pamphlets and do propaganda among soldiers while on leave.

B. Punjabi has begun to work. I have hunted up all the workers who were sitting idle and uncoordinated. Sections of Ahrars and Sikhs have come up. Provincial office is fully organised with Ludhiana Sheikhupura, Sialkot, Patiala, Lahore.

Printing of bulletins in Urdu, Gurumukhi and English have been organised. Separate arrangements have been made for propaganda amongst students, Sikhs and Muslims. Army Department has its own publicity arrangement, which published leaflets in five languages. Work in the Army is going on nicely, enclosed report will show how our pamphlets have been received. Army Department has established nine branches.

Gandhiji's fast is servings its own purpose. Lahore responded well. All colleges were closed on the first few days. Now is the time to push on work vigorously.

Sabotage Department has now begun functioning and you will hear something in the coming weeks. Now I am in a position to give you a rough monthly budget for work in Punjab.

According to present calculations, I am not expecting to get more than Rs. 4000/- here per month. So, you should be ready to give us Rs. 8000/- per month. Now when Punjab is coming up, we should work with full vigour. When once Punjab masses take up, Punjab will be in the forefront and it will affect the personnel of the Army all over India.

I have contacted workers in Jammu and work will begin there shortly. For broadcasting a gentleman has offered the materials free. We have only to bear the recurring charges. I have not yet seen them. Next I will be able to tell you in detail about them.

What about those Districts of Punjab that are close to Delhi. I would prefer, if you can arrange, work in them from Delhi. In that please let me know in details what districts I have to leave from my account.

P.S. Situation is developing rapidly and it is going beyond my resources now.

About Sind. If you send me the contacts, I can go there and find out how things are working there.

APPENDIX 'C' TO DMI/4746

Translation of Manuscript Letter in Both Urdu and Gurmukhi Script Found in Forward Area in Arakan

Dear Army Brother,

Today, the 16th February, the Jap Army have brought an Indian soldier named Peyarai of Meerut Dist., No...... Copy ......, ...Regt. On inquiry it was found that on the 14th February he, with Lieut ...., Subedar .... and 15 soldiers went on patrol. He was arrested by the Jap soldiers and sent to me.

According to his statement most of his companions wish for independence and want to join our side. But they are frightened by untrue British propaganda that the Japs used to kill prisoners and for this reason the majority do not come over to our side.

This is just British propaganda. We soldiers of lthe Indian Army were all captured in Malaya and Burma, we have been given Independence and are working an Independant Army to fight for the Independence of India.

You are all come to sacrifice your lives for Rs. 20/- or 25/- a month. For the cruel British you have left your dear parents, brothers, and relations. Do you not know that this cruel government hanged thousands of lovers of their country? Our leaders were sent to jail and bombs were dropped daily on innocent Hindus, who were ill-treated in various ways. It is better for you that you should all sacrifice your lives for the independence of your motherland.

Any brothers, who gets this letter is requested to convey this message to all Hindu, Muslim and Sikh soldiers who come close to us. You can come straightaway without fear after hiding your arms in the jungle. If you bring arms with you the Japs will suspect you to be enemies. The hiden arms will be of use to us very soon. When you come to this side show a white flag and keep your hands up whenever and wherever you meet Jap soldiers. Then tell them to take you to Capt. Mohan Singh, Indian National

Army. The Japs will bring you straightaway to me. Then you will be an independent soldier of the Independent Army under me. Officers will be given their respective ranks.

Brothers, what more am I to write to you. Please take my short letter to be a lengthy and important one as the time is very short. Do not lose this present opportunity. Time is going to be changed very soon or we will be loser.

Get up and wake.

Yours obediently,
Sd/-
Capt. Mohan Singh
Indian National Army.

APPENDIX 'D' TO DMI/4746

Extract from "Security" History of 'X' Battalion

1. The Battalion includes one company of Sikhs (mostly Jat), and one company of Jats.

 The Sikh company first came to Security notice in September 1940 when a reservist, backed by three others, tried to make the wearing of steel helmets a religious questions. One of these reservists had already been noted corresponding with a Sikh N.C.O. who had been imprisoned for playing a leading part in mass desertions of Sikhs from another unit on the eve of its departure overseas. Following on a police report of a statement by a man on leave that secret meetings were held in the unit by subversive elements. Security investigations resulted in seven suspects being removed. While the investigations were in progress three Sikhs (reservists) deserted under suspicious circumstances. There is little doubt that this trouble was linked with Kirti Communist plot, which formed the background to the 3/Ist Punjab desertions, the R.I.A.S.C. mutiny in Egypt, and the C.I.H. mutiny.

2. A close Security watch was kept on the unit and a Sikh N.C.O. was detected receiving Young Communist literature from another Sikh N.C.O. who had been earlier discharged as an undesirable. Except for this minor incident, the Security "clean up" of unit appeared to have been effective, although an ex-Subedar Major came to notice about this time, belonging to the same village as the purveyor of Communist literature, and two notorious Ghadrites who had returned from Fiji. This V.C.O. had left the unit in June 1940 (some three months before the steel helmet trouble) in an apparently disgruntle from of mind as he considered that his services (described by his C.O. as mainly trouble making and intrigue) had not been adequately recognized by Government. A unit report in September 1941 suggested that the influence of this V.C.O. apparently lingered on in the unit.

3. In January 1941 there were three instances of Sikhs receiving sure subversive pamphlets by post, but the C.O. eventually decided that these were "put up" shows, the motive being to obtain discharge. A number of other incidents, connected with the receipt of subversive literature (also a Sikh desertion with arms) occurred between January and June 1941, from when, following the discharge of suspect, no further incidents were reported until the receipt of an anonymous letter by the C.O. in December 1941. This was to the effect that as it was possible that the unit would soon go on service and many men were in debt, they should receive their credits in the Provident Fund in order to enable them to discharge these debts, and that otherwise the men might refuse to go overseas. Actually out of 300 men sent on leave prior to going on service only one failed to return.

4. **Bihar, May 1942.** Five Sikh sepoys deserted one taking his rifle and bayonet. Next day one Jat N.C.O. and four sepoys deserted. No evidence of subversive activities came to light and Jat and Sikh patrols from the unit are said to have done their utmost to apprehend the deserters. About the same time a very large number of letters were received from relatives requesting leave for men on compassionate grounds. Prior to its move to the ARAKAN area in June-July 1942, the Battalion showed a high incidence of sickness.

5. **ARAKAN rear area, July 1942.** A Jat line sentry deserted with arms.

   September 1942. Another Jat desertion with arms and ammunition occurred. Three days later on V.C.O. and seven other "Escapees" from Japanese hands reported to a detachment of the Battalion. The party included one Naik subsequently catogorised as "Grey". The escapees were said to have been immediately handed over to Bde. HQ for interrogation.

   November 1942. Congress agents were reliably reported to have contacted some men of the Battalion in Chittagong and to have been assured that they would join the movement when well advanced. The C.O. and Brigade Comdr. were fully in the picture, but as the unit had moved into the forward area further trouble was not anticipated.

6. **Field Censorship Report:**

   January-February 1943—The unit was specially mentioned as a unit which "as a whole" complained of delays in payments of family allotments.

7. **February 1943**. A patrol from this unit reported that they had found two letters stuck in trees, one in Urdu and the other in Gurmukhi, addressed to Indian troops and signed by Capt. Mohan Singh of the I.N.A. (quoted in Appendix 'C'). The Sepoy mentioned was reported as captured by the enemy on 12th February 1943 east of Rathedaung. He returned from Japanese occupied territory on 7th March, 1943 with the party of possible I.N.A. Personnel, and is now under interrogation.

8. A point which may, or may not, have significance is that one of the I.C.Os who was transfered from the 4/19 Hyderabad Regiment, subsequent to the trouble in that unit in Singapore in July 1940, was posted to 'X' Battalion.

9. A further possible line of investigation which is being followed up, lies in statements recently obtained from a fanatical young Sikh agitator who stated that he has been employed in subversive troops under Subhas Chandra Bose's instructions. One of the units which he claimed to have established contacts is 'X'' Battalion.

APPENDIX 'E' TO DMI/4746

Extracts from a letter from a K.C.I.O.[1] dated 13-3-1943

18th March, 1943

I have already stated that the I.N.A. is not to be feared as a fighting force but purely because of the Psychological effect it may have on the Indian portion of the Army as well as Civil population of this country. When dealing with this problem we must be absolutely clear about certain basic facts. However unpleasant they may be they are realities which must be faced. I say that without being unduly pessimists about this. These facts are as follows:—

(1) Every Indian (soldier included) desires a higher political status for India. The difference is only in degree. The extremists want complete Independence - the moderates Dominion status and the last group will be satisfied with something approaching Dominion status. This produces a feeling of dissatisfaction which does not always or even nearly always amount to disloyalty at present but under certain circumstances it might even develop into disloyalty. This fact is most important and must not be lost sight of.

(2) The second fact is a natural corollary of the first one in that from the point of view of the British every Indian is a possible 5th Columnist (this is difficult to write about). The number of people I have met both official and non-official who indulge in defeatist talk and take up an attitude of indifference about the Japanese menace is alarmingly large.

Indians from the British point of view may be classified into the following three categories:-

Category 1 : Strongly anti-British and some even pro-Japanese. This type are prepared to be actively hostile. They are only

1. K.C.I.O. King's Commissioned Indian Officers usually came from well-to-do families. They had their education in British public schools and later on in the British Military Academy at Sandhurst. They were pro-British in their leanings and some of them joined the I.N.A. with the intention of deserting it at the first opportunity.

a small minority.

Category 2 : Indifferent. They are the type who will adjust themselves to Jap masters if circumstances shape that way. This is the largest group and herein lies real danger.

Category 3 : Strongly pro-British and will fight the invader as readily or even more so than the British. This again is a small group but let us hope not smaller than Category 1

The above classification applies to all Indians, soldiers and civilians. The most dangerous group is Category 2 because it is by far largest group and is composed of people who have not any character (unfortunately a quality whicn is not possessed by the average man in these times). An average Army or civil officer and man would fell into this group. Most of the people here are time servers who will serve any master. Many amongst them are very vocal in their profession of loyalty and devotion to the British. It is an unfortunate fact that they have to be generally speaking accepted at their face value by the British. Loyalty is not quite as general as it believed by Senior British Officers. A number of people are loyal but they will only remain so long as it suits them.

That we have to tell people something about the INA and IIL there is no doubt about it because if we do'nt tell them they will learn about it from other sources, i.e., radio and whispering agents. My own opinion is that we must tell the barest minimum and ensure that the knowledge of these organisations does not give direct or indirect incouragement to the enemies of Britain in India[2].

2. But subsequently it was decided not to give any information about the I.N.A. in all the official correspondence, the use of the word I.N.A. was stopped, instead, it was mentioned as J.I.F.C. (Japanese Inspired Fifth Columnist)

8

Order by Shah Nawaz Khan from Headquarter I.N.A. Bidadari Regarding the Re-Organisation of the I.N.A.[1]

22 March, 1943

Sub.—Policy regarding re-organization of the I.N.A.

Herewith 2 copies of "Policy regarding Re-organization of the I.N.A." for necessary action, please.

(Sd.) Shah Nawaz Khan, Lt.-Col. C.G.S., Office of the D.M.B., I.I.L.

Copy to—

Iwakura Kikan.

Policy regarding Re-organization of the I.N.A.

1. All the formations in the I.N.A. will first re-organize within themselves. Units and sub-units will be completed in strength by a process of amalgamation. Any deficiencies will be made up from the reinforcement camp. These will be demanded as far as possible, as complete units and sub-units. Say, for instance, after re-organization Gandhi Regt. 4th Bn., is deficient of three platoons of Sikhs and one Section of Jats, Comd. Ghandi Regt. will place his demand on the Army Commander, who will forward it to the D.M.B., who, in turn, will place them on the O.C. reinforcements. System of going direct and selecting men from the reinforcement camp is strictly forbidden.

2. Reinforcement camp is being formed as soon as circumstances, permit. All the volunteers for the I.N.A. from prisoners of war camps in Syonan, and from the mainland will be concentrated there and organized on the same basis as the corresponding units of I.N.A.

3. Comd. reinforcement is entirely responsible for the organization, training, disciplines and administration of all such men under his command. He will maintain a complete record of each individual coming to his camp, showing the date of joining, original unit, place from where he came and how finally disposed of.

1. I.N.A. Trial Papers.

4. It is notified for the information of all concerned that owing to the very small number of P.M. and Sikh volunteers coming forward to join the I.N.A., Jat and Gujjar Companies may have to be accepted in their place.

5. Army Commander is requested to forward to these H.Qrs. deficiencies by Regiments, as envisaged by this letter as soon as possible, please.

6. This letter will take effect immediately as no more volunteers are expected to rejoin their units from Separation Camps.

Sd./-
Shah Nawaz Khan,[2]
Lt.-Col. C.G.S.,
Office of the D.M.B., I.I.L.
Syonan, 22/3/1943.

---

2. Lt. Colonel, Shah Nawaz Khan, came from a wealthy Loyal Muslim family of Rawalpindi, whose members had served the British Raj. He was born in1914. After a few years in school, he joined the Prince of Walse Military Academy from where he passed to join the Indian Army in 1935. He went to Singapore in January 1942. Joined the Indian National Army, was devoted to Subhas Chandra Bose and was member of the Provisional Government of India, took command of the 2nd Division of the I.N.A. and fought against the British along with the Japanese. Was tried by the British for Waging War against the king in what is known as I.N.A. Trials, Red Fort. After independence joined the Indian National Congress and served as a Minister.

9

An Appeal by A. Yellapa President I.I.L. Singapore to Indian Youth in Malaya to Come Forward and Fight for the Liberation of India[1]

29 March, 1943

One Organisation, One Leader and One Fight and Our Poorna Swaraj is Assured

Indian comrades must be aware of the official permission granted by the Malai Branch of the Indian Independence League to start the Indian Youth Movement all over Malai as a section of the Indian Independence League. In this connection, we would like to point out to our readers that this is the result of our steady action which some of our self-interested leaders misinterpreted and cried to level charges against people who were not responsible for it at all. Not realising their own shortcomings, that it was indeed the most selfish thing to-supress the youth, who undoubtedly form the backbone of a nation, the members of the Territorial Committee[2], Malai passed the following resolution at a meeting held at Penang some time ago.

"That this committee, having considered a scheme for a youth Movement on which it has been withholding action pending an opportune moment, views with grave concern the attempt that has been made to organize an Indian Youth Movement :—

Comrades there cannot be any better opportune moment than this to organize ourselves and to strength our cause. If any particular committee or section of people neglected us and oppressed us for no reason at all, we are solely to blame, for we relied too much on them and thought that they were sincere in their undertakings. They may be sincere, but definitely

1. *The Young India*, March 29, 1943.
2. This refers to the Territorial Committee, which were formed after the Bangkok Conference with the specific aim of supervising the working of the Indian Independence League within the countries of South-East Asia.

they have proved themselves unworthy, as the resolution clearly indicates. Why should there be any objection for a good work done to strengthen our cause? Why view the move with concern? It matters little, who does it, but if it is for the good of the cause, it should be welcome with satisfaction. Any one who tries to bring in the question of discipline and under its cover seeks for name and fame and self aggrandizement, is deliberately trying to harm the movement.

Our object is to fight our way and purify the activities of the Indian Independence League. Now that permission has been granted, we hope that the youth workers themselves should be very careful, so that they do not become a group of pro-British elements and targets for criticism. Instead, they should organise themselves into a strong and healthy body to fight our way till India is liberated from the yoke of British slavery. We should not deter from our main objective. We will fight till India is free. Our purpose is not to seek name and fame, but to work for the holy cause under one leader.

I thank you for accepting me as the President of the Indian Independence League, Syonan Branch. It is needless for me to emphasize the fact that the President of the I.I.L. Syonan Branch and the members of the Youth Section should understand the seriousness of the mission that we have undertaken and work as one indivisible unit for our deliverance. You all know that the most sincere worker amongest us today is Sri Rash Behari Bose, that great patriot of India and our leader and you also know that he has been and is still striving hard to lead us from darkness to light eternal.

Strong language should not be our strong point. Therefore, in the name of our sacred Mother Country in the name of the thousands of Indian martyrs who had laid down their lives in their struggle for freedom, in the name of our leaders in their struggle for freedom, in the name of India and in the name of those women of India whose brothers, husbands and fathers have undergone untold sufferings as a penalty for their love of freedom let us vow that we will organize ourselves as well-disciplined youths and march forward with Indian National Army for the fulfilment of our Mission under the able leadership of Sri Rash Behari Bose. May the almighty guide us in our struggle.

Yours in service,
A. Yellappa

10

Statement by Rash Behari Bose; Informs about the Revised Plan for the role of the I.I.L. and I.N.A. in the Light of the Resignation of the Members of the Council of Action[1]

5 April, 1943

Owing to a series of "Crises" and resignations, the general public has begun to entertain doubts regarding the Indian Independence Movement.

Our present state of inaction, however, is due to certain weakness inherent in the organisation which has guided the Movement so far. We have to examine the background and the surrounding circumstances under which the old system came into being and I find these factors to be radically changed.

Whereas in June, 1942, India was pressing for Independence from the British, today she is fighting for against Britain, both morally and physically. It was to increase the physically pressure against the British war-effort that Mahatma Gandhi recently risked his very life.

The collapse of the British war-effort would have meant the retreat of the Anglo-American forces now in contact with the Japanese forces on the Indian Border. The extent to which the British forces return is the extent to which Japanese forces advance; and that contact cannot be broken till one side is defeated. What is obvious to us, is obvious to the Indian National Congress. The Congress has considered the consequence and made the choice.

The safeguards and assurance for which we asked in June 1942 are now not necessary. Our aim is only to convert the potential strength of the Congress into an actuality and help the Congress in proclaiming a National Government. The League is NOT a state but only the begetters of a state. The future constitution of India as the relation of the Indian National Government with Japan will be decided by the Congress itself.

1. Indian Independence League Papers, F. No. 45/3 See also S.A. Das and K.B. Subbaiah, **Chalo Delhi**, Kaula Lumpur 1946, pp. 105-108.

In the past we have followed a system of collective responsibility and elections, similiar to that adopted by the Congress in peacetime to wrest political control by a process of Evolution. Our object is Revolution.

In the past the resignation of a member or members has resulted in the dislocation of Vital Departments, Civil or Military. This may be tolerated in peace time but never in time of War.

My immediate concern is to maintain the League as a fighting organisation, so that even if individuals indulge in a process of trial and error, the departments go on discharging their vital functions.

The following interim plan has therefore been drawn up to put the League on a war-footing.

I. Guiding Principles

1. Freedom cannot be won by a universal longing for it.
2. The success of each Branch of the I.I.L. will be judged from the number of young men it can produce, educate and train as potential fighting men for the Independence of India, and not from the numbers of Office bearers who can argue, or resign.
3. No Nation on earth holds a square foot of territory by any right of argument. The frontiers of a country are held by the human effort of the nation.
4. We must in the interests of the Nation, conserve that human effort by avoiding any action showing divison or lack of solidarity.

II. Functions of the League Branches

The Indian Independence Movement is a people's Revolutionary Movement and Not literary Clubs or debating societies. The League Branches, therefore, have three main functions:

1. The Political Awakening of the Masses with a view to producing a body of the patriots with a revolutionary spirit.
2. To obtain the financial and moral support of all those who cannot take active part in the movement.
3. To undertake due share of social uplift and relief work without getting involved in local Administrative problems.

To give concrete shape to Item No. 1, a Youth Section will be started immediately on receipt of this communication.

A women's section with its own President is to be started wherever practicable.

A Movement for boys and girls under 17 will also be started. In all National Schools Hindustani will be taught, patriotic songs will be sung and significance of daily saluting of National Flag will be taught. (Uniform same as Seva Samiti in India, i.e., Boy Scout or Girl Guide Uniform with Tricolour Scarf).

To body of spirited young people so produced will help in the other two activities of the League.

III. Naujavan Section (Youth Section)

Object: To train Indian Youths in East Aisa to:

1. Become revolutionary soldiers in the fight for India's Independence.
2. Behave as free citizens who with their example will foster the spirit of independence among the inhabitants of occupied territories.

It is suggested that where the Vice-Presidents of the Local Branches are willing to serve the National cause actively they themselves may take over the Youth Section otherwise suitable young men will be appointed by the presidents concerned.

Syllabus : The following is issued as a guide. Time Tables and period of training will, of course, vary according to the facilities in each centre.

(i) Elementary Drill and Route Marches.

Weapon training, Rifle, Pistol, Grenade

(I.N.A. Japanese side have consented to provide staff to work at different centres).

Relief Work: Nursing, Stretchers bearing, First Aid, A.R.P. Hygeine.

Meeting: National and Social Dreams.

Bicycle trips to places 30 or 40 miles away cooking of own food.

(ii) Physical Training and Labour. Building of Wooden Bridge, swimming, digging slit trenches, rowing and games.

(iii) Education: Teaching of Hindustani.

Significance of the War of Greater East Asia.

Geography, topography, maps with special reference to India.

Weak points in British War organisation and Civil administration in India.

History of British aggression in India.

Study of lives of Congress Leaders.

Study of Nippon-government will be encouraged.

(iv) National Discipline: Obey before you command. Building of character, self reliance, right living, right thinking, love for country. Ordinary Military discipline, Punctuality.

(v) National Culture : Common manners and customs. Army salute. Common good, common dress, Khaki shorts or trousers, rubber shoes with shirts. Head dress, Khaki Gandhi cap with double fold. Tricolour rectangle 5" × 2" on the left arm.

Note. Women's and Boys' and Girls' sections will choose suitable subjects from the above syllabus.

Organisation

As the Youth Movement is the potential reserve for the Indian National Army, the League "Naujawan Sections" will adopt similar organisation.

Unit of 10 .... Section
4 Sections .... Platoons
4 Platoons .... Company
5 Companies .... Battalion
3 Battalion .... Regiment.
3 Regiments .... Formation.

For the present each Branch should aim at a maximum of one Company at the discretion of the Territorial President. The training will be the entire responsibility of the League Branch and should be carried out on the most economical line, e.g., those who can afford should be encouraged to meet their own expenses. (The Naujawan Section is a popular Movement run on the lines of the Boy Scout Movement).

A tour inspection will be arranged by this headquarters during the month of April.

Training Centres for Youth Workers

In order to start a really strong youth movement a nucleus of trained workers is necessary.

An experimental school for training 50 such workers will be started at Syonan (Azad Institute Syonan) with effect from the 1st April, 1943.

The first course will last for two months at the end of which these trained workers will be available for posting to various centres.

A infiltration course for 100 young men from all territories will start on the 1st May, 1943, at the Swaraj Institute, Penang. Duration three months. From among the present Graduates from the Swaraj Institute Penang, some will be selected by this Headquarters for immediate posting as trained workers for the Youth Sections in various Branches.

The Burma Branch is running its own training centre at Rangoon on the lines of the Azad Institute Syonan. Military Staff has been borrowed from the Burma Detachment of the I.N.A.

Pocket Money

Pocket money at the rate of S. 800 will be given to all students at the Azad School. Syonam and the Swaraj Institute, Penage, as well as to the civil volunteers at the training school at Kuala Lumpur. Rations and uniforms will be free.

Military Training

The main centre of civilian volunteers for the training as regular soldiers is at present at Kuala Lumpur.

Duration of Course

Four months.

1000 volunteers will be ready for absorption in the I.N.A. by the end of May.

Recruiting will be done through the Branches of the League from their Youth Sections. The Malaya Branch can apply to this Headquarters for Medical Officers when required. The Burma and Thailand Branches can obtain assistance from the I.N.A. Detachment of Indian Army detachments stationed there.

In view of the limited training staff and the expenditure involved. NOT more than 5000 recruits can be trained at one time. If accommodation is available the Kuala Lumpur school will be expensed to accommodate these 5000. Otherwise more centres will be opened to accommodate that number.

The following approximate numbers should be kept ready by the middle of May.

Thailand	1000
Burma	1000
Malaya	1000
Hong -Kong and Shanghai	1000
Borneo and Sumatra	1000
Java, Philippines, Celebes	1000
	6000

All Branches will please estimate and inform this Headquarters of the number of recruits likely to be forthcoming from their territories during the year 1943.

Finance

The present scheme for actual military training throughout East Asia for the next 1¼ year is for 20,000 volunteers to be trained in four batches. Ultimate object is to train maximum number available in East Asia.

Syllabus

1. Preliminary training with the object of becoming tough guerrilla fighters :–
2. Drill. Physical training (P. T.) Route Marches, Weapons (Rifle, Bayonet, Tommy Gun, Pistol, Bombs and Hand Grenades).
3. General spiritual training, i.e., making them proud of themselves as Indians and determined to achieve and maintain the freedom of their country.

Training Staff

For a batch of 1000 volunteers the following are required.

Major	1	Medical Officer	1
Captains	2	Asst. M. O.	1
Subalterns	3	Asst. M. O.	1
N.C.O.s	20	Nursing Ord	5
Sepoys	100	Clerks	4
	126	Amb. N. C. O.	1
		Total	139

These have been seconded for duty with the Volunteers by the Indian National Army.

Absorption in the I.N.A.

(a) Headquarters, I.N.A.

(b) Guerilla Regiments
(c) Special Service Group
(d) Intelligence Group

With their civil experience these volunteers will be more useful in these rather than in the Field force Group.

(e) Reinforcement Group

(f) Field Force Group...

It is obvious that all cannot be absorbed in the I.N.A. owing to the limited number of arms now available. Some of the remainder will either go to other schools such as the officers. Training School or the Civil Administration School (See below) or go back as fully trained instructors for training the youths in each territory in East Asia. The names of all trained personnel will be put on the list of reserve volunteers to be called up when required.

The system is analogous to the conscription system obtaining in other countries.

Other Activities of League

It is proposed to start the following institutions as soon as accommodation and staff is available.

1. Officers' Training School

For the training of future officers of the Indian National Army. Vacancies will be allotted both to the Civilians being trained at Kuala Lumpur and to candidates from the Indian National Army.

2. Staff College

For the higher training of senior officers of the I.N.A.

3. Civil Administration School

For the political training of officers both civil and military. The civilian will be chosen from among students of the various training institutes. Special cases can be recommended by the Territorial Presidents.

Reorganisation of Headquarters.

In order to cope with the immediate task in hand the following interim organisation of the headquarters came into from w.e.f. 1.4.43 when headquarters will be established at Road, Syonan.

11

British Assessment of the Indian National Army and its Activities[1] (Extract)

17 April, 1943

6. Recent information shows that a Gurkha O. R., who was taken prisoner during the Burma campaign early in 1942 and was in Japanese hands for over six months, volunteered for "contact work" in Burma, in the course of which he rejoined our forces at Magwe with other fifth column volunteers. Subsequently he deserted, taking with him a Jamadar and two O. Rs., who had been persuaded to join the enemy by one of the G.O.R 's fifth column companies. He then surrendered to the Japanese and again joined a fifth column party at Yunangyang and accompanied it to Mandalay and Maymyo. Later he returned to Rangoon, where he was detailed to form one of a fifth column party which left for India at the end of August 1942, with instructions to collaborate with Congress workers and help them in destroying communications, dumps, etc.

7. This account of the G.O.R.'s history since first being taken prisoner by the Japanese is believed to be substantially true. It is the first definite instance which has so far come to notice of the success of a Japanese–inspired "contact party" in Burma in winning over men from our forces in the field. Incidentally, although most of the personalities involved in this episode were Gurkhas, this does not invalidate the conclusions reached in paragraph 3 of Survey No. 13 of 1943. where the reactions of Gurkhas to I.N.A. propaganda were discussed. It is perhaps significant that neither the G.O.R., the successful propagandist who accompanied him, nor any of the soldiers who were seduced from their loyalty in this affair came from Nepal. The two Japanese agents are line boys from Almora and Dharmasala respectively, the Jamadar is also a Dharmsala lineboy, while one of the O. Rs. is a Darjeeling Gurkha and the other a Dogra.

---

1. Military Department F. No. L/WS/1/1576. India office Library and Records, London.

8. In addition to the above report, it is known that fifth column parties consisting of men from a Sikh Regiment and from the Burma Army also returned to the Japanese after being sent out on contact work among Indian Troops during the first Burma campaign, thus demonstrating the success achieved by the original contact party which set to work from Prome.

9. There is evidence from the Arakan front that the enemy has already attempted to use his fifth column tactics against Indian troops, easing his approach on the I.N.A. principle. In March 1943 attempts to suborn the loyalty of Indian Troops in forward areas took the form of notices in Urdu and Gurmukhi signed by Captain Mohan Singh, stuck at trees where they would be found by our patrols; leaflets have also been dropped by Japanese aircraft, one of them being headed "Singapore– the cradle of Indian Army revolt" exhorting Indian soldiers to join hands with their "comrades from Malaya". Sikh and Punjabi battle–cries were heard during an enemy attack, and voices called to our troops in Indian vernaculars; there is also reason to believe that "contact parties" were assisting in the interrogation of prisoners and in efforts to persuade them to join the I.N.A.

10. In this connection it was recently discovered that one of the I.N.A. leaders had advised the Japanese that suitable Indian prisoners taken in Arakan should be given immediate instructions and propaganda treatment and returned to the British lines as quickly as possible. In this way it was hoped that they would rejoin their units so rapidly that they might appear merely to have got temporarily separated during action, and would not be suspected of having been in enemy hands. As an example of these instructions being put into effect, it is interesting to learn that three I.O. Rs., who were taken prisoner by the Japanese early in March, were released to spread anti-British propaganda only a fortnight later. One of these prisoner had a pass signed on behalf of the Iwakuru Kikan, certifying that he was employed by that organization and asking all concerned to afford him the necessary facilities to enable him to carry out his task. This is the first known instance of Indian prisoners taken on the Arakan front being released for propaganda purposes. These men are being interrogated.

12

Welcome Address by A. Yellappa at the I.I.L. Conference at Singapore; Emphasis the Need for Activating the I.I.M. and put it on War Footing[1]

27 April, 1943

Mr. Presidents, Delegates from East Asia and Friends,

On behalf of Indians of Syonan–I welcome you all to this city and I hope you will kindly forgive me for having delayed the proceedings for about half an hour. The rain in the morning upset all our programme.

Now, we have a Conference in Bangkok some time in June last year. Since then the events in India have changed. As you all know in India the British have rejected our "Quit India" policy. They are murdering our Brothers and sisters in numbers, machine–gunning them. It is our duty, Gentleman, to find out ways and means to revolutionise the Indian Independence Movement. It is no use having a democratic Constitution and having discussions on the Constitution. It is now for us to revolutionise this Movement and put the whole thing on a war footing.

We have heard, Gentleman, General Iwakuro, who came here on the 25th, and again he came in our midst yesterday and he has been repeating the same thing. He told us last time that we must have the spirit of sacrifice. We must have a sense of unity and we must make up our minds and find out where we stand. And he also said that among Indians there are some people who are real workers, some are half and some a quarter. But I can assure you Gentlemen, that every Indian, whether he is from the North, South or any part of India, every Indian wants to be free. It is the instinct of every human being to be free but the methods to be adopted differ,. Some may be longing to be free, some want to be free but want somebody else to do the work and some are real workers. We are not going into any discussion into these things, but our President will address you at length.

1. I.I.L. Papers. F. No 45/3.

My humble submission is this that we have today gathered here on a very important mission, that is to find out ways and means to put the whole Movement on a war footing. We are not fighting, Gentlemen, for leadership, we are not fighting as to who should be the leader and who should be sub–leaders, "We are fighting for a cause, and today we have only one leader, that is Sri Ras Behari Bose (Applause) and unless and until we have complete faith in him, and we are prepared to work with him there is no use having conferences. If we are not satisfied with something or other, it is for us to approach him and tell him—he is always amenable to reason and he is always approachable—and I do not want to waste your time by saying more. At this Conference today, we have a Subjects Committee meeting. The President will tell you the programme.

I thank you all for having come to this city and honoured us.

13

Opening Address by Rash Behari Bose at the I.I.L. Conference; Appeals to the Delegates to Join Hands for Achieving Indian Independence with Japanese Help

27 April, 1943

Comrades and Countrymen,

It is with mingled feelings of joy and regret that we are meeting today to discuss ways and means for the liberation of our Motherland. This is the third time within a short period of one year that we are meeting for one and same purpose. I used the words "feelings of joy and regret" – joys because our enemy is being consistently defeated by the Imperial Nippon forces and thus the British Chain of Imperialism which is strangling India is being weakened daily and our hopes of Independence are brightening; regret, because the actions of some of my colleagues have marred temporarily the speedy progress of our Movement. But with the help of Almighty God all the difficulties have been overcome, the whole Movement has been rejuvenated and placed on a more solid ground than hitherto and I can assure you that if I continue to receive your full support and co-operation our success is at hand.

Before going any further I shall repeat my words of warning in the very opening chapter of my speech at the Bangkok Conference. I wish to reiterate the same words, as I hope that it will not be necessary for us to meet again before the liberation of India. I said thus: However, if I have obeyed your command and taken this chair in spite of my knowledge of the intricacies of the problems that may confront me. I have been prompted to do so by my great faith in your spirit of co-operation and your sincere desire to put your heads together and to come to useful decisions without wasting much of your time on unnecessary discussions and arguments. I was prompted by the experience of the Tokyo Conference to give those words of warning but, despite all that, the result of the deliberations of the

1. I.I.L. Papers F. No. 45/3. See also K.S. Giani, *op. cit* pp. 140-142.

Bangkok Conference is well known to you. To remedy the short-comings of the last Conference, it has been necessary for me to call you the representatives of different territories in East Asia, and also the representatives of the Indian National Army. Let us put our heads together once again and work out a plan which should be very short and effective in our organisation and the progress of the Movement. It is a time for action and not words, so you must avoid all lengthy arguments and jugglery of words. Before working out a plan you must remember two points, (a) that Japan is at war and we can expect only what can conventionally be given to us because their needs are above ours and (b) we are preparing to get into action very soon, so the constitution should be as brief and simple as possible.

I do not wish to take up much of your time by reading out to you the history of the Indian Independence Movement, but I would like to mention a few facts which should always be remembered by every Indian. The foundation of Indian Independence was laid in 1857 when the most ruthless policies of the British resulted in a catastropic breakdown in the social and economic life of the Indians and the dissatisfaction of the people against British domination finally reached the bursting point when almost the whole country revolted to oust the British from India. This battle for Indian independence was described by the British as the Indian Mutiny. But was that a mutiny? I say NO, it was a holy war against the inhuman treatment of Indians by the British. It failed because there was no capable leader to lead the Movement to a success. Six thousand of our compatriots were hanged just because they were asking for their birthright. But since that day the seeds of Swaraj have been nourished by the blood of thousands of our beloved and respected leaders. Just a few days ago mass meetings were held in all the territories in East Asia in memory of the martyrs of Jalianwala Bagh. Let us pay respect to the memory of all those numberless known and unknown comrades who laid down their lives in the cause of their Motherland. The time is fast approaching when in every city and town in India we shall find a worthy monument erected in their memory so that posterity will pay homage to them and look upon them with pride.

You all know that great changes have taken place both in and outside India since the Bangkok Conference last year and so it is essential that we should also speed up our activities to keep pace with the progress of world events. You all know that the "Quit India" resolution was passed by the Congress Committee in the presence of Mahatma Gandhi on 8th August last year, and immediately after the meeting of Congress Committee,

Mahatma Gandhi and the President of the Congress, Maulana Abdul Kalam Azad and all the other leaders were imprisoned. It was then that the active struggle of unarmed people commenced against the armed forces of Britain. Thousands upon thousand have been thrown into prisons. Defenceless people have been shot dead and they are still being murdered daily. Villages have been bombed and machine-gunned and the properties of the innocent confiscated. But the war continues unabated and it will continue until India is free. It is therefore imperative that we should do our bit at this end to lighten the burden of our compatriots at home. Now is the time for action and not for talk. Our people are suffering under the tyrannical rule of the British in India and it is the duty of every Indian in the East to be ready to sacrifice his all when the call of his country comes.

Friends, The War of Greater East Asia is a gift from God for us Indians and every day which follows, looks brighter for Indians. Practically all the Far East has been cleared of the Anglo–Saxon races and their allies and it will not be long before India will also rank among the Free nations of the world. I have been working in Japan for decades so I can see that Japan is in a position to stand by the oppressed Asians and to liberate Asia. I was anxiousty awaiting the day when Japan would fully realizing the great significance of creating a free and united Asia and would feel convinced that it was in the interests of Japan itself, as also for the rest of Asia if not for the world as a whole, that the octopus grip of the Anglo-Saxon Imperialism in the East must be destroyed root and branch.

I was fully convinced that Japan alone was in a position to take the honour. I knew well that she was not in the habit of taking any serious steps unless she had fully weighed her strength and was convinced of her success. The ultimate result of her action is well known to you all. Realizing the full significance of the situation, China joined hand with Japan and declared war on the Anti-Axis powers. Japan on the other hand as a true friend took the lead and relinquished her extra-territorial rights in China which was consequently followed by all other friendly nations. The dream of Dr. Sun Yat Sen, the father of China, has been realised through the help and co-operation of Japan.

Another important happening since the Bangkok Conference is the declaration made by His Excellency General Hideki Tojo, the Premier of Japan, promising Burmese people their independence within this year. One cannot over-emphasis the good intention of Japan towards all Asiatic people and the case of Burma is an outstanding example my brothern in Burma on this very auspicious occasion.

Let us not forget that the greatest living Indian, Mahatma Gandhi who undertook twenty-one days first, partly to inspire the Indian masses to redouble their fight against the British and partly to disclose the most heinous of crimes committed by the inhuman British against the unarmed and defenceless people in India. To survive a fast of twenty-one days in a prison at the age of 74 is in my mind no less than a miracle. Mahatma Ji scored a great moral victory over the British. Let us pray that God may spare him long and lead us to success.

I am proud to say that the Indian National Army has been re-established on more solid and firm foundation and when the time comes, your comrades-in-arm will fight to the last men in the cause of their country. They deserve our great respect for the service is still awaiting our decision. No one can doubt the bravery of our soldiers in a righteous fight for a rightous cause. Our sympathy goes to the families and friends of those Indian soldiers who erroneously believed that they were fighting for a right cause and lost their lives in Africa and Asia. They have been misled by the same propaganda of lies by the British which is responsible for the tinge of suspicion in the minds of so many of us.

I bow my head to the bravery of our soldiers and we should have no doubt that with their whole-hearted support we are going to win our final fight against British Imperialism. Let us stand shoulder to shoulder and let us march hand in hand to success.

Another important activity of the League was the creation of the Bharat Youth Training Centre at Kuala Lumpur where almost a thousand civilians are being given advanced training in the military art by the members of the Indian National Army. The existing camp is more on an experimental basis than a regular training camp. It is anticipated that when necessity arises for the training of the mass youth volunteers in East Asia for active service as part and parcel of the Indian National Army, the existising centre at Kuala Lampur will be greatly extended and a few more centres will be opened to meet the requirements of the Army at convenient localities. Plans for such establishments are under ways and it is expected to start the work in the near future. I hope Indians in East Asia will be ready to come forward as volunteers and will undergo the necessary military training under the capable hands of the members of the Indians National Army to make themselves fit to serve the cause of their country. I want to congratulate the youths now undergoing military training at Kuala Lumpur for their sense of sacrifice, patriotism and their love for their Motherland. I appeal to all able-bodied Indians in East Asia to follow the example of these brave and true nationalists.

You all know that youth is the cream of a nation and as such Indian Youth is the cream of Mother India. I am very glad to say that I am greatly moved by their enthusiasm and resolute determination to make any sacrifice demanded of them for the victory of our battle for freedom. Youth has always played a great and noble part in all revolutionary movements. And in the great Indian revolution it is the youth of the country that is playing a most significant role. Youth is impulsive, daring, resourceful, determined and ready for any sacrifices; and it is to the youth of India that Mother India looks for actions—decisive action that will break the shackles of British Imperialism. It is self sacrificing courage of India's young freedom fighters that has reduced the British power in India to sheer importance. And it is the united effort of the youth of India that will bring victory and glory to our Motherland. It was thus imperative to create a Youth Section of the Indian Independence League all over East Asia. This important section is the nucleous of the Indian Independence Movement and is the main reservoir for supply of manpower for India's National Army. They will be the warriors of Indian Freedom and in this great battle before us there is no distinction between civilian and military. We are all Indians, we are all freedom fighters and together we shall march to liberate our sacred Motherland. Azad School has been opened for the training of fifty young Indians and all those who are found fit after an extensive course of two months will be distributed as instructors for the training of the youths of the country. I congratulate all those who have been selected for training and welcome all others who are prepared to fight in the cause of Indian Freedom.

Last but not least I would like to mention the creation of the Women's Section of the Indian Independence League. It is highly significant that our sisters are taking keen interest in this Movement and are prepared to make any sacrifices side by side with their Indian brothers in the case of their Motherland. Freedom lies at the feet of a mother. Mother make heroes. Mother produce martyrs. It is through the encouragement of mothers that the youths of a country make sacrifice. Mothers are the backbones of a country's nationalism. They are the inspiration of the masses and the encouragement of the desperate.

I appeal to you my friends who have come to participate in this Conference, to divorce all party-feelings, suspicious and prejudices and make every effort, so that when you conclude your session you have a most effective and workable plan of action for Indian freedom, so that we can start our work immediately after this conference and march ahead. I hope you have realised the shortcomings of the last two Conferences and will keep aside all old and complicated ideas which are nothing mere than mere obstacles in the progress of this revolutionary movement and will work out a simple and straight forward plan which will leave no room for future disturbance. This is a revolution and there is an international conflagration all round us and I know you will all agree there is no time for discussion and argument. So I advise you once again to sit down and the create something which will revolutionize the whole Movement. The masses are iching for action but our existing constitution is so cumbersome and impracticable that we cannot move an inch. All plans should be made on the basis of self sufficiency because this is our Movement and the major part of it should be workable by us.

In the name of four hundred million starving Indians for whom you have pledged to lay down your life, I appeal to you once again to create the atmosphere of brotherhood, trust each other and have mutual understanding far this common end of ours. Your plan of action should be such that, as for as possible, only full time workers could be permitted to function—people who will be ready to make decisions day and night and from day to day, people who should be ready to serve anywhere and in any capacity, people who will be ready to bear all personal inconveniences of sleeping on the ground, going without food, and travelling on foot or travelling by whatever conveyance may be available. Every League Branch should be so constructed and organised that every worker from the Chairman downward should, as far as possible, be a full time self-sacrificing person who should be prepared to bear all hardships and should be prepared to work in the firing line when called upon to do so. Every League official should try to undergo a complete course of military training. May God help you in your efforts.

Finally I thank the Japanese Government on behalf of the Indians in East Asia for extending every facility and co-operation in every part of the occupied territories to my countrymen. But for Japan's whole-hearted support in the cause of Indian Freedom, it would not have been possible to achieve what has so far been achieved.

I also sincerely acknowledge the friendly attitude of all the allied governments and their people and take this opportunity of thanking them for their co-operation and assistance in the cause of our Country's Freedom.

14

Iwakuro's Speech at the I.I.L. Conference Clarifies Japanese Policy Towards the I.I.M. and Congratulates the Delegates for Re-organising the I.I.L. and I.N.A.[1]

27 April, 1943

Because of the situation that has considerably changed since the Bangkok Conference which was held in June, 1942, and in order to meet the existing circumstances, you have decided to convene a meeting of all the representatives from the various territories in the East Asia in order to lay down the guiding principles anew for the Movement, and I certainly consider that the action taken by you is indeed an appropriate one. Let me offer you my hearty congratulations and express my most sincere wishes for your success.

The Greater East Asia War has developed and has reached a final and decisive stage and the whole world is absorbed in this desparate struggle. Unless we win this war, that is the Greater East Asia war, it is more than obvious that all Asiatic peoples, all Asiatic races cannot be emancipated from the bondage of the Anglo-American tyrants; and if we fail in bringing about freedom of the Asiatic racess, I am sure, that the independence of India will be doomed into the same fate.

The reasons why Nippon is offering her unstinted support for the Movement are as follows:

1. India is one of the fellow Nations in Asia.
2. Her struggle to drive out the Anglo-American influence from India falls in line with the aim of our Greater East Asia War, and thus Anglo-Americans are our common enemies in the fullest sense of the expression.
3. Through cultural relations and Buddhism, we, Nipponese, have had traditional respect and affection for India, for more than 2000 years

1. *Ibid.*

and it has indeed been unbearable to us to see the present slavery that India is undergoing under the rule of Great Britain.

Needless to say, His Excellency Premier General Tojo's several declarations have been based on these very sentiments. It therefore goes without saying that Nippon has no desire to control India in place of Britain. Nippon has no ulterior motive whatsoever in India, politically, militarily or economically.

Let me recall the events of the past year. It is regrettable that certain sections of the Indian Community have been responsible for impairing the harmonious relations that have existed between us and the Indian Community. I cannot help but notice that there is also a certain section of the Indian Community who deliberately misconstrued our intentions. You will not blame me if I feel that we have been more than insulted. However, I am sure, that these people form only a small section of the Indian Community.

Such people's misunderstandings can be attributed to the following reasons:

1. They know nothing about Nippon and the Nipponese people.
2. They do not possess a correct knowledge of China and Manchukua.
3. Some people have misunderstood our temporary measures.

   You know we are fighting an enormous War and we have taken many emergency measures and some people have mistaken such temporary measures to be permanent measures.
4. There are many who are being misleading the enemies fabricated propaganda.

We have been trying to clear such misunderstanding with the utmost patience. However, I feel that our patience has already been exhausted and it is high time that we should draw a clear line between those who are anxious to co-operate with us for the achievement of our common goal and those who are disinclined to do so.

There are three categories of people:

1. Those who are anxiously desiring the Independence of India and require our assistance believing in our sincerity. They are our friends and fellow workers. To such friends we most certainly will not stint any kind of assistance and support.
2. Those who cannot yet liquidate their pro-British feelings or those still entertaining doubts about Nippon's sincerity or those who are

not satisfied with the present policy of Nippon. Such people should be considered as elements of more or less of enemy nature and such people should be treated accordingly.

3. Those who are still wavering and playing the game of "Wait and See". In my opinion such people should also be treated in the same manner or those of hostile nature.

I firmly believe that the Indian Independence League and the Indian National Army are organised and managed by only such people as those belonging to the first category. I trust that the League at this Conference consisting of representatives of such people should lay down new guiding principles and so reform the League as to make it perfectly workable in true co-operation with us which, of course, must be based on mutual trust.

I wish you again every success.

15

Proceedings of the I.I.L. Conference held at Singapore in April 1943 to Revive the Indian Independence Movement (I.I.M.) after the Resignation of the Members of the Council of Action. Reaffirms the Resolution Earlier Passed at Bangkok and the New Constitution of Indian Independence League[1]

27 April, 1943

Indian Independence League Conference of Delegate From East Asia Held at Syonan

Plenary Session

The meeting started with the singing of Vande Matram and a National Song by Indian Girls. Major General Iwakuro then addressed the gathering. The Chairman of the Reception Committee, Sri A. Yellappa made a speech welcoming the delegates. The President, Sri Rash Behari Bose, then delivered his Presidential address. After the speech was over he said that he wished to nominate the following gentleman to form the Subjects Committee.

1. Dr. Lukshumeyah
2. Dr. Majumdar
3. Sri B. A. Mallal
4. Sri K. A. Narayanan
5. Sri J. A. Thivy
6. Sri A. Yellappa
7. Sri B. Prasad
8. Sri D. Pandey
9. Sri Mahtani
10. Sri A. M. Nair

1. *Ibid.*

11. Sri D. N. Khan
12. Lt Col. Bhonsle
13. Lt Col. Kiani
14. Lt Col. Loganathan

Dr. Lukshumeyah spoke reiterating the confidence of the gathering in Sri Rash Behari Bose and requested the delegates to accept the proposal. The Committee nominated was unanimously approved. The President then announced that the Subjects Committee would not meet at 2.30 p.m. as shown in the programme but would meet at 10.30 a.m. on the 28th.

Copies of some draft resolutions were distributed to the members of the subjects committee and the meeting ended.

Resolutions
(Syonan 28.4.1943)

Whereas it is the objective of the War of Greater East Asia to destroy for over the British and American Imperialism in Asia and thus emancipate the Asiatic people from Anglo-American yoke; and

Whereas it gives an opportunity for India as an Asiatic country to realise the goal of complete independence ; and

Whereas the representatives of the Indians in East Asia hold conference at Tokyo and Bangkok in March and June 1942 respectively and resolved that the object of the Indian Independence Movement shall be the complete independence of India free from any foreign control or interference of any nature whatsoever; and

Whereas in conformity with such resolution and for the carrying out of that objective a written Constitution of the Indian Independence League was framed as a result of the resolutions passed thereat; and

Whereas the Indian Independence Movement has been organised all over East Asia in accordance with the resolutions passed at the above said Conference; and

Whereas now the British Government in India has rejected the "Quit India" demand of the Indian Nation and has thrown Mahatma Gandhi and other revered leaders of India into prison and is pursuing an inhuman policy of mass murders and wholesale arrests throughtout India and is perpetrating such atrocities as the bombing and machine-gunning of innocent and defenceless population of India; and

Whereas the Anglo-American forces in India are deliberately using India as a base of operations in their war to perpetrate the Anglo-American exploitation of Asiatic Nations; and

Whereas the objective of the War of Greater East Asia cannot be achieved unless the Anglo-American forces of aggression in India are annihilated; and

Whereas the conference of Indians in East Asia records its profound conviction that a state of emergency exists and that therefore nothing short of direct and immediate military action against the Anglo-American forces in India would help the Indian Nation to achieve its goal of complete Independence of India.

This Conference therefore to meet the existing circumstances and in conformity with the wishes of the Indians in East Asia passes the following resolutions to take the place of Bangkok Resolutions of 1942.

1. That this Conference reaffirms that the complete independence of India free from any foreign control or interference of any nature whatsoever is the object of this Indian Independence Movement as it is that of the Indian National Congress, and resolves that the Indian Independence Movement shall be guided by the principles indicated below:

   (a) That Unity, Faith, Sacrifice, shall be the motto of the Indian Independence Movement.

   (b) The Movement should be carried out in a revolutionary manner including military action.

   (c) That India be considered as One, and indivisible.

   (d) That all activities of this Movement be on a National basis and not Sectional, Communal or religious basis.

   (e) That the framing of the future constitution of India be only by the representatives of the Indians in India.

   (f) That the sympathy, co-operation and support of Japan is essential for securing the object of this Movement, namely, the Independence of India.

2. That the Indian Independence League owes allegiance to India.

3. That the Indian National Army is the army of the Indian Independence League and all officers and men of the Indian National Army as well as members of the Indian Independence League shall over allegiance to the League.

4. That this conference reiterates the true significance of the National Flag of India, the correct interpretation of the elements of the Flag being a follows:

Saffron—Courage and Sacrifice
White—Peace and Truth
Green—Faith and Chivalry
Chakra—Home of the masses

5. That for the purpose of financing the Indian Independence Movement the President, Indian Independence League, East Asia, be authorised to raise funds from Indians in East Asia.

6. That the entire Indian Independence Movement be placed on a War Footing immediately and that the Constitution of the Indian Independence League be so altered as to enable it to discharge its vital war duties with the utmost speed and efficiency, and

7. That this conference resolves that the written Constitution of the Indian Independence League passed at a Conference in Bangkok of Indians in East Asia in June, 1942, be amended and that the written Constitution approved and passed herein be adopted in its place.

8. That this Conference adopts the following Constitution for the Indian Independence League organisation.

9. Constitution Of The Indian Independence League—(Passed at a Conference in Syonan-to of Indians in East Asia in April, 1943 (2603) when the written Constitution passed at a Conference in Bangkok of Indians in East Asia in June 1942 (2602) was amended.)

   (i) This Act may be cited as the Constitution of Indian Independence League in East Asia.

   (ii) In this Act:

   "President" shall mean the present President of the Indian Independence League in East Asia, Sri Rash Behari Bose or his successors.

   "Chief Executive" shall mean the President.

   "Headquarters" shall mean the Office of the President.

   "Territories" shall include:

   Japan and Manchukuo

   Phillipines.

   Thailand.

   Malai.

   Burma.

Borneo Celebes.

Hong Kong, Canton and Macao.

Other parts of China including Shanghai.

Indo-China.

Djawa.

Sumatra.

Andamans.

(iii) The Indian Independence League shall consist of :—

(a) A Chief Executive (President)

(b) Council of Action

(c) War Council

(d) Territorial Committees

(e) Local Branches

(iv) Local Branches

(a) Local Branches of the Indian Independence League may be formed at a public meeting of Indians in any locality who shall elected committee. The President may nominate a Chairman from among the Committee Members.

(b) Vacancy or vacancies on such Committee or in the office of the Chairman shall be filled up by the Territorial Chairman with the approval of the President.

(c) All Indians above the age of 18 shall be entitled to be members of such Branch on compliance with the Rules framed from time to time by the Committee subject to the Approval of the President.

(d) No such Branch shall be recognised as a Branch unless the President accords and continues to accord to such Branch due recognition; provided, however, that all Branches of the Indian Independence League now in existence and recognised in the various territories in East Asia shall until otherwise decided upon by the President be recognised by the Indian Independence Movement.

(v) Territorial Committee—Representatives elected by the Committee of the Local Branches in each territory shall form as Territorial Committee for the effective working of the

Movement within the territory, subject to the approval of the President. The President shall nominate the Chairman of the Territorial Committee.

(vi) The Territorial Committee in each territory shall supervise and control the work of the Movement within its territory through its Chairman, subject to the approval of the President.

(vii) Chief Executive. (President)—The President shall be the Head of the Indian Independence League in East Asia and shall have powers to nominate his own successor. The successor or successors of the person nominated by the President shall be elected by the Council of Action and the War Council.

(viii) The President will formulate ways and means for the effective carrying out of the policy laid down at this Conference and shall deal with all new matters that may arise from time to time and which may not be provided for by this Conference and his decision shall in every case be final and binding on each and every member of this Indian Independence Movements.

(ix) For the proper and efficient carrying out of the work, the President shall have power to create as many departments as are necessary and expedient and to appoint and dismiss Administrative Officers and staff whenever he deems fit so to do.

(x) The President shall have power to alter, amend or rescind any previous decisions made by him, including any decision arrived at in this Conference.

(xi) The President shall have general superitendence and control over all Branches of the Indian Independence League in all territories and over the Indian Independence Army.

(xii) The President shall decide the military policy in consultation with the War Council.

(xiii) War Council—War Council will consist of the President, Director of Military Bureau, the Army Commander whenever available and one or more advisers nominated by the President as the exigencies of the situation may require.

(xiv) Council Of Action—The President will nominate two or more members, who and the President will constitute a Council of Action. The members of the Council of Action as nominated by the President will functions only in an advisory capacity and will give advice as and when required by the President.

(xv) Head Quarters—The Headquarters of the Movement shall be at any such place as may be decided upon by the President from time to time.

10. That this Conference pays its humble homage to the countless Indian patriots who have laid down their lives in India's war of independence in and out of India and expresses its deep admiration for the heroic fight now being waged by the Indians against the Anglo-American armies of occupation in India.

11. That this Conference expresses its sincere gratification at the war policy of Nippon and conveys to the Imperial Government its best wishes for the continued successes of the Imperial Japanese Armed forces, and records its grateful appreciation of the various Declarations and pronouncements as made by His Excellency General Hideki Tojo, the Premier of Nippon, expressing the preparedness of the Imperial Nipponese Government to give its unstinted support to the cause of complete independence and full sovereignty of India.

12. Further this Conference places on record its deepest appreciation of and grateful thanks for the co-operation, assistance and support extended to this Movement and its objective by the Imperial Government of Nippon.

13. That this Conference conveys to all the powers fighting against Britain and America its sincere congratulations and prays that their efforts may meet with complete success.

14. That this Conference gratefully acknowledges the sincere and friendly attitude the Government and people of Germany, Italy, Thailand, China, Manchukuo and other friendly powers have adopted towards our struggle for freedom and places on record its deep appreciation and thank for the offer of assistance and co-operation extended by them to this Movement.

15. This Conference offers hearty congratulation to the Burmese Nation to whom the Imperial Government of Nippon has promised to grant independence within this year.

16

Minutes of an Interview between Members of I.I.L. Malaya and Col. Kagawa; Clarifies the Relations between the I.N.A. and the Japanese

1 May, 1943

Present: Lt. Col. Kagawa[1]
Lt. Kunizuka[2]
Dr. Lukshumayya
Sri B. A. Mallai
Sri G. Maganlal
Sri S. N. K. Nagappa Chettiar
Sri J. A. Thivy[3]
Sri S. Shanmugam
Sri A. Yellappa
Sri K. M. Kannampilly
Dr. D. K. Majumdar
Dr. N. K. Menon
Dr. J. Samuel

Col. Kagawa said that it was a good opportunity to discuss the problems of the League organisation in Malai and asked those present to tell him of any difficulties they were experiencing in their territories.

Dr. Samuel replied that the *Gunseibu* in Penang did not show much recognition of the Indian Independence League in its dealings. Col. Kagawa

1. Colonel Kagawa Yoshio was Staff officer in Hikari Kikan.
2. Lieut. Kunizuka, was an interpreter with Fujiwara Kikan and subsequently with Iwakuro Kikan, played a major role in persuading Mohan Singh to form the Indian National Army. He has recorded his experience with the Indian Nationalist in the book entitled *Rainbow Across the Sky* in Japanese.
3. J.A. Thivy, (1904-1957), born in Malaya. After studying in England, became a prominent lawyer, joined Indian Independence League and was its Vice-President, was minister in the Provisional Government of India. After War, founded Malayam Indian Congress and was its President; was diplomatic representative of India in Malaya, then Indian High Commissioner in Maurtious; served also as ambassador to Greece and Hague till his death in 1957.

asked for concrete examples. Dr. Samuel gave as an example the difficulties experienced in holding meetings.

Col. Kagawa asked what the position was in the other states.

Sri Shanmugam replied that there were no difficulties in Malacca.

Dr. Majumdar said that in Negri Sembilan also there were no difficulties.

Sri Thivy said that in Perak they had to inform three departments. In the case of sub-branches they had to inform the departments even for committee meetings, and minutes nad to be submitted.

Col. Kagawa asked whether there were any other difficulties being experienced.

Sri Thivy said that the indifference shown by the Government to those who go against the League made the position of the League rather difficult. He gave as an instance the attitude of the Government towards those who had refused to pay their quota to the Indian Independence Fund.

Col. Kagawa asked whether the allotments made by Sri Bose were fair.

Dr. Lukshumayya replied that it depended on whether the collections were to be repeated or not.

He said that Sri Bose had empowered him, as chairman of the Malaya Branch, to reduce the amounts where he considered such a reduction fair and necessary. He had already reduced the amounts allotted to some states, and he was going to suggest to Sri Bose that it would be better to have smaller contributions at intervals.

Col. Kagawa asked whether they could think out any better methods of collection.

Dr. Lukshumayya said that he was working on it. Unequal proportions in different states made the collection difficult. In Syonan for instance no collection had yet been made.

Col. Kagawa requested those present to study the best ways for the future. In Japan contribution to political parties always voluntary.

Sri Yellappa said that the Bose had seen the Mayor of Syonan a month ago but the Mayor had not yet given the necessary permit to start collection. As soon as the permit was got they could start.

Sri Nagappa Chettiar said that most of the Malay officers were anti-Indians. In the Survey Department in Kedah for instance only Malays are employed. Even the Indians who were employed in that department previously had not been taken back.

Sri Narayan said that they were having no difficulty in Selangor.

Col. Kagawa wanted to know whether there was any possibility of communists taking advantage of the League organisation to advance their activities.

Dr. Lukshumayya said that there were practically no communists among Indians.

Col. Kagawa said that the British did not like the League Movements. They might use the Chinese to discredit the Movement or make use of it.

Dr. Lukshumayya said that no signs had yet been seen of any such action in the Mainland. In Penang there was one instance of some records being discovered when a house was raided, of a plan to discredit the League or to cause bad blood between the League and the Japanese.

Col. Kagawa said that they had a confidential report that about 80 Indian soldiers, who had taken part in the Malain campaign were leading the communities in their activities.

Dr. Lukshumayya asked whether these soldiers were communists by persuation or simply robbers.

Col. Kagawa said that at present they were only robbers but there was danger of their being influenced by the communists.

Dr. Lukshumayya said that they had been watching to see if the communists would attack the League leaders. So far there had been only one case when Sri Thivy was shot at.

Sri Shanmugam said that there was one important question which he wanted to discuss. There was a recent announcement by Premier General Tojo that Indians were no more enemy nationals, but this was not being given effect to in all places. For instance, in some states attorneys of principals in India were allowed to operate business while in other states they were not. If the Kikan could help in having a uniform policy throughout the territory, it would be of great assistance. Col. Kagawa said that it was a problem very difficult to solve in a general way. He suggested that it would be better to tackle individual cases one after the other as they arose. He also said that if the attorney had proper document, it would be easy to settle.

Sri Yellappa said that on 6/7/02 instructions were given by the government regarding Asiatic people, to the effect that all those who left Malai before the 8th of December were not to be considered as aliens. Yet in a few cases this rule was not being applied.

Col. Kagawa said that he would like to know the rules regarding this and also the instances from each state.

He then explained the campaign on the Indo-Burma border. After that he gave an account of League activities as he conceived them. He said that when the Indian National Army and the Japanese advance into India, all organisations in India may be destroyed. The British may adopt the scorched earth policy. Who will then put back the organisation into existence? Essential repairs of a strategical nature will of course be carried out by the Japanese army, but other things will have to be looked after by the Indians themselves. The Indian Independence League will act as an intermediary between the Congress and the Japanese. If the Indian National Army and the Japanese occupy any portion of India, it is possible that there may be a revolution in other parts of India. Then the Indian National Army and the Indian Independence League should go in advance and take the initiative to take advantage of the situation. For that the League should have trained men. Such training cannot be done overnight. It must be done beforehand. One can say when the operations will start. It might come as a surprise. But must be ready when operations start. For instance in the case of propaganda, if Japanese are sent to do propaganda, it will not be good. The League must have large numbers of people— specialists in broadcasting, writing pamphlets, leaflets, etc. For instance, in broadcasting the League should select fit people and send them to broadcasting stations, and have them trained during the peace time. The League will require the service of technical experts. It must get details of men in Malai who are qualified and mobilise them when the time comes. The League must train young men to fight. We can expect to get plenty of arms from the enemy. Thus every Indian will be utilised in the Movement. Suppose the Indian operations start and the League has no organisation for it, there is bound to be trouble between the Indians in India and the Japanese. If the League could prepare a scheme, the Japanese will give all facilities. Col. Kagawa said that these were his dreams. He requested those present to discuss these points with the President.

Before leaving he said that with the transference of the Headquarters of the Kikan from Bangkok to Syonan, the Malai Branch of the Kikan had ceased to exist but that the policy and principles would be still the same. He also announced the change in the name of the Kikan from Iwakuro Kikan to Hikari Kikan.

17

General Staff Branch Instructions to the British Officers to Check the Subversive Activities of the I.N.A. Against the Indian Army[1]

3 May, 1943

1. Replies from H.Q. Eastern and Southern Army Central Command to these HQ letter no DMI/4746 of 18/3/43 have been considered. These and certain other connected problems have been under active consideration and certain decisions on matters of policy have been approved by H. E. the C-in-C. These are set out below under their various headings.

Disposal of stragglers from Burma who have prima facie never actually been prisoners in Japanese hands.

2. Numerous cases are coming to light of stragglers from Burma who maintain that they have never actually been prisoners in Japanese hands, but who have spent varying periods in enemy occupied territory before returning to India. In some cases these men are self-confessed deserters in action who have returned to India disguised, as civilian refugees and have remained in their villages or elsewhere for periods upto months before reporting to their units of regimental centres. In some cases they have only reported because they have heard that their presence has come to light and they are being searched for. There are many variants and by no means all initially deserted. In some cases personnel have reported back to their units without disclosing the fact that they returned to India in refugee guise and remained at large for some time, but have subsequently served satisfactorily for some time before the facts came to light.

3. While primarily disciplinary cases, the possibility cannot be ignored that some of these men may have developed subversive tendencies

1. F. No. 601/10569/H.S. Ministry of Defence.

during their sojourn in enemy occupied territory. They are potentially the most dangerous form of enemy agents. There is the additional consideration that knowledge that there are a number of such cases who have hitherto "managed to get away with it" must be fairly widespread and cannot but have a bad effect on morale and discipline and encourage such conduct.

4. It has been decided that where such cases come to light each should be considered on its merit and disposed of on the basis of expendiency on the following lines:

(a) Trial by Court Martial where a definite case can be established and there are prospects of exemplary punishment.

(b) Dismissal and detention under Defence of India Rule 26 where trial is not expedient but prima facie the individual will be danger to security if left at large.

(c) Dismissal where the facts warrants this, but trial by Court Martial is not likely to be successful and it is concluded that the individual is likely to be less of a danger out of the Service than in it.

(d) Retention in the Service where the individual has "got away with it" for some time and his subsequent service has been satisfactory or the circumstances otherwise justify this, the question of whether he remains with his unit or is reposted being decided on its merits.

(e) Retention in the service with summary reduction in rank where the facts justify this and where action as in (c) or (d) would have a bad effect on others.

The question of setting up central machinery to investigate and dispose of such cases is under consideration and orders will be issued in due course by adjutant General's Branch.

Action against members of "contact", parties apprehended.

5. "Contact" parties consist of individuals who after capture by or desertion to, the enemy are sent back to our lines with instructions to encourage desertion or to build up I.N.A. cells in units and training centres. They may also include civilians from enemy occupied territories.

6. Trial by Court Martial on capital charges should be resorted to in the case of military personnel in well-sustained cases, the decision being left to G. O. C. - in -C. the Army/ Command concerned. Death

sentences should be carried out by hanging in Civil jails, or in reoccupied territories under arrangements to be made by the Civil Affaris Service. Civilian accused should be handed over to the Civil Authorities for trial under the Enemy Agents Ordinance if within Indian territorial limits, otherwise their cases may be disposed of by the courts set up under the Civil Affairs Administration in reoccupied territory.

7. In coming to a decision as to whether it is expedient to resort to trial, the following factors should be considered:-

(a) Probability of conviction and of a sentence sufficient to obviate the individual subsequently becoming a menace to security. In the case of civilians should trial result in a finding "Not Guilty" but the circumstances otherwise warrant it, would still be possible to detain under Defence of India Rules. In the case of military personnel dismissal by administrative action would be necessary before such detention could be affected. In cases therefore where conviction is doubtful for want of legal evidence, it would be preferable in the interests of security to dispense with trial and to forward the individual on to C. S. D. I. C. for disposal in accordance with existing practice.

(b) Whether the value of conviction and punishment as a deterrant to others outweights the value of information that might be obtained from the individual or from using him (if willing) as evidence in other cases. We now have a great deal of information on I.N.A. organisation and methods outside India, i.e., in Japanese occupied territory, but information as to the organisation, if any, within India, and of contacts in Indian units, is of very great importance with view to preventing the spread of contamination. We have not yet reached the stage where we can dispense with any potential source of this latter type of information.

8. Normal publicity should be given through Service channels by publication unit, formation and Indian Army orders, promulgation of findings and sentences on parades in the unit to which the convict belongs/being resorted to at the discretion of G.O.C.-in-C. Armies Commands.

Publicity and Counter Propaganda on I.N.A. and I.I.L. Questions.

9. This has been considered under three main headings:-

(a) To Troops

(b) To the General Public

(c) To the enemy including I.N.A. and I.I.L. personnel in enemy occupied territory.

To Troops

10. In HQ letter DMI/4746 of 18/3/43, it was ruled that, for the present, the dissemination of information about I.N.A. and kindred activities should be confined to British Officers, and to selected Indian and Viceroy Commissioned Officers (V.C.O.'s). It has now been decided that we should put the situation plainly to all Indian ranks and prepare them to meet a method of attack of which they are at present largely unconscious. Commanding Officers should be authorised to explain the situation frankly to all I.C.O.S. V.C.Os and men, omitting only details likely to be of use to the enemy, such as the extent of our knowledge of the detailed organisation and personalities of the I.N.A., details of our own organisation and methods for discovering and dealing with agents and of the degree of success they are achieving. Commanding Officers should however be given details of members of their regiments known to be active members of the I.N.A. and be permitted, at their discretion, to pass these on to their Subedar Major and Unit Security Officer, to assist the latter in their task of keeping the Commanding Officer informed of developments with in the unit.

11. The Subject of Japanese efforts to suborn the loyality of the Indian Army should be dealt with on the following general lines:–

(a) Description of Japanese treatment of prisoners of war, including such items as forced labour, semi-starvation, violations of caste, propaganda, flattery and promises.

(b) The effects of this treatment in dividing prisoners into three categories:–

(i) Those who have joined the I.N.A. and promised to help the Japanese and intend tc keep their promise;

(ii) Those who have joined the I.N.A. with a view to help the Japanese and do not intend to keep their promise;

(iii) Those who refused to join the I.N.A.

(c) The methods adopted by the Japanese to exploit those in (B) (i) and (ii) including lectures, training is espionage, propaganda, sabotage etc., and return to India in contact parties.

(d) No descredit attaches to a man unfortunate enough to be captured who agrees to join the I.N.A. or undertake any employment offered by the Japanese *with the sole object of:*

(i) *returning to India at the earliest opportunity and who immediately on return reports the full facts and whole truth immediately to the nearest HQ., or*

(ii) *otherwise deceiving the Japanese.*

(e) Those who feel that they can successfully undertake the role of deceiving the Japanese and the Indian traitors in their pay should do so.

(f) We now have means of ascertaining the names of those who promise to assist the enemy and *actually become active enemy agents;* whether they remain in enemy occupied territory or re-enter India.

(g) Steps will be taken to stop the family allotments and to confiscate the property of those who are known to have become traitors. When apprehended they will be brought to trial on Capital Charges.

In passing on information to troops, the terms "I.N.A." or "Indian National Army" should not be used except in a derisory manner, and attention should be drawn to the facts of the so called "Burma Independent Army" which the Japanese disbanded as soon as it had fulfilled its role of betraying Burma to the Japanese. Care should be taken to prevent these titles being given currency as describing this traitorous movement.

12. An essential corollary to the frank treatment of the question outlined above are measures to encourage the moral resistance of Indian troops to I.N.A. and I.I.L. propaganda, whether the latter is applied to them while with our own forces or in the event of their being captured. Special measures of an All–India nature to assist in this are under consideration and further instructions will follow.

To the General Public

13. It has been decided that for the present there should be no over publicity in India outside the Armed Forces regarding the I.N.A. or

I.I.L. as organisation. No attempt will however be made to conceal the fact that individuals are known to have become traitors, but such publicity will be incidental to publicity to the troops (described above) and to counter propaganda directed to the Japanese and INA–IIL themselves (described below). No use will be made of the terms "INA" "IIL", "Indian National Army" or "Indian Independence League" in giving publicity to any action taken against members of these organisations. Nor, except in exceptional cases, will publicity be given outside the Services of the names of individuals against whom action is taken or who are known to be in these organisations. The question of general publicity measures is however, under reference to Provincial Governments who may consult commanders of Armies/Commands as to their views on the matter.

To the Japanese, the I.N.A. and the I.I.L.

14. Hitherto no direct propaganda or Counter Propaganda specifically refering to either I.N.A. or I.I.L. has been included in broadcasts or leaflets directed to the Japanese Army or to Indians in enemy occupied territories. It has now been decided to initiate a campaign both in Japanese and in Indian languages designed to :–

   (a) Undermine the confidence of the Japanese in the I.N.A., especially in its leaders;

   (b) Undermine the confidence of the I.N.A. in itself, in the Japanese and in its leaders;

   (c) Play on the fears of genuine members of the I.N.A. / I.I.L. by stressing :–

      (i) that the families of Indian Officers and men in enemy hands are being well looked after and family allotments or allowance are being paid regularly hitherto without exception,

      (ii) that we know that certain (unspecified) disloyal I.C.O.s, V.C.Os. and men are actively helping the Japanese and trying to persuade others to do so.

      (iii) that steps are now being taken to stop the family allotments or allowances, and to confiscate the property of, individuals known to be helping the enemy.

15. With regard to para 14 (a) and (b), the daily broadcasts, in Japanese and Indian languages directed to the Japanese Army and to the Indians in enemy occupied territory will be used to indicate that–

    (a) Our troops are now being instructed in the methods used by the enemy to soborn their loyality.

    (b) They are being encouraged, the event of their being captured, to accept enemy offers, with a view to deceiving the enemy and escaping with information both about the enemy and Indian traitors assisting them.

    (c) Number of individuals have already escaped by these means and the great majority of these sent back to India by the enemy have reported immediately and given full details of :–

        (i) Their instructions;

        (ii) The Indians helping the Japanese and those ostensibly doing so but actually deceiving them;

        (iii) All they know about enemy strategies, dispositions and intentions;

        (iv) Composition of future parties.

    (d) A number of I.C.Os., V.C.Os. and men have been decorated for the gallantry, resource and skill they have displayed in deceiving the Japanese and the Indian traitors and in escaping.

16. It has also been decided to drop leaflets designed to reinforce the broadcasts and with the object if encouraging genuine escapes and also "desertions" from the I.N.A., especially in forward areas. These will include promise of safe conduct to actual members of the I.N.A.

17. In both broadcasts and leaflets, actual names of escapes or "deserters" may be given in certain specific cases where considerable effect, either of encouragement to loyalists or uneasiness to disloyalists or to the enemy, would result from disclosure. Normally however the object will be to leave the enemy and the Indian traitors uncertain as to the actual extent of our knowledge of success.

18. It is realised that broadcasts in Indian languages on this subject, though directed to enemy "occupied" territories will inevitably be heard in India itself. This will inevitably result in a certain amount of general publicity in spite of the policy of restricting this to the Services for the present. To minimise this "spill over" to the public

of India, G.S. I. (q) broadcasts will avoid all specific reference to either I.N.A. or I.I.L. organisations.

19. It is intended to introduce the propaganda policy outlined above with effect from 15th May and to leave the enemy in no doubt, of our intention to encourage prisoners to join the I.N.A. from that date.

20. Paragraphs 2 to 7 of this letter are issued with the concurrence of the Adjutant General in India.

18

Implementation of the Recommendations of the I.I.L. Conference, Held at Singapore on 27 April by the I.I.L. Malaya Branch[1]

8 May, 1943

The Conference of the Committee of Representatives from Territories all over East Asia held at Syonan from 27th to 30th April, effected vital changes in the Constitution of the Indian Independence League. The main trend of the changes was towards putting the organisation on a war footing, giving full dictatorial powers to the President. A copy of the new Constitution is sent herewith for your office. You will notice that there is a change in the designation of the President (of the Territorial Committee, State Branch or Sub-Branch). Kindly have all rubber stamps changed from "President" to "Chairman" and make other necessary alterations according to the Constitution.

Propaganda

More intensive and widespread propaganda is necessary now more than ever. In the earlier days, enrolment of labourers owing as members was not feasible to the fact that in many parts Estates had not yet resumed work, and even in the case of those, Estates which had reopened, the labourers were getting only a few days work. In some States, however, as a result of negotiations with the Syonan Gomu Kumisai, labourers have been assisted to join the League. In Johore for instance each labourer gets 5 day's extra work to enable him to become a member of the League. Such or similiar attempts should be made in each state to make it possible for the labourers to join the League and even if they cannot immediately join, League officials and workers should make it a point to keep up and strengthen their contact with the labourers.

Membership in most states seems to have come to a standstill. In all popular movements like ours a period of slackness is common after the

1. I.I.L. Papers., F.. No. 45/3.

original enthusiasm, but we should be always on the watch to pull up the organisation from stagnating in a state of complacency. Increase in membership is not merely to effect an increase in finance. Our efforts towards organising the movement in Malai cannot be considered to have succeeded until every Indian, man or woman, is a member of the League.

Finance

The Malaya Branch has recently made to all Branches substantial contributions towards organisation expenses. Apart from this it has also been decided to reduce the contribution from the branches from 25% to 5% of membership fees each month starting from Ist May, 2603. This has been done to allow to each Branch more money to carry on its work within its territory with greater vigour and intensity. Branches must, however try as far as possible to make themselves financially self–supporting. All expenses which are not essential to the advancement of our cause must be cut out. Funds for distress relief must be raised locally by each Branch and sub-Branch.

Youth Section

Almost all Branches have now organised Youth Sections. It has come to our notice recently that there is in some circles an erroneous impression that this is a Movement separate from and independent of the League. The Youth Section is one of the sections of the Indian Independence League and, as such, is a part and parcel of our movement. The Azad School at Syonan is now training a number of youths from all over Malai. These people will be sent out after training as Instructors and we are confident that with their arrival the Youth Sections in all Branches will proceed with their work with intensified activity.

Messages

We have received instruction to the effect that messages will be accepted only if they are from Indians to Indians. Branches are therefore requested not to accept any more messages from non-Indians or from Indians to non-Indians. All the messages of this type remaining with us awaiting broadcast will be sent back to the Branches to be returned along with the fees to the parties concerned.

Syonan
8th May, 2603

Indian Independence League
Malaya Branch
Secretary

19

Statement of S. C. Bose After his Arrival in Tokyo; Requests Indians in East Asia to Take up Armed Struggle Against the British in Collaboration with Japan

19 June, 1943

Ladies and gentleman!

"At the outset, I may say that it is for me a very great pleasure to offer you my cordial greetings, since I have been for a long time connected with journalism in my own country."

"You may be wondering what has brought me to this part of the world at such a time. For long years, British jails India and Burma have been my residence. But the fact that today I am standing before you in the heart of Nippon, instead of sitting idly in a prison house in India, is symbolic of the new movement that is now sweeping over my country. It was in accordance with the will of my countrymen that I left homeland more than two years ago and whatever I have done since them, is also in accordance with their will".

"During the last World War, our leaders had been bluffed and deceived by wily British politicians that is why we took a vow more than 20 years, my generation has striven for freedom and has eagerly awaited the hour that has now struck–the hour that is for the Indian people the dawn of freedom. We know very well that such an opportunity will not come again for another hundred years and we are, therefore, determined to make the fullest use of it".

"You have so often heard of the war that is being waged for freedom and democracy. But you can very well imagine what my countrymen think of those Powers that talk of freedom and democracy and deny the same to one–fifth of the human race–the Powers that reply to the demand for liberty by terror and brutality and by massacre of unarmed men, women and children. British imperialism has meant for India moral degradation,

---

1. *Nippon Times* 20 June 1943. The above Statement was read at the Press Interview which Subhas Chandra Bosh granted to newspapermen at the Imperial hotel, Tokyo.

cultural ruin, economic impoverishment and political enslavement. Is it any wonder, therefore, that the Indian People have at last solemnly received to end the British yoke?

"The present world conflict means for the Indian people struggle between the forces that want to maintain the status quo and those that are determined to overthrow it. Can any one blame us if in such a conflict, our sympathy lies with those Powers that stand for change for New Order? And when these Powers support our demand for freedom, it is but natural that our sympathy for them should deepen into enthusiastic support.

"Inspite of all that, Anglo-American propaganda has been saying to the contrary, believe me when I say that the overwhelming majority of the Indian people desire to see the Tripatriate Powers emerge victorious. The victory of the Tripatriate Powers will mean the defeat of Anglo-American imperialism, the dismemberment of the British Empire and the restitution of India's lost liberty."

"The Tripatriate Powers have rendered the greatest help to India's struggle by waging war against our eternal foe. And they have earned our lasting gratitude by offering us-not only sympathy, but support and assistance. Nevertheless, it is our duty to pay for our liberty with our own blood".

"The freedom that we shall win through our sacrifice and exertions. we shall be able to preserve with our own strength. We, therefore feel very strongly that we should actively participate in the war against our common foe. The enemy that has drawn the sword, must be fought with the sword".

"Civil disobedience must develop into armed struggle. And only when the Indian people receive the baptism of fire on a large scale, will they qualify for their freedom".

"Since, I left India more than two years go, I have travelled all over the world and I have, therefore, been able to study the world situation quite objectively. I have also seen something of the inside of Japan, Germany and Italy. I am not blind to the difficulties that still lie in the path of the Tripatriate Powers—but I also know their strength and the sources of their strength. I am not, therefore, impressed at all by all this loud task of a second front, whether in Europe or in the Pacific, of landing in Europe or of an offensive on the Indo-Burma frontier".

"If noisy, bumptious propaganda could win a war, the Anti -Axis Powers would have had their victory long ago. We all know that in this World War, time is not working in favour of the Anglo-American Powers as it did in the last. Winston Churchill was constrained to admit it publicly the other day at Washington. From my own study of the general war situation, I have the 100-percent conviction that, however long those struggle may last, there can be but one outcome; namely, the absolute victory of the Tripatriate power and their Allies".

"Another point in which you may be naturally interested is as to what the Indian people think of Japan. Japan was the first Asiatic Power to stem the tide of aggression that had been sweeping over Asia in the 19th century. Japan's victory over Russia in 1905 was the starting point of the Asiatic renaissance in the 20th century and as such, it was hailed enthusiastiscally by the Indian people, as it was by the Japanese. Japan was, and is, a historical necessity for the revival of Asia".

"It is true that Indian public opinion regarding Japan changed considerably after the outbreak of the China Affair in 1937. But the out break of the War in East Asia has fundamentally altered the situation".

"Today, Japan is fighting our enemy. On the other hand Chungking is an ally of Anglo-American Powers. Moreover, General Chiang Kai-shek has been giving his full support to the British domination of Burma and India".

The average Indian is not interested in ideological questions. He is interested only in the political and economic emancipation of his country. Consequently, whoever sympathizes with and supports India's Independence is automatically India's friend and ally. Last but not the least, the adoption by Japan of the new China policy, has made the Indian people ask why General Chiang Kai-shek does not to try to arrive at an honorable understanding with Japan and why he is allowing himself to be used as a tool by the Anglo-American Powers.

"India and Japan have, in the past, been bound by deep cultural ties which are about 20 centuries old. In recent times, these cultural relations have been interrupted because of the British domination of India. It is, however, certain that when India is free these relations will be revived and will be further strengthened".

"Moreover, in view of the active support and assistance which Japan has been giving and will, in future give to India's struggle for independence, it is but natural that the grateful Indian people will enthusiatically welcome close political and economic cooperation with Japan, when they are masters of their own homes and of their national destiny".

"In this connection, I should add that the statements made by Prime Minister General Hideki Tojo on India since March, 1942, and repeated by him before the Imperial diet on June 16, 1943, have made a profound impression on India and have greatly helped to improve as the days roll by".

"Industrial production-satisfactory though it is will be pushed up further in order to cope with and overcome any possible advance made by the enemy. And lastly, one can see with his own eyes that there is an immense reserve of manpower which can be drawn upon at any time, if the necessity arises."

"Ladies and Gentlemen, For all these reasons, I feel absolutely confident of the ultimate defeat of the Anglo-American Powers, of the break-up of the British empire and the liberation of 398- millions of my countrymen".

20

Japanese Reaction to the Arrival of Bose From Germany

20 June, 1943

Subhas Chandra Bose, eminent Indian nationalist, is now visiting Japan, it has been revealed. The Japanese nation is happy to bid him cordial welcome, for he is a man whose record and life aim are such as command the respect of all true Orientals.

As the greatest Indian leader outside the prison- infact the only Indian leader of first rank who is not, in some British jail- Mr. Bose represents the shining hope of the four hundred million peoples of India for freedom. Twice the president of the national congress party, he finally resigned to found the Forward Bloc which demanded immediate and complete independence from British rule without condition or compromise. Undaunted by the material power of the British Empire, the leader has long been courageously pitting his intelligence and his spirit against the physical might of the alien rulers of the country in a manner which calls forth admiration.

It is significant indeed that this man who is the personification of India's hope for independence has found it feasible to return from Europe at last to direct at closer quarters the movement for the liberation of his homeland. It is an indication that thė victories of Japan and the Axis are presenting the Indians with an opportunity such as they, have never have again to throw off the yoke of the British rule. The hour of destiny for India may be close at hand, if only all the Indian people will realize it as Mr. Bose and other clearsighted leaders realize it so well.

To the Japanese people, the presence of Mr. Bose at the time cannot help but emphasize the contract between India and the countries, which Japan has been able to help more directly. Fresh in the memory in Prime Minister Tojo's announcement of only five days ago that the Philippines would be accorded independence within this year, while a few months

1. An Editorial from *Nippon Times*, 20 June 1943.

ago there was his similar statement with respect to Burma. The spectacle of Burma and the Philippines rising as independent sovereign nations while older, larger and potentially infinitely more powerful India lies helplessly in chairs is one which must arouse in the breast of every Indian a tumult of emotions which defies description. But as fellow-Orientals, the Japanese people can sympathize with the Indians in the humiliation and indignation they must feel over the contrast between their lot and that of the Burmese or the Filipinos.

The contrast in essence, however, is not so much that between Burma and the Philippines on the one hand and India on the other as between Japan on the one hand and Britain on the other. Japan as an Oriental nation, is naturally sincere and anxious to help promote the welfare of all the nations of this part of the world. Britain on the other hand, as a distant imperialistic Power can have no interest is any Oriental country except as an object of exploitation.

No amount of sophistry can hide his fundamental difference between the attitudes of Japan and of Britain. Jan Christian Smuts, the Prime Minister of Union of South Africa, in an attempt to quiet the carping criticism of British imperialism on the part of some Americans, wrote recently in the American magazine Life that the reason India has not been able to become a "free" commonwealth like Canada or Australia is that the Indians have not been able to agree on the terms of a national constitution. What Smuts deliberately hides is the fact that if there is lack of agreement among the Indians, it is the British who have created and have consistently fomented that disagreement in accordance with their policy of divide and rule. At any rate Smuts' arguement is beside the point, for what the Indians want is not the fictitious "freedom" of being a British "Commonwealth" but complete independence from all British connections. On that point there is agreement enough among all the Indians, and as for the constitution of such a truly independent India, it should be one concern of Smuts or any other torch-bearer of British imperialism.

The British also like to say that "freedom" of the illusory kind which they always mean will be granted to India after the war if the Indians prove themselves "worthy" of it by fighting for Britain now. It may be remembered that the same promise was given during the last World War, with what results everyone knows. Such an attitude on the part of Britain not only indicates most clearly the insincerity of the British, but it also reveals that they have no little confidence in their own strength in the war that they must resort to bribery in an attempt to secure the help of the Indians. In contrast, Japan is not making vague promises of future independence to Burma and the Philippines on condition that they help Japan in the war. Japan is granting complete independence to Burma and the Philippines while that war is going on, for Japan has no doubt as to the outcome of the struggle. Japan is acting now on the premises of certain victory, while Britain, hedging on the outcome of the war, is merely promising action in the future on the premise of her doubts.

As the Indian people fret on their condition and their prospects for independence, they may well take to heart Prime Minister Tojo's words of five days ago when he said, "For this plight of India I feel at once sympathy and indignation. Japan is firmly resolved to exhaust all means in order to help expel and eliminate from India Anglo-Saxon influences which are the enemy of the Indian people, and enable India to attain full independence in a true sense of the term. I confidently look into the day, which I trust will soon come, when the ardent and widespread desires of the Indian people are fulfilled and they regain, freedom and prosperity". This is Japan's message of goodwill to the Indian people.

21

Copy of a Platoon Lecture Prepared by the I.I.L. Entitled "Our Mission" in Life as Indians First and Last[1]

21 June, 1943

My brothers,

From the lectures you have had so far, I am sure all of you have no doubt or misconception in your mind, regarding the history of our movement both in India and in East Asia, our policy and the principles, which we are pledged to abide by. We have also studied in details all the requisite characteristics we should cultivate, for the attainment of our object, including the spirit of Bushido in Nippon. During the course of our study hitherto, we have learned to evaluate correctly our merits and defects, assets and liabilities in an unprejudiced, unbiased manner. We are quite conscious of our original status and attainments from the cultural, economic and political aspects. We have learnt how and to what extent we have been degraded from every point of view after the British advent in India; and to what depths we have sunk in every aspect. You would now be in a position to understand the imperative necessity for such knowledge and training, concerning the political and spiritual aspect of our movement in order to enable us to achieve our mission in life.

We are all Indians, first and last, both in the army and in the civil. It is vitally essential that all of us should develop this outlook constantly at every opportunity. We must root out completely from our minds all ideas of provincialism, sectarianism and other aspects of individualism. Such an outlook is more essentially required in our action than in our thought and speech. We are engaged in a war of supreme and momentous importance not only to ourselves, but also to the entire world today. The problem of

1. European Manuscript Collection No. A73 India Office library and records, London copies of some of these platoon lectures are also available amongst the Indian National Army papers at the National Archies of India. For some other lecture see Appendix; These were meant to create patriotic sentiments amongst the soldiers of the Indian National Army and were given regularly. Each one of the officers was given a copy also.

India today is a problem of bread and salt, of famine and nakedness of disease and dirt, and of degradation and death to the Indians. The causes of such a downfall of India from her glorious past we have studied in details. We have no doubt in our mind that it is essentially due to British imperialistic domination of India, for well over two centuries. We know also the secret of the means of remedying India's pitiable state. The only thing that remains to be done is to translate our ideas into action.

We have to survey all aspects of our mission in life. The problem of India is a world problem. There will be no end to this war as long as India remains the bone of contention. There can never be any lasting peace in this world as long as India remains a subject nation, as long as every fifth man in the world is a slave under British domination, as long as forty crores of humanity are shouting aloud for freedom, as the cry of their souls, and as long as British imperialism continues to perpetuate such slavery of the souls, captivation of the spirit and physical torture of pain, hunger and suffering due to starvation and total neglect of responsibility of the British rulers of India even to preserve the very existence of Indians as a nation, let alone promote their happineess and welfare. Before the advent of the British, peace and plenty reigned in India. After the advent of the British, there was apparent a seemingly outword peace in India due to their technological unification of our country by railways etc. for purely political advantages and objects; but, all the same, our souls are shouting aloud and clamouring for freedom of thought, speech and association. How can ever there be real and lasting peace under these circumstances? Hence we, Indians, feel very strongly that all subject nations must be liberated, if any object has to be served by the colossal wars, that are now being conducted on a scale, unprecedented and unknown in history so far, and of an importance which is most genuinely world-wide, in extent and intensity. It is advisable for warring nations to take note of these facts, declare their respective war aims unequivocably and to carry out their campaigns accordingly. In precept and practice, Dai Nippon has carried out all these noble principles in so far as it relates to her campaigns in the Far Eastern theatre. What of England, whose sole aim is to get all the others to do the fighting for them in all the theatres of war, where they desire to perpetuate their imperialistic preserves at the expense of other nations, either subject or free. The British have not declared their war aims so far, nor will they ever do so.

What is our outlook in life, as Officers and men of the Indian National Army. We are real revolutionaries. Hence our outlook is much more pointed and specific. We have defined duties assigned to us in this noble mission we have under taken to achieve. We have pledged our lives to do so. Nothing on earth is going to deter us from achieving our object. No earthly possession or wordly remuneration is going to unhinge our grim determination. We are quite conscious of the fact that the British have used the 'Golden Key' to suit their purpose, wherever deemed feasible, by the offer of suitable bribes such as titles, rewards, high posts, jagirs, etc. Just playing to human weakness. Alas! Most of us have been involved in our economic grip, no doubt: and hence passive sufferers in the struggle. But some of us have gone out of our way to oblige the British rulers of India with a view to help ourselves, which conduct is unfortunately detrimental to our nations' interests.

The British no doubt work on their time-honoured dictum of Walpole that 'Every man has his price'. These victims of our nation, with the motive of self-aggrandizement, have been directly responsible for our subjection and slavery to a very large extent. Would that we can remove the curtain and open the eyes of these fattening and glittering unfortunates, and retrieve their stagnant and misguided mentality? It will be a great day when we can make them see the day light of truth and clear up all their misconceptions.

The idea of reward or remuneration is totally inconsistent with that of a revolutionary mentality. Once we accept any thing in this life of ours, however, deserving we might have been, the recipient of the gift automatically becomes the paid hireling of the donor. Hence even the very thought of a similar nature, in a revolutionary is quite untenable.

We have to enlighten ourselves by a study of the origin and growth of revolutions in the past in different parts of the world. It was always a question of struggle between the' haves' and the 'have nots'. Those who had not, desired, naturally to have things , vitally essential for them. In the annals of the world history, the first upheaval between the masses and classes occurred in Europe between the Plebians and Patricians in Rome. Christian religion during the mediaeval period retrieved the masses of Europe, who were steeped in ignorance and barbarism. Christian missionaries were able to achieve this result, by preaching to the masses the gospel of faith, hope and charity. However, during the Middle Ages the masses in Europe were the slaves of the barons. The Renaissance in Europe did not contribute enough to the liberation of the masses. The next upheaval was during the French Revolution, when the message of liberty, equality and fraternity was proclaimed from the housetops. In reality this was a middle-class revolution. Yet, it was this attempt made by the French people in 1793,with the object of equalizing the wealth among all the people of France, by the different means in their power that tended towards socialism. Henceforward, the adherents of socialism propounded their theories of uplift of the masses. By this time Capitalism had already made its mark; and suffering labour under capitalistic domination was able to feel their inherent power and strength. All these ideas gradually gained ground and trouble broke out in many countries from time to time between the suffering masses and the dominating and pleasure-loving capitalistic classes. Such a struggle took the shape of strikes, lock cuts and other forms of protests which resulted in the trickling through a little more of the capital, the sole property of the owning classes, down to the masses in the shape of increased wages, diminished working hours and other elements of amenities of life. All such events in different parts of the world gathered strength in the minds of the masses and culminated in the Proletariat Russion Revolution in 1917. The advanced Labourities and communists in all countries have the dream of a Proletariat Revolution throughout the world. Such revolutionary ideas have captured the minds of many of our youngmen in India. The suffering masses in India are already seething with revolution.

India, in her glorious past, had her own politics, economics, sociology and all that is essential for the growth and expansion of a race. The ancient Indian Village Social System, as in vogue in India, has won the admiration of all the modern socialists. Karl Marx, the well-known exponent of Socialism, has devoted a whole chapter on the Indian Village Social System, in his book. Das Kapital. However, the ancient Indian civilization underwent many changes through time, due to various reasons. The priest class were in the ascendant, to start with, with the drawback of exclusiveness and monopoly of knowledge. Then came the power of the solider, and the rule of the military, with its more liberal views of life but with the ideas of pomp, power and territorial aggrandisement. Next came the capitalist civilisation, with its ideas of progress of science and culture and utlisation of that knowledge, but with its inherent defect of accumulation of wealth in the hands of the few and corresponding suffering and poverty of the masses. Hence the struggle of the masses all over the world, even for the bare elements of life's amenities, which have been deprived to them by the possessing classes. Hence the upheaval all the world over, with a view to solve the problem of distribution, for a fair and equitable division of the benefits of science among the suffering humanity at large. Hence the coming into existence of a new order in Asia and in Europe. Hence the idea of co-prosperity sphere and Pan-Asiatic co-operation, interdependence and Federation.

In so far as India is concerned, such an upheaval among the masses is nothing new to Indian history. It is only a revivification of the ancient system of India, for the benefits of all the forty crores of our suffering humanity. That is the end and aim of all our agitation. That is the ultimate objective of all our leaders. That is the Summum Bonum of our Purna Swaraj. There is no word in English literature to describe the correct meaning of Purna Swaraj. It includes complete freedom of our mind, body and spirit, freedom of our thought, speech and action, freedom of association, freedom to enjoy all the bounties of our motherland, freedom to promote happiness and comfort of our masses, with advancement of human knowledge for the welfare of humanity at large. The term Independence is not complete in itself; because India does not desire to live in isolation. What India wants is inter-dependence of all nations, on the terms of equal and mutual reciprocity. Then only the forces of freedom and progress would assert themselves all over the world. Then only the happiness of humanity at large would be ensured and the Utopian millenium would come in to being.

What have we got to do to achieve this nobel mission of ours? We have to rejuvenate our minds completely. We want a complete transformation of our thoughts and activities. For this purpose, education in the origin, course and progress of our national evolution and spiritual training are essentially required. That is what is being provided for you by the Department of Enlightenment and Culture. Have we forgotten the past when the rise of the Marhattas, the Sikhs and the Rajputs moulded our society and politics? Do we not remember that our sense of duty was realised to the maximum extent by our Rajput heroes and heroines? Are we not conscious of the fact that our saints of Maharastra gathered all the spiritual forces which culminated in the ascendancy of Shivaji who succeeded in creating a nation out of the various scattered groups? Have not our great reformers, like Buddha, Ramanuja, Ramananda, Nanak, Chaitanya, Kabir and other risen against the priestly tyranny of our religion and caste system? Are we going to be caste-ridden and religion-driven, steeped in orthodoxy and superstition? Do we not realise that one of the causes of our downfall is a total neglect of our masses, amounting to a national sin against man and God? How can we over associate ourselves with the British system of Government which is determinated to humiliate India before the world?

So, what have we got to do, in order to fulfil our mission in life, the attainment of Purana Swaraj for India? First and foremost we have to feel fro.n the heart. Through the heart comes inspiration. Love opens the most impassable gates. Love is the gate to all secrets of the Universe. Do you feel that millions of our countrymen have been starving for over 200 years, due directly to British domination and exploitation of India? Do you feel that millions of our friends and relations in India are dying of hunger and starvation to-day? Does this thought not make you restless and sleepless? Does it not generate in your minds an intense love for your motherland? Does it not make you realise your sense of duty to your Motherland? Have you not thought of some practical solution in order to soothe the sufferings of the starving and voiceless millions of India, which are progressively increasing from bad to worse, day by day? Have you not yet developed the strength of character and will power, to overcome all obstructions in your path. However insuperable they might be? Come what may in this world, your grim determination should be to pursue your objective, until you achieve your goal. Let fortune support or thwart you, let others blame or praise you, let death come to you to-day or a hundred years hence, let the rest of the world support or desert you, none of these events should count in any way with you at all. You should never swerve from the path of truth righteousness, your sense of duty to yourself, to your friends and relations, to the land of your birth and in fact to humanity at large, in order to support the freedom forces in this world, to establish the new order of inter-dependence of all individuals and of all free nations. You should never rest until slavery and subjection are completely removed until domination and exploitation are totally annulled. It is absolutely imperative that all ranks in the I.N.A. in particular should develop that steadfastness in their life's mission. If your thoughts are sincere, true and correct, if your love for your country is really what it should be, then it is certain that your ideas would permeate the most impenetrable obstacles around you and would pulsate the whole world in your favour. Such is the force and driving power of thought, of sincerity and of honesty and purity of purpose.

We are not stones and trees. We are not inanimate matter. We are all human beings possessed with life, commonsense and power of discrimination and judgement. Why should we behave.

22

Message of Congratulation From the Japanese Premier, General Tojo to the Indians Assembled at Singapore to Welcome Bose: Reiteraties Japan's Desire to See India Free[1]

3 July, 1943

On the occasion of welcoming the Great Leader Sri Subhas Chandra Bose, the Indian Independence League in East Asia held a meeting of the committee of Representatives of Indians in East Asia at Syonan, which has been liberated from British bondage. With this welcome to Subhas Bose, you are taking a long stride towards decisive action with renewed and grim determination to achieve India's Independence.

On this occasion, I extend my most sincere congratulations because it is a happy augury not only for India but for all East Asia also.

Since the outbreak of the Greater East Asia War, the Imperial Japanese forces have annihilated the enemy wherever he was found, and within a very short time, battered all the Anglo-American strategical points in this part of Asia.

At the same time, the bonds of unity among Japan, Machukuo, China and Thailand have been strengthened, and they are irresistably advancing towards the goal of the establishment of the sphere of co-prosperity in East India.

With unshakeable faith in ultimate victory and the triumph of justice for which Japan is fighting, the accumulated wrongs and misdeeds of the British are going to be wiped out. Thus the brilliant dawn of Greater East Asia has arrived.

This is the golden opportunity for India to liberate herself and such a rare opportunity will never occur again.

With the outbreak of the Greater East Asia War, Indian Nationalists in India rose against their British rulers, and India has thus already attained

1. K.S. Giani, *op.cit.* p. 11.

spiritual independence. The British Empire which is gasping for a last breath, will in desperation choose any means to put off the day of their impending doom, and America is also stretching its devilish hands towards India.

In a situation like this, it is by no means an easy task for Indians to achieve India's complete independence; but four hundred million Indian should unite into one solid body and win their own freedom and independence with their own blood and toil.

The sincere wish of Japan for the fulfilment of India's long cherished ambition of "India for Indians" has been proved beyond doubt by the repeated declarations of the Government of Nippon.

Nippon is inflexibly determined to exhaust all her means to help Indian achieving her independence which is the earnest desire off Indians.

It is Japan's sincere wish that the active movement for the achievement of India's Independence must be intensified both inside and outside India, and the Anglo-American forces must be driven out of every corner of India as early as possible. The world situation is becoming more complicated and taking advantage of this, the Anglo-American enemies will no doubt intensify their intrigues. Traditionally Nippon is a country, which invariably keeps faith where friends trust each other, and so is India.

I sincerely wish that Indians will not be deceived by Anglo-American intrigues and miss the God sent opportunity to win their freedom, I trust that Indians, with firm faith in the victory of Japan, Germany and Italy, will fight for justice and righteousness shoulder to shoulder with us.

I firmly believe that this is the only way that Indians can hasten the glorious day of their Freedom, and I sincerely wish them every success in their brave fight.

23

S.C. Bose's interview with the Press; Outlines his Concept of full Freedom and Explains the Reasons for Achieving it with the Help of Tripartite Power[1]

3 July, 1943

Q: What prompted you to come to Japan?

A: There are two reasons: The first is a general reason, namely, that I believe in a personal contact with all the Tri-partite Powers; the second is a special reason, namely, that here I shall be nearer my country, and therefore there is a possibility of working more effectively from these quarters.

Q: To what extent do you think, your broadcasts to India are being, listened to by the people?

A: So far there has been no general prohibition or confiscation of radio sets, though in some cases the local authorities might have done it. Generally speaking, it is rather difficult in India to prevent from listening over the short-wave band: first because the British authorities want to be heard from London, New York and Cairo; and second because we do not use on a large scale sets only with the medium and long wave bands. Therefore, in case the British authorities prohibited short wave bands, people would not be able to listen even to Indian broadcasts on medium and long wave bands. For instance, when I was in prison in 1940 they kept me confined alone: I strongly protested against this solitary confinement, and allowed at last to listen over the radio. But I was allowed at last to listen over the radio to music programs. But I was able all the time to listen to broadcasts from Berlin and Italy.

Q: What prompted you to leave India in 1941?

A: I had three aims, first to find out the correct war situation and general international conditions, which was impossible to judge from inside

1. *Nippon Times*, 4 July 1943.

India, and thereby to judge what the results of the war would be; second, I wanted to get into contact with the Axis Powers and to see for myself their attitude regarding India; and whether it was possible to cooperate with them against the common enemy; third I wanted to make contact with Indians abroad in order to organize them, so that they also would help our fight for freedom. I may say all these three objectives have been fulfilled.

Q: Do you think that help carried to the independence movement to India from abroad can work Independently from the trend of the movement inside India?

A: No, we must work in complete harmony, with the same aims and by a common strategy. This is possible only when someone who has worked inside India comes out and contacts with people outside. It was for this that I had to take the risk of escaping from India.

Q. Perhaps it will be more risky to re-enter India? In fact you stated that no power on earth can prevent you from doing so. Do you mean by that campaign will start from inside India, even if prepared abroad?

A: Well, the campaign is really prepared inside India. But we have to give necessary directions so that people inside can expand the movement in accordance with the general war situation. When we have on the whole a more favourable war situation, then we can intensify the campaign at home. If not, we must go slowly. We have to wait until there is crisis for England in the general war situation-then act both by action from inside and pressure from outside. The time will come when I will have to re-enter India.

Q: What is meant by action from inside and pressure from outside?

A: The main thing is for us to fight. We must do our utmost to free ourselves and only when we have done our best, can we ask others for help. Even if help is offered to us we cannot accept it unless we can also do our share. By pressure from outside I mean two things; pressure of general war situation and also Indians outside India giving all possible help.

Q: Will not your effective campaign from abroad prompt the British Government to come to terms with the Congress as a result of which there might be split caused within the Congress itself, one

side following you and another following the compromised views? If such a situation arises, what would be your attitude?

A: The possibility of a compromise is always present, and we are determined to carry on our flight even if a part of our countrymen enter into a compromise with Britain. That a compromise has not already taken place between Mahatma Gandhi and the British Government is due to two reasons: first our party in the Congress has intensified the anti-British feeling throughout the country to such a degree that unless the British Government agrees to transfer full power immediately to India. Our leaders will not be able to persuade their people to accept the compromise; second, Churchill himself, is wrongly against making any concession now to the Indian people, because he wants to make up the war losses by exploiting India even more after the war is over.

Q: Please outline the meaning of "Purna Swaraj" and the course of its evolution during the past 20 years.

A: Before 1930 the goal of the Congress was swaraj. But the conception of swaraj and what relation India would have with Britain did not result altogether from the constitution of the Congress. "Swaraj" means "self–government", but the meaning of this phrase was rather vague: it was interpreted by us as complete independence, whereas older people thought it was possible to have swaraj in the form of dominion status, as Canada and Australia, and still remain within the British Commonwealth. In 1928, at the annual session held in Calcutta, Mahatma Gandhi moved a resolution that our demand be for dominion status. This was opposed by me, and after a long debate my resolution was defeated by 900 to 1,400 votes. But really speaking, many people voted against some because M.G made it a question of confidence. We had already organised a party within the congress, the Indian Independence League, and throughout 1929 we spread propaganda all over the country. In December 1929, at the Congress session held in Lahore, the situation was so changed that, had Gandhi opposed full independence, he would have been defeated. So at Lahore Gandhi himself came forward and moved a resolution by which complete independence, or purna swaraj should henceforth be our political objective. Now, in principle, it is impossible to reach any compromise therefore we have been holding that any talk of such a compromise means going against the Congress principles.

Q: What part is America playing in the present situation in India?

A: America has now lost the moral influence she had before she entered war. Everybody in India now realizes that America, under Roosevelt's administration has developed a new imperialism. As a result she has been sending to India her representatives and armed forces, so that in spite of the British Government being in India, the American Government is gradually going to get control of our country.

Q: At the interviews you give to foreign correspondents, much attention was called to your declaration that you were ready to abanden non-violence.

A: As far as civil disobedience campaign is concerned, there is no reason for abandoning it since it has proved so effective. It is our task to do more. But all the time, during these last 40 years there has been a big secret movement advocating and even employing violent tactics and lately in the congress, too resorted in some cases to them. The abandoning of non-violence is nothing new. But now the point is to adopt it on a big scale.

Q: Turning to external factors, let us make two suppositions, either the Japanese Army remains stationery on the Burmese-Indian border, or it advances into India. How would you act to meet these two respective conditions?

A: We desire the Indians themselves should take the initiative in the fight against British rule, whether it be an armed struggle, or a civil disobedience campaign. At the same time, they should utilize any new development in the war situation in any part of the world.

Q: It has been often said that the Indian problem is social reorganization and modernization more than independence. What do you think about this?

A: The political movement for independence has been in reality the strongest factor in bringing about social and educational reforms, as well as the development of national economy and industry. But we know from the actual experience that until we have gained complete freedom. It is impossible to bring about radical reform. Men in the Congress have most progressive ideas on such questions, and once India is free politically, they will be the best qualified to carry out a full programme of reform.

Q: What have you understood to be in the conception of the Axis Powers regarding India?

A: All the Axis Powers support the unconditional independence of India. It is for the Indian people themselves to decide what kind of political and social order they want to set up, and in this matter none of the Axis Powers will interfere in the least. For our part is but natural that we desire close relations with the countries that has helped us in your struggle for liberty.

24

Address by Rash Behari Bose while Handing over the Command of the I.I.M. to S.C. Bose; Explains that the Victory of the Axis Powers would Definitely Lead to India's Freedom[1]

4 July, 1943

"It is indeed a great pleasure for myself and for you all that we meet today, so soon after our last conference in Syonan. But events are marching fast these days and our Movement for the sacred cause of Mother India has made enormous strides in the two months since our Conference at the end of April. To day we are on the eve of the most vital the most decisive phase of our fight for the freedom of our Motherland, and I am confident that we are on the threshold of victory.

Friends, it is now one year and a half since the Indian Independence Movement was organised in East Asia. For all practical purposes, that historic day, December 8th 1941, when Japan unsheathed the sword of righteouseness to destroy the Anglo-American Imperialism and to liberate the Asiatic Nations from bondage...... that historic day marked the inception of the Indian Independence Movement in its present form. You do not expect me on this occasion to review the progress of our Movement, to enumerate our efforts, our successes and our failures. You know we started from scratch with nothing but our indomitable spirit of service to our Motherland. But soon we found sincere friends and powerful allies and our Movement gathered strength, thanks to your efforts and cooperation, thanks to the patriotic fervour of Indians throughout East Asia. And our most sincere gratitude is due to our Japanese friends, the Government of Japan, the local Military Authorities in every part of East Asia and to the Japanese Nation in general.

1. Sopan, *Netaji Subhash Chand Bose, His Life and Work* (Bombay-1946) pp. 293-300.

Friends and Comrades-in-Arms, as you all know very well, we have had our share of trials and tribulations, some trivial other serious. But thanks to your grim resolve in the battle for India's freedom and to your patience and devotion to duty, our movement survived all obstacles in its way and emerged with increased strength and solidarity. Today the Indian Independence League is an All-East Asia Organization an organization which is almost on a war footing. The League's Branches throughout East Asia are functioning smoothly and every Branch is contributing its share to the success of the great event's. I want to thank you form the _very bottom of my heart for all the support, assistance, and co-operation extended to me by you and your colleagues, as well as by compatriots throughout East Asia is the fulfilment of duties and responsibilities you have entrusted to me.

Friends, I told you that we are now on the eve of a new phase of our fight for India's independence. For decades India has been struggling against British domination and exploitation. Thousands of Indian patriots have laid down their lives in the cause of India's freedom; and even at this very moment, all India is at war with Britain. As Mahatma Gandhi, our revered leader has stressed "This is a fight to the finish". And with the help of Almighty God, the fight will be finished with the glorious victory of India and ignominious defect of India's enemies, the Anglo-Americans.

Friends, a casual glance at world events today will show you what I mean. Within India the Anti-British revolution has been going on for nearly eleven months. The British boasted that they would crush the revolution in no time but they have failed and failed miserably, inspite of all the ruthless terror and repression they unleashed on India's freedom-fighters. Beyond the frontiers of India we Indians in East Asia are girding for battle to supplement the efforts of Indian Nationalists at home. And in support of us for the assistance of India we have powerful allies, the Japanese. It was only the other day while I was in Tokyo that Prime Minister general Hideki Tojo. re-affirmed Japan pledge of all out aid to India in her fight against the Anglo-American forces. And you will remember that Premier Tojo also made the categorical declaration that it is Japan's policy to assist India to attain full independence in the true sense of the term.

Friend and Comrades-in-Arms, now you see why I am confident that India's victory is a certainty. As I have told you very often, the odds are in our favour—I mean in India's favour—and against our enemies, the Anglo-American enemies of India. This is our God-sent opportunity—an opportunity that we must take advantage of. For decades India fought

Britain single-handed, but today, India has powerful allies. Japan and her Axis partners in Europe are India's friends and allies. India is with them in this war. Victory of the Axis Powers means slavery of India for hundreds of years to come. Therefore as Indians our duty is clear. For the sake of India's freedom, for the sake of justice and decency is this world, for the sake of a better order of human life and intercourse, we Indians must work and fight for the victory of Japan and the Axis Powers. For, as I have just said, victory of Japan and the Axis powers means victory of India, the freedom of four hundred million Indians, the glory of Asia and a new order in the world.

Friends, when I left Syonan for Tokyo towards the end of May, I told you that I would be back in about six weeks. And I am here now. I want to thank the Administrative Committee of the Headquarters for the most efficient manner in which they had carried on the work during my absence and, want to thank you all for the warm reception you accorded me on my return.

Today we meet here just two days after my return from Tokyo and naturally you would expect me to say something of what I saw and heard in Japan. Well, I was impressed by many things I saw and heard during my brief sojourn in Japan. I was greatly impressed by the great sympathy for India's cause on the part of the entire Japanese Nation from His Excellency the Premier down to the man in the street. Freedom of India is stressed on all sides and the entire Japanese Nation is prepared our and out in helping India expel the Anglo-American enemies and to win the National Independence. And you know for yourselves that Japan is fully confident of her ability to help us crush the Anglo-Americans in India. And was for the sincerity of Japan's policy we have before us the historic example of Burma which will be independent very soon and that of the Philippines which will emerge as a free country within the course of this year 1943.

Friends, this is India's golden opportunity—an opportunity the like of which may never again occur. We take this opportunity and we save our Mother land, we save the four hundred millions of our compatriots from the alien tyranny that has been crushing their body and soul for over two hundred years. On the other hand, we miss this opportunity and we betray our Motherland. We condemn our four hundred million brethren and the future generations of India, to slavery for ever. Now or never is our opportunity, now or never is India's chance for freedom.

Friends and Comrades-in-Arms, you might probably expect me to say somethng more of what I saw in Japan. Well, I saw in Japan a great and powerful Nation in its grim resolve for victory. And remember what I told you just a little ago; Japan's victory means India's freedom. India's victory and glory.

In Japan, I saw mighty forces at work forging, weapons of war, assuring victory of the Asiatic cause. The unity and determination of the people of Japan are mervellous, their war-efforts at their zenith, factories work day and night turning over war planes, tanks, arms and ammunition. The huge factories and workshops which once carried on peacetime manufacture, are armament factories now which means the entire industry of Japan is a war industry. The entire labour of the Japanese Nation is now war-labour. New docks and shipyards in various parts of Japan turn out war-ships and merchant vessels to further strengthen Japan's invincible Navy and intrepid merchant marine. Training of soldiers, officers and airmen goes on throughout the country and millions of youngmen are joining the armed forces. And as for the food situation in Japan, I got exactly the same food that I got last year. There is plenty of rice, fish, meat and vegetables. One year and a half of war has not in the least affected Japan's food situation, thanks to the excellent planning and control by the Government. In one word, I found Japan, united as one man with no thought but of war and victory-victory of the holy war of liberation, victory that would mean freedom and prosperity for India and all Asia.

Friends and Comrades-in-Arms, you might now ask me what I did in Tokyo for our cause, what present I have brought for you. Well I have brought for you this present (turning to Subhas.) Shrijut Subhas Chandra Bose needs no introduction to you, to India or the world. He symbolises all that is best, noblest, the most daring and the most dynamic in the youth of India. As an all India leader in the fight against British Imperialism, he stands as a class by himself. He is a brilliant leader and an uncompromising fighter. He has dedicated his life to the cause of Mother India and he richly deserves the name of "Desh Sevak Subhas". Eleven times he has been to British political prisoners but all that suffering and sacrifice have only strengthened his dynamic will to wage the battle for freedom until victory is achieved. Friends, this is one of the happiest moments in my life. I have brought to you one of the most outstanding personalities of our secred Motherland to participate in our campaign for the freedom of India. The spontaneous and enthusiastic welcome which the two million Indians in East Asia have extended to Subhash is an unqualified assurance to him—and to me and to India-that Indians in East Asia have whole heartedly placed themselves and all they have at his command.

Friends and Commander in-Arms! In your presence to-day. I resign my office and appoint Deshsevak Subhas Chandra Bose as President of Indian Independence League in East Asian.

25

Address by Col. J.K. Bhonsle, Director Military Bureau Welcoming Bose as New President on Behalf of the Army; Hopes that his Leadership will Inspire the People and Guide them Successfully to the Achievement of India's Freedom

4 July, 1943

Sri Subhas Chandra Bose, Sir,

Two days ago I, on behalf of the Indians of East Asia, had the proud privilege of welcoming you amidst us, today, as a soldier, on behalf of the Indian National Army, I greet you.

Your brilliant achievement's as one of the greatest leaders of contemporary India and the sacrifices that you have made for the cause of the motherland, are so well known to every one that there is no need for me to narrate them here.

To us you are a new hope, your arrival has instilled a new spirit among our soldiers. So far we had an ideal and a cause to fight for, now we have a leader who will inspire and guide us successfully to the achievement of our goal.

The battle of Indian Independence started in 1857 and has gone on incessantly ever since. So far victory has been denied to us. During every phase of our struggle there was something lacking. We had no armed force to fight the might of the British Empire. We had the leaders of the highest caliber, our men and women showed courage and valour unparalleled in the word history. Unarmed and unaided from outside they defied the British Empire. Through shear tenacity of our purpose we managed to get a few concessions out of the grudging Britishers, but final goal of complete Independence was still not achieved.

To win a victory it is necessary to engage the armed forces of the enemy in a battle and destroy them. To carry out this operation you must have an organised armed force of your own.

1. K.S. Giani, *op.cit.* p. 15.

To day India has an army pledged to fight for the liberation of India. We are determined to fight any one who tries to dominate India. India is ours and must belong to us. Our friends can come there and deal with us as friends, but no one other than Indians shall ever rule her again. We have tasted the misery of slavery long enough. We will be free and shall remain free.

The sacrifice and sufferings of thousands of the brave Indians who have laid their lives at the altar of freedom and the prayers of the starving millions of Indians have borne fruit today. The combination of cincumstances has created a most favourable situation for India.

Telling blows by the Axis Powers have broken the might of the Anglo-American Imperialism, the people of India are up in revolt and with the help of Nippon we have organised ourselves in East Asia to fight for our motherland. We have been given a promise of all out aid by Nippon and the other Axis Powers have given us the assurance of their support.

We are ready and pledged to our motherland. We only await your orders. You are our leader, we have trusted our destinies and the destiny of India in your hand. When you think the opportune time to strike has come, on your orders we shall march forward.

Ours shall be a grim but a glorious fight. I am sure—may certain—our soldiers will give a good account of themselves. We will meet the enemy in the field and destory him there and rid the sacred Bharat Mata from the evil influences of Anglo-American Imperialism for ever.

Vande-Mataram.

26

Bose's Speech at a Huge Rally at Singapore While Taking Over the Command of the I.I.M. from Rash Behari; Requests all Indians to Rise and Fight for the Liberation of Their Enslaved Motherland

4 July, 1943

"From the bottom of my heart, I thank you, Mr. Rash Behari Bose, the representative in East Asia of the movement for Indian Independence, for appointing me leader in East Asia of the movement. I have accepted that post and I humbly pray the god will give me strength to carry out my duties, and hope sincerely that I will be able to satisfy completely my compatriots inside and outside of India. If you accept the experience that I have gained in India and out since the outbreak of the current great war then you too will understand as I, do that the god above is protecting us from the many cases of persecution and oppression and is leading our efforts toward victory and freedom. By this fact my optimism and confidence has increased a hundred fold.

"My friends the time has finally come for the freedom loving Indians to rise. In war time and in emergency, however military discipline as well as the indomitable loyalty to fall for a great cause, if of the greatest, necessity. Therefore I would like to call upon all of my compatriots in East Asia to prepare fully to go into the intense fighting lying before us with solid organization under one centralize control and leadership. I believe deeply that you will not act contrary to my expectations.

"I also believe firmly that freedom loving Indians throughout the world who have continued to work actively for Indian Independence will all give their support to the present movement. And the Indians at present in enemy countries and who therefore are unable to work actively for Indian Independence also support us spiritually. This is the first time in recent world history that Indians in various foreign countries have been

1. *Nippon Times*, 5 July 1943.

united into one centralized organizations aiming at the attainment of common goal. What is further to be noted is that patriotic Indians outside India are working as one for their motherland in perfect harmony with complete contact with their comrades in India. Since I left India in 1941, carrying with a truly important mission. I have had frequent occasions to declare openly, bluntly that my mission is based on the will of the absolute majority of my compatriots. And in spite of every device the secret police contrived to prevent me from doing so, I have maintained continuous contact with my compatriots at home.

"Not only that, I can tell you here that in the last 12 months a great number of representatives have made contact from all directions with India. Some of these representatives where captured, some were shot to death. But when the time comes we will without fail avenge them fully. The greater number of these representatives, however escaped being captured, and especially, according to recent reports, are carrying out action satisfactorily. That is, the patriotic Indians in foreign countries are working actively as fitting representatives of the fighters for Independence in India. I would like to repeat that what we have done until today, and what we will do in the future for the independence of India have not been contrary to what compatriots desired. I say that definitely again to all Indians.

"Then how can we gain independence? There was a time when we hoped that Britain would be forced under an international crises to accede voluntarily for its own good to Indians demands for independence. But those friends who held that veer today no doubt feeling the sorrow of this futile dream. It is clear that Britain, during the war and after, will continue to exploit India. The Wavell is about to be sent to India as Viceroy is only for that a reason.

"A certain section in India seems to be extremely dissatisfied over the appointment of Wavell. They probably wanted some one like Hali-fax for that post I can not agree with such a view. By Wavell's appointment I see, like the handwriting on the wall a prophecy of the future. Wavell's carries with him a fate of being the last British viceroy in India. The new viceroy has the duty to increase Britain's political and economic exploitation of India but as result the hate of Indian masses will become further aggravated and united revolutionary power will take a long step forward being more powerful.

"However, Britain, at the same time she puts into force a brute dictatorial rule, without fail, plan to accomplish a compromise. Such a plan will only be a trick, a ruse and nothing more. It follows that you, our compatriots inside India, must see through to the truth and prepare just as you did in April, 1942, when special envoy Cripps proposed futfile promise.

"In his recent address given at the Guild Hall, London, Prime Minister Churchill use the term "British Common Wealth", and that has clearly revealed his attitude towards India. Of course, it is natural for the imperialistic British Prime Minister to adopt every possible effort to main the integrity of the British empire. Whatever proposal he might make to India, it form nothing but the wish to cheat the Indians. It will absolutely meaningless to think of compromising with the British empire will soon disappear from the face of the earth.

"You who have learned the history of the movement for emancipation in all countries of the world know that for the attainment of independence two conditions are necessary. The first is a favourable international situation and the second is the sacrifice.

"The first condition has been already realized. If India had to fight the British Empire with her bare hands, our task must have been very difficult. But Japan, Germany and Italy are now fighting our enemy and giving him fatal blow, and thus our burden is greatly lightened. These three nations are also determined to continue the war until the imperialism of the United States and Great Britain is destroyed. Thus we are in a favourable position.

"My friends, these two years, I had been continuing to travel to see the real condition of the world war. This study has convinced me that however long the war might continue there only one result—the complete victory of Japan, Germany and Italy, and their allies. Of course, there will be various difficulties before the British-American imperialism is totally smashed.

"Then in a long war, there will be certainly temporary changes in the war situation. I am well aware of the fact, that at present the United States and great Britain are enjoying temporary advantages in certain unimportant fronts. But the entire war situation and particularly strategic conditions are very favourable to Japan, Germany and Italy.

"As time pass the United States and Britain will suffer continued defeats, as you will see. Though the British Empire possessed vast national strength, it has been asking for aids from all quarters. This it is natural for us to ask for sympathy and co-operation as far as possible.

"All past emancipation movements in world history had foreign supports to attain success. In case of India, Japan, Germany and Italy have become our natural allies and therefore, in case of necessity there is nothing wrong in willingly receiving their sympathy and aid.

"Some of you seem to have been influenced by British propaganda and doubt the sincerity of the attitude of the Japan, Germany and Italy toward India. It is quite natural for nations fighting British imperialism to support all demands of India. Then, putting Britain aside for a moment, it will be good for Japan, Germany and Italy, or the whole world, that India will become free. The three nations announced their attitude toward India several times in the past.

"The Government of Japan, through Prime Minister Tojo, announced its policy towards the Philippines, Burma and India because of hypocrites, their propaganda organs said that the Japanese attitude lacked sincerity. Prime Minister Tojo bravely announced to the whole world that the Independence of Burma would be given not after the conclusion of the war but within the present year. That was fatal blow to the British and American propaganda.

"The attitude of the Japanese Government toward the Philippines and Burma is proof of her sincerity and justice. As one of you, I can find no reason to doubt the attitude of the Japanese Government.

"Japan is a strong nation who successfully repulsed foreign invasion. Unless Asiatic peoples who had become slaves are liberated, Asiatic countries would never be safe from the threat of invasion. Japan knows this fact better than any other Asiatic nation.

"Further more, in Japan today there has arisen strong Asiatic consciousness and there is an atmosphere of desiring to cooperate with Asiatic races for their emancipation. These favourable development are giving all enslaved Asiatic people an opportunity to liberate themselves and to establish a new order based on liberty and justice. If there is any one who doubts this point, I feel like saying to him, "Believe me". In view of my loyalty or atleast patriotic sentiment toward India, even enemies cannot say that I am betraying my Motherland.

"As I have said at Tokyo recently, the British Government persecuted me all the time, but it was unable to crush my conviction and principle. Who can move my principle? Craftly British political parties could not cheat me, and no body else can.

"All Indians must bear in their mind that when the United States and Britain should be victorius, India will be left in the state of slavery and will be exploited more than ever.

"Thus the only hope for India to gain independence and freedom rests on the victory of Japan, Germany and Italy. Thus we must work so that our flight, the Axis' victory and the freedom of India will be brought together.

"My friends, we are now given the most favourable international situation. Therefore for attaining freedom, it is only necessary to exert sufficient endeavours and to make sacrifices. In this respect, our efforts in the past were not at all unsatisfactory.

"You will remember my declaration made last May, 85 years after the First Indian Independence war, following the departure of Sir Stafford Cripps from India, that Indian resistance had entered an important stage.

"We passed a number of mile posts as we advanced on our road to independence. One of them was the intensification of non-violence and non-obedience movement. Another was the launching of a drive to cause disturbance in India following the arrest of Mahatma Gandhi in August last year. August 1942 is a most important period in the history of the independence movement in India. During that month the men in the movement abandoned their passive attitude in the drive in favour of an attitude of active resistance. It was during this month that the mass of men in India made up their minds to use some other method than non-violence and non-obedience in order to achieve their ideal of their independent India. It was clear that the time had come for the Independence movement to enter the new stage.

"The thing the Indians at home and abroad have to do today is clear. They have to build a structure enabling them to work for an independent India under unified direction.

"The aim of this structure is to organize the Indians in a manner which will enable them to rise in arms against British Imperialism when the time to do so has come. I have an idea of mobilizing all our resources effectively, an idea which impels me to organize a provisional government is to direct the effort to revolutionize India and realize the ideal of an independent India.

"In order to gain its end the provisional government will prepare the Indians at home and abroad for an armed struggle with American and British Imperialism. An armed struggle for an independent India represents the last phase of the national effort of the Indian people since 1885. The provisional government will have finished its work when American and British imperialism is swept out of India. A permanent government reflecting the will of the Indian people will then be set up, to it the provisional government will transfer power.

"When we are fully prepared for our final armed resistance, it will be possible for us to fight at the side of Japan, Germany and Italy. By participating in the war against the common enemy we should be able to qualify as the people of free and independent nation. Blood shed in the cause of great and holy principle is the price we have to pay for freedom and independance. When we the Indians are ready to shed blood in this way they will have laid firmly the foundations of a structure of national unity. It must be remembered that in sacrificing ourselves to acquire freedom we shall be getting the power to preserve the freedom once it is gained.

"Friends, I wish to express my hearty gratitude to you who repose trust in me and who have signified your intention of giving endless support to me. I have an unshakeable confidence in our ability to win in the struggle for freedom. But it will be dangerous for us to make light of the enemy. I warn you that there will be ups and downs before the ideal we are after is a reality. The enemy is strong, and he will stop at nothing to check us. I imagine that you will find yourselves starving and in frightful difficulties in the final stages of our fight for freedom.

"Freedom will be yours only when you have passed the trial. I have a firm conviction that you will overcome difficulties which are sure to confront you along the way to freedom and be successful in bringing freedom and happiness to your mother country which is impoverished and in the state of slavery".

Inqiulab Zindabad! Azad Hind Zindabad

27

Bose to the INA Soldiers : Outlines their Duties Towards their Motherland[1]

5 July, 1943

Soldiers of India's Army of Liberation and my Comrades,

To-day is the proudest day of my life. To-day it has pleased Providence to give me the unique privilege and honour of announcing to the whole world that India's Army of Liberation has come into being. This Army has now been drawn up in military formation on the battlefield of Singapore, which was once the bulwark of the British Empire. This is not only the Army that will emancipate India from the British yoke, it is also the Army that will here-after, create the future national army of Free India. Every Indian must feel proud that this Army—his own Army—has been organised entirely under Indian leadership and that when the historic moment arrives, under Indian leadership it will go to battle.

There are people who thought at one time that the Empire, on which the sun did not set, was an everlasting Empire. No such thought ever troubled me. History has taught me that every empire has its inevitable deadline and collapse. Moreover, I had seen with my own eyes, cities and fortresses that were once the bulwark, but which became the graveyards of by-gone Empires. But standing to-day on the graveyard of the British Empire, even a child is convinced that the almighty British Empire is already a thing of the past.

When France declared war on Germany in 1939 and the campaign began, there was but one cry which rose from the lips of German soldiers "To Paris, to Paris." When the brave soldiers of Nippon set out on their march in December, 1941, there was but one cry which rose from their lips "To Singapore, to Singapore." Comrades! My soldiers! Let your battle cry be "To Delhi, to Delhi." How many of us will individually survive this war of Freedom, I do not know. But I do know this that we shall ultimately win and our task will not end until our surviving heroes hold the victory-

1. *Nippon Times*, 6 July, 1943.

parade on another graveyard of the British Empire—the Lal Kila or Red Fortress of ancient Delhi.

Throughout my public career, I have always felt that, though India is otherwise ripe for independence in every way, she has lacked on thing; namely, an army of liberation. George Washington of America could fight and win freedom, because he had his army. Garibaldi could liberate Italy, because he had his armed volunteers behind him. It is your privilege and honour to be the first to come forward and organise India's National Army. By doing so, you have removed the last obstacle in our path to freedom. Be happy and proud that you are the pioneers—he vanguard—in such a noble cause.

Let me remind you that you have a two-fold task to perform. With the force of arms and at the cost of your blood you will have to win liberty. Then, when India is free, you will have to organise the permanent army of Free India whose task it will be to preserve our liberty for all time. We must build up our national defence on such an unshakable foundation that never again in our history shall we lose our freedom.

As soldiers, you will always have to cherish and live up to the three ideals of faithfulness, duty and sacrifice. Soldiers, who always remain faithful to their nation, who perform their duty under all circumstances, and who are always prepared to sacrifice their lives, are invincible. If you, too want to be invincible engrave these three ideals in the innermost core of your hearts. A true soldier needs both military and spiritual training. You must—all of you—so train your selves and your Comrades that every solider will have unbounded confidence in himself will be conscious of being immensely superior to the enemy, will be fearless of death and will have sufficient initiative to act on his own in any critical situation, should the need arise. During the course of the present war, you have seen with your own eyes what wonders, scientific training, coupled with courage, fearlessness and dynamism, can achieve. Learn all that you can from this example and build up for Mother India an absolutely first class modern army.

To those of you who are officers, I should like to say that your responsibility is a heavy one. Though the responsibility of an officer in every army in this world is indeed great, it is far greater in your case. Because of our political enslavement. We have no tradition like that of Mukden, Port Arthur or Sedan to inspire us. We have to unlearn some of the things that the British taught us and we have to learn much that they did not teach. Nevertheless, I am confident that you will rise to the occasion and fulfil the task that your countrymen have thrown on your brave shoulders. Remember, too, that the British have suffered defeats on so many fronts, largely because of worthless officers. And remember also that out of your ranks will be born the future General Staff of the Army of Free India.

To all of you I should like to say that in the course of this war, you will have to acquire and experience and achieve the success which alone can build up a national tradition for our army in future. An army that has no tradition of courage, fearlessness and invincibility cannot hold its own in a struggle with a powerful enemy.

Comrades! you have voluntarily accepted a mission that is the noblest that the human mind can conceive of. For the fulfilment of such a mission, no sacrifice is to great—not even the sacrifice of one's life. You are to-day the custodians of India's national honour and the embodiment of India's hopes and aspirations. So conduct yourselves that your countrymen may bless you and posterity may be proud of you.

I have said that to-day is the proudest day of my life. For an enslaved people, there can be no greater pride, no higher honour, than to be the first solider in the army of liberation. But this honour carries with it a corresponding responsibility and I am deeply conscious of it. I assure you that I shall be with you in darkness and in sunshine, in sorrow and in joy, in suffering and in victory. For the present. I can offer you nothing except hunger, thirst, privation, forced marches and death. But if you follow me in life and in death—as I am confident you will—I shall lead you to victory and freedom. It does not matter who among us will live to see India free. It is enough that India shall be free and that we shall give our all to make her free. May God now bless our Army and grant us victory in the coming fight!

Inquilab Zindabad! Azad Hind Zindabad!

28

Communique by I.I.L. Headquarters Announcing the Aims and Objects of the I.N.A. Under the Leadership of S.C. Bose

5 July, 1943

The I.I.L. in East Asia has organised an Army. This army will be known as the Azad Hind Fauj or the Indian National Army. The Azad Hind Fauj has sworn allegiance to the cause of India's complete independence. The officers and men of Azad Hind Fauj have dedicated their times to the secret task of expelling the British from Indian and establishing an India. for the Indians. After the above communique, the spokeman of the I.I.L. made the following statement:-

"You have just listened to the official announcement of the Indian Independence League Headquarters, that the League has organised an Army which will be known as the Azad Hind Fauj or the Indian National Army. You have also heard that this Azad Hind Fauj or the Indian National Army has sworn allegiance to the cause of India's complete independence and the officers and men of the army have dedicated their lives to the sacred task of expelling the British from India and creating an India for Indians.

I wish to make it clear to the world that the Indian National Army has been organised solely by Indians and consists of picked soldiers from Indian Volunteers who have taken a solemn oath to achieve the complete independence of India by fighting the British and wiping out of India all traces of the two centuries of British Rule. They are anti-British in very fibre of their being and they are inspired by the spirit of independence. They have dedicated their lives to the cause of India's freedom; they have no thought of personal comforts luxury or profit, their one motto is "Freedom or death" to quote Mahatma Gandhi's dictum; and they are ready to lay down their lives in the fight for India's complete independence.

This is the first time in India's history since the advent of the British that a truly National Army has been raised.

1. K.S. Giani, *op.cit.* pp. 23-24.

The sole aim of the I.N.A. (Indian National Army) is to destroy the British Power and influence in India and to make an India for Indians.

As I said earlier the I.N.A. is a picked fighting force from Indians selected on the basis of volunteer system. The men of this force are burning with the anti-British spirit of independence.

The anti-British spirit permeates the entire I.N.A. it is organised on a system best adopted to the Indian genius and is in tune with the revolutionary war which the I.N.A. is expected to wage when the time for action comes.

The training of the I.N.A. is also adopted to Indian spiritual and cultural heritage and Indian military traditions. A strong anti-British spirit and the spirit of independence are the bases of the moral spiritual training undergone by every single soldier of the I.N.A. from the commander down to the soldier. Their training goes on from morning till night. As soldiery the entire I.N.A. is best upon beating British tactics and it is well trained and equipped so to do.

The uniform of the officers and men of the I.N.A. also conform to the Indian Spirit, Indian genius and Indian environments.

The British have been ruling over India by sedulously following their policy of "Divide and Rule". They carried this policy in to the Indian Army also thus keeping alive the difference of race and religion in the Indian Army and thus preventing the growth of National consciousness in the Army. Fully realising the diabolical nature of this "Divide and Rule" policy of the British the organisers of the Indian National Army have laid the axe at the very root of this traditions. All distinctions of class, caste, creed and religion have been abolished in the Indian National Army which has been organised on truly National lines. There are no water-tight compartments based on the religious faiths of the members of the I.N.A. Every man of the I.N.A. feels that he is an Indian first and Indian last. His goal is liberation of India from British rule; and his motto is unity, faith and sacrifice.

The officers and men of I.N.A. are undergoing an intensive training course of enlightenment and culture to fit them spiritually for the sacred task before them.

Spartan living is one of the marked features of the I.N.A. and Indian manners and customs have been given an honoured place in the general conduct of the I.N.A.

To wipe out every trace of denationalisation deliberately fostered by the British by the compulsory use of English language and to establish strong bonds of affinity between the officers and men, the Indian language has been adopted as the medium of communication between officers and men at the barracks and on the field.

I would most emphatically stress once again that the I.N.A. is entirely of the Indians and for the Indians. And only task to which the I.N.A. has solemnly decided itself is the winning of India's complete independence.

Nippon has repeatedly pledged all-out aid to India to achieve her complete independence free from any foreign control or interference.

In conformity with this pledge the relations between the I.N.A. and the Nippon Army are those of two allied armies."

Re-organisation of the I.I.L. by S.C. Bose in the Light of the New Wave of Interest Shown by the Indians in East Asia after his Arrival[1]

13 July, 1943

In view of the new responsibilities that the Indian Independence Movement has to face in the near future and in view of the wave of enthusiasm that is visible among Indians in East Asia, it has become necessary to reorganise the Indian Independence League. The first step in this direction is to reorganise the Headquarters of the Indian Independence League. For this reorganisation, some of the existing Departments have to be expanded while other new Departments have also to be set up. I am giving below the scheme of reorganisation. I shall watch carefully the result of this reorganisation and in the light of experience, I may make further changes—if and when necessary.

Departments

1. Military Bureau, 2. Recruitment, 3. Training, 4. Supplies, 5. Finance, 6. Publicity, Press and Propaganda, 7. Health and Social Welfare, 8. Overseas, 9. Women, 10. Reconstruction, 11. Education and Culture and 12. General Secretary.

Department of Recruitment

This Department will organise Recruitment for the Azad Hind Fauj (Indian National Army) all over East Asia in a systematic way. This is a new Department.

Department of Training

The existing Youth Department will be absorbed in this new Department. The work of this Department will be to provide some kind of training for all recruits throughout East Asia until the Army is in a position to take over these recruits and put them into military barracks.

---

1. S.A. Das and K.B. Subbaiah, *Chalo Delhi*, Kuala Lumpur, 1946, pp. 149-156.

The existing Training Institutes will be managed by this Department and if necessary, more may be started. The present staff of the Youth Department will come under this Department and fresh appointments will be made, if and when necessary, according to the amount of work that has to be handled by the department. The Head of the Youth Department will become the head of the Department of Training.

Department of Supplies

The function of this new Department will be to collect supplies from all over East Asia for the Indian Independence Movement in general and for the Azad Hind Fauj (Indian National Army) in particular for present and future use.

The existing Stores at the Headquarters of the Indian Independence League will henceforth be managed by the Department of Supplies.

Department of Health and Social Welfare

The existing Welfare Department will be absorbed in this Department. The new Department of Health and Social Welfare will have two sub-departments-namely: (a) Medical, and (b) Social Welfare.

The existing Welfare Department with its staff will be absorbed in the sub department of Social Welfare. The head of the Welfare Department will become the Head of the Sub-department of Social Welfare. The medical Sub-department will be under a junior Medical Officer. The whole department of Health and Social Welfare will be under a Senior Medical Officer.

Overseas Department

The work of this new Department will be:

(a) To direct and stimulate the work of theh Branches

(b) To establish new Branches where necessary

(c) To maintain regular contact between the Headquarters and the different Branches.

Women's Department

This will be a new Department. The work of this Department will be to organise Indian women throughout East Asia and direct and stimulate their activities in connection with the Indian Independence Movement.

This Department will also recruit women for the Army and will organise a Red Cross Department form among Indian women and girls.

Reconstruction Department

The work of this new Department will be:

(a) To prepare plans for the future—particularly in connection with future administration in India.

(b) To train men for future administration, etc.

Education and Culture

This will be a new Department. The function of this Department will be to direct the educational and cultural activities of Indians in East Asia to provide for additional facilities in this connection, in so far as it is possible for the League to do so.

General Secretary's Department

The functions of this Department will be—

(a) To maintain liasion with the Hikari Kiran[2]

(b) To co-ordinate the work of the different Departments

(c) To perform any special duties that may be assigned by me from time to time.

This Department will have a sub-department, to be called the House Sub-department. This sub-department will deal with problems arising out of the daily work of the Indian Independence League Headquarters, e.g., (a) Transport and Petrol, (b) Buildings and their equipment, (c) Light, Telephone, etc. at the Headquarters, (d) Medical Staff, and (e) Arrangement for the stay of guests coming from outside.

When the work of the House Sub-Department increases it may be necessary and advisable to convert it into a full-fledged Department.

Establishment

Questions dealing with establishment (e.g., appointments, allowances, transfer, etc.) will be dealt with by me. The Department concerned will, however, make recommendations from time to time.

Existing Staff

The existing Staff will all continue to work for the League in future. Transfers from one Department to another may, however, be made, if found

2. Major General Iwakuro had departed form Malaya to take up another appointment leaving the Kikan in charge of his successor Col. Yamamoto, the Kikan came to be known as "Hikari Kikan," "Hikari" meaning light and glory.

to be necessary, in order to give effect to the re-organisation scheme outlined above.

Detailed Instructions

Detailed instructions with regard to the working of each Department will follow.

Sd/-
Subhas Chandra Bose,
President,
The Indian Independence League
East Asia.

The following circulars were issued by the Departments of Recruitment and Training to provide detailed instructions for the working of each department:

Indian Independence League Headquarters.
(Department of Recruitment).

Subject: Recruitment

You may be aware by now that the Headquarters of the Indian Independence League have been re-organised and that, in order to effect the Total Mobilisation of our manpower and resources, several new department have been started. In accordance with this plan, this Department has come into existence and it is the earnest desire of our President that at least 300,000 men, (including women volunteers) be recruited for the coming fight for India's freedom.

Regarding the training of these recruits, the newly formed Training Department will address you separately. I shall only tell you this that we do not want to call up these recruits at once. In fact, the training will be done in three stages. In the first stage, recruits should not leave either homes or their professional work—and they should do only morning or evening drills. In the second stage, they will be brought into camps for whole-time training—when these camps are started in diffferent parts of East Asia. In the third stage, they will be brought in to military Barracks when they will become full-fledged members of the Azad Hind Fauj (Indian National Army).

It will be considered a breach of discipline if any recruit suddenly gives up his professional work, or leaves his home, before he is called up for whole-time training.

To carrry on the recruitment of volunteers for the Indian National Army in a systematic way, the following machinery is being set up:—

1. Under each Territorial Committee, the Chairman of every I.I.L. Branch will be the Recruiting offficer for his own area.
2. Under each Branch, the Chairman of every I.I.L. Sub Branch will be Assistant Recruiting officer and will be responsible for recruitment within his area.
3. The Recruiting Officer (Branch Chairman) will supervise and co-ordinated the work of the Assistant Recruiting Officers. In case any Assistant Recruiting Officer fails to do his work properly, the Recruiting Officer will have authority to remove him and appoint a new Assistant Recruiting Officer in his place—after obtaining the approval of the chairman of the Territorial Committee.
4. The Chairman of each Territorial Committee will be the Chief Recruiting Officer for his area. He will supervise and co-ordinate the work of the Recruiting officers within his area. In case any Recruiting offficer fails to do his work properly, the Chief Recruiting Officer can remove him and appoint a new Recruiting Officer in his place—after obtainning the approval of the Secretary of the Department of Recruitment of the I.I.L. Headquarters.

Duties Regarding Recruitment

1. Each recruit should fill in an enrolment form and hand it over to the Assistant Recruiting Officer.
2. These forms should be collected and sent to Headquarters through the Recruiting Officer and the Chief Recruiting Officer.
3. Owing to extreme emergency, old forms are being made use of, until revised forms are printed by this Department.
4. In case of shortage of printed forms, typed enlistment forms may be used by any Recruiting Officer or Assistant Recruiting Officer.
5. Each Officer, either R.O. or A.R.O., who is directly responsible for recruitment should keep a register of all the recruits who have applied for enlistment within his area—together with all particulars regarding each recruit.
6. Every C.R.O., R.O. and A.R.O., will please note that there will be no age-restriction for recruits applying for enlistment. Printed forms of enlistment which contain age restriction should be amended accordingly.

7. Each Assistant Recruiting Officer should arrange for the Medical Examination of each recruit within his area. If necessary, he will, take the help of the R.O. in this connection and the R.O. will if necessary, take the help of the C.R.O. in this connection.

8. The forms of enlistment duly filled in should be forwarded to Headquarters, together with the Medical Officer's report.

9. No recruit should be rejected by the Medical Officer simply because he does not come up to the Army Standard— Provided he is otherwise physically fit.

10. Each Branch or Sub-Branch as the case may be, should meet the expenses in connection with recruitment.

11. Enlistment forms together with the Medical Officer's report should be sent to Headquarters regularly once a fortnight. The first instalment of enlistment forms should be sent up as soon as possible.

12. In order to facilitate and expedite the work of recruitment the Headquarters will send to each Territorial Committee one or more Military Recruitment Advisors. The C.R.O., R.O. and A.R.O. are requested to make the fullest use of these Advisers.

Secretary,
Department of Recruitment

Indian Independence League Headquarters
(Department of Training)

Subject—Training

In view of the total mobilisation in which Netaji requires not only the youth but all able-bodied men to serve irrespective of age, the existing Youth Department has been absorbed in the Training Department.

2. The training being imparted to the Youth Sections by the I.S.I. and the Azad School Graduates at the local centres in Malaya will be continued under the directions of the "Member in Charge Training" of each branch or sub-branch.

More Instructors for local training will be sent to Malaya Branches on demand by the Malayan Chairman.

The demand from other territories should state the approximate number of recruits likely during the next 3 months.

3. The system of training will mobilise the manpower of East Asia in three successive stages:-

1st Stage—Local training in the nature of part time instructions for 2 hours in the morning or evening, every day as far as possible.

This is the responsibility of the territorial Branch and its Sub-Branches. Recruits should neither leave their profession, nor their homes.

It will be considered a breach of discipline if any recruit suddenly gives up his professional work, or leaves his home, before he is called up for whole-time training.

Instructors for this purpose will be provided from I.N.A. and from men trained in Central Camps.

Officers of the Azad Hind Fauj (I.N.A.) who are on recruiting or other duty will be utilized wherever possible to supervise such training and to help the Local Chairman in matters of Military Training and Organisation.

2nd Stage—Central Training in Central Camps under the direct Control of this Headquarters.

(i) Ordinary Camps; (ii) Special Camps.

(i) Territories will be informed of their quota for ordinary camps as and when Camps are ready. Although no high educational qualifications are needed, the best men from local training Centres must be selected to make up this quota.

The first ordinary Central Camp will open in Malaya on or about August 15. The total quota of 5,000 is allotted to Malaya. Detailed instructions later.

(ii) **Special Camps**—The highest possible educational qualifications are needed for candidates for Special Camps.

Three such Camps, the Azad School, Syonan, the B.Y.T.C., Kuala Lumpur, and the Swaraj Youth Training Institute, Rangoon, are already in existence.

Another Camp, the Azad School, Penang, for 100 volunteers will open during the first week of August 2603. As other territories will not be able to send candidates in time the quota of 100 will also be required from Malaya.

Other territories should proceed with the task of sifting good material and must send in applications as soon as possible.

3rd Stage—Training in Azad Hind Fauj.

This will begin as soon as the Army is in a position to absorb the men permanently.

When the system is in full swing volunteers from the 1st and 2nd stages of training will provide a large reservoir for the I.N.A.

4. *Conditions and Allowances*—In addition to free clothing, board and lodging, men in all central camps will receive a normal pocket allowance.

5. Training Syllabus and Organisation for the 1st Stage and will remain the same as given "Interim Plan" dated 13-4-2603 except that more emphasis will be laid on Physical Fitness Route Marches, and Military Training.

A simple specimen programme for the month of August is given below:-

Once a week : Route March Distance to be incresed from 5 to 15 miles.

Daily : P.T. : 45 mins., Spiritual Training : 20 mins, Drill : 45 mins, Instructions for next day and rest 10 min.

Total : 2 hours.

Sundays and Holidays : Special lectures for spiritual and political training.

6. *Finance*—The expenses in connection with training will continue to remain a territorial responsibility as far as the 1st Stage of training is concerned.

Secretary,
Training Department.

30

British Propaganda Against the I.N.A. and I.I.L. after the Arrival of Bose in East Asia

23 July, 1943

1. Since 1.1.43 G.H.Q. has been producing daily propaganda talks which are addressed via All India Radio to Japanese troops and to Indians in occupied territories. The Japanese talks form part of a short joint programme, the rest of which is produced by the Far Eastern Bureau, British Ministry of Information, located in Delhi, who contribute news, news commentaries and music. The Indian language talks form part of a similar programme conducted by All India Radio. During the first few weeks "answers" from enemy controlled wireless stations indicated that these talks had at least been 'noted' by the enemy, who evidently feared their effect. Soon afterwards, decrees were issued forbidding listening to Allied broadcasts, and thereafter, as was to be expected, answers were no longer given to our talks.
2. On 15.5.43 a special campaign against the J.I.F.C. was opened in G.H.Q. radio programmes. About five weeks later, Subhas Chandra Bose appeared in Tokyo and gave a series of broadcast speeches. It was suspected at the time that this move was made partly as a counter-propaganda measure - a suspicion which has since been confirmed by Bose himself. He is reported to have stated at a recent press interview in Singapore that one of his two main objects was "to deal once and for all a crushing blow upon the enemy propaganda conducted against the Indian Nationalists working abroad, and also against our friends who have been helping us in our work for India's freedom".
3. In the anti-J.I.F.C. campaign the aim has been to :—
   (a) Discourage the Japanese from sending further contact parties to India.

1. War officer 208/803. P.R.O. London.

(b) Encourage any parties that are sent to give themselves up on arrival in our lines.

(c) Give food for thought to genuine traitors.

(d) Give encouragement and confidence to those who join the J.I.F.C. but remain loyal.

(e) Encourage Indians to pretend to co-operate with the Japanese in order to deceive them.

(f) Foster distrust between Indians and Japanese.

(g) Impress the Japanese with the futility of relying on a few despised traitors and terrorists.

4. With these objects in view, our talks have been based on a limited number of definite themes. It must be remembered that these themes are treated from so many different angles that a short synopsis of this kind cannot include all the arguments and appeals used. The first of the following lists gives the line taken in addressing the Japanese in relations to J.I.F.C. and other Indian questions, the second covers propaganda addressed to members of the J.I.F.C. themselves in Hindustani, Punjabi and Tamil. In addition in the broadcasts in Japanese, consistent attacks on the morals of the troops after made by "Plugging" certain definite themes. Japanese prisoners captured in Arakan have admitted that these broadcasts are listened to by the troops.

5. Japanese—

(a) India remains completely indifferent to alternate threats and blandishments of Japanese propagandists, and to the antics of Indian traitors in Japanese pay.

(b) Indians realise that the way to Indian freedom and independence is by co-operation with the Allies. They have seen too many examples of Japanese conquests to believe any talk about Japan helping India to independence.

(c) The Japanese are being deceived by the majority of Indians who join the J.I.F.C. and the rest are men whose reputations bring them nothing but scorn from true Indian Nationalists.

(d) All Japanese efforts to employ Indians as spies and saboteurs have failed miserably, because these men always report back to their units and give valuable information about Japanese dispositions, etc.

(e) Japan relies on the support of Congress, but this party has always been strongly anti-fascist and anti-Japanese. In any case it has lost much of its influence in India by now.

Indians realise that Congress has been the main obstacle to their attainment of unity and independence.

(f) Japan's pro-Congress propaganda makes no appeal to the many minority parties and communities, nor to the martial races.

(g) All our troops are being encouraged to pretend to co-operate with the Japanese.

(h) Japanese susceptibility to flattery shown by the success of the German Fifth-Column in Japan, as well as by that of the Chinese and Indians in occupied territories who "pretend to co-operate".

6. Indian Languages—

(a) We know all about the J.I.F.C. organisations - who are the real traitors and who are still loyal, etc.

(b) Although refusal to work for the Japanese in any circumstances is highly meritorious, Indians in occupied territories can best assist us by pretending to co-operate with the Japanese and so finding opportunities for escape. Hints on how this can be done and examples of escapes are given.

(c) Exposure of Japanese propaganda methods with examples of broken premises, exploitation of religious sentiments, misinformation etc. Our knowledge that only very few Indians are deceived by this propaganda. "Deceive the Japanese but do not be deceived by them" is constantly repeated.

(d) Distrust between the Japanese and Indian leaders. The stories of the Indian conferences held in Tokyo and Bangkok, murder of certain delegates, etc.

(e) The wretched positions of these traitors who have become Japanese puppets, and the fate of those who have tried to defy the Japanese and insist on the rights of Indians, showing that the Japanese have no intention of allowing independence to India.

(f) Descriptions of traitors and their past records, showing that all are criminals and thoroughly corrupt swindlers. The fate in store for such non-contrasted with the welcome accorded to these who use the J.I.F.C. as a means of escape and report to our authorities.

(g) Examples of Japanese rule in Korea, Formosa, Manchuria, China, etc. after false promises of independence. Determination of Indians to prevent the same rule in India.

(h) Behaviour of the Japanese Army in Burma. Fate of the Burma Independence Army, which was never armed or assisted by the Japanese as promised, and was finally disbanded. Forecast of the Japanese treatnent of the J.I.F.C.

(i) The aims and aspirations of true Indian Nationalists and how these would be defeated by the Japanese.

(j) Hints of anti-Japanese organisations among Indians in occupied territories, including 'messages' to contact, etc.

7. In this campaign, a definite policy has been worked out regarding the tone of the appeal and the general "atmosphere". It has been maintained throughout that those talks are given by representative Indian Nationalists who know Japan, and who therefore know what Japanese rule in India would mean. They address the Indians in occupied territories as friends and brother nationalists (except, of course, the proved traitors). The aim is to maintain an entirely Indian atmosphere, references to the British being few and far between, and usually of a general nature in speaking of the allied Nations. It should be fully realised that only Indian propaganda can have any effect on who are exposed to a constant barrage of India for the Indians with the help of Japan", especially when this is preached by a man of the caliber of S.C. Bose.

8. It is not easy to produce radio propaganda for audiences whose reactions are practically unknown and whose attitude of mind probably varies from sympathy to violent antagonism, by the recent Japanese reactions described above, coupled with letters of appreciation that have been received by A.I.R. from listeners in India,

give some reason to hope that the right lines are being followed. Covert channels are also being used where possible to reinforce this "overt" propaganda.

9. The fact that these overseas programmes are partly "run by the Army" has not been and should not be made public.[2]

---

2. British reactions to the formation of the I.N.A. are reported in the Weekly Intelligence Summary by the General Headquarters. Anti-Japanese propaganda was designed to create mistrust in the Japanese mind about the sincerity of the Indian soldiers. For details F.No. 601/7378/Historical Section, Ministry of Defence, New Delhi.

Japanese Image of the I.N.A. as given by Nakazawa

25 July, 1943

The spectacular review the Indian National Army recently held in Shonan, the city that was once Singapore is now an old story. The world already knows that the Indian National Army is a mighty force composed of patiotic Indians, that is the vanguard of the provisional Indian Government, which is being organised that it is fully equipped, well trained and efficient army, having artillery, engineering and communication units as well as infantry and that is constantly augmenting in prepration for the war of independence.

The world also knows that it is functioning under political as well as military leadership, as it recently claimed as its commander Subhas Chandra Bose, President of the India Independence League, and the greatest active leader India has today.

Yes, the review is an old story, but in that old story, we find the facts, which are not necessarily new, but which are worth remembering.

Passive Resistance Over

One of these facts is that India's days of passive resistance are over, and the Indians are now determined to win their freedom at the point of bayonets. This, however, does not mean that the principle of non-participation and non-violence, which Gandhi preached and practiced all his life, has lost its influence, but rather that the principle is to be applied in a more effective manner. It is the case of giving bullets of the predatory animals that could not be mitigated or banished by the Bible.

Another fact the old story brought out is that India is not alone in her fight for freedom. The numerous greetings and encouragements the National Army received on the day of review proved the fact that all the

1. The above assessment was given by Kn. Nakazawa, the press correspondent of *Nippon Times* after seeing the Indian National Army Parade at Singapore *Nippon Times* 25 July 1943.

right thinking nations in the world are solidly behind India and as per Japan, she is ready and willing to do all in power for the liberation of the country.

It was in Japan that Subhas Chandra Bose made his first request for assistance, as well as first declaration of Independence. It was in Japanese territory that the first Indian National Army was organised, and had its review. All these, many other similar sets, proved beyond the shadow of doubt that India considers Japan as other supporter in the cause.

India knows that only a winner can give her real assistance in the venture of her type. It may be that India had realized the fact that the true champion of Independence is not England or the United States, but Japan. She saw how splendidly Japan's effort to establish the Greater East Asia Co-prosperity Sphere is progressing, and, especially how some of the nations in the sphere are gaining the Independence with the aid of Japan, Burma, for instance, is in a fairway to attain her freedom.

The Philippines is another nation to realize shortly her hope of independence. She, who, only a little while ago was groaning in the vice of American imperialism—whom the United States squeezed dry, and then, try to cast out under pretence of giving her freedom, is now joyfully preparing herself for the day of independence.

Not only these candidates for the honour of independence—all the nations in the Co-Prosperity Sphere are working together, harmoniously, diligently and contentedly for the peace, progress and prosperity of their own.

Looks upto Japan

Seeing these things, India must have concluded that Japan is the true liberator of oppressed nations, and that she is the country to which India must apply for support.

Whatever the reason may have been, this reason this recent attitude India is, worth remembering in that it reveals the fact England and the United States are not the friends of independence.

Still another fact, that was brought out in connection with the review that the Indian National Army is the beginning of the Provisional Government. This Provisional Government will be free from the domination and corroding influence of England. It also will be different from the exiled government in London, for, while those exiled governments are idly waiting, and hoping against hope, for the day of deliverance to come, the Provisional Government will form the centre of the Indian activities abroad, and render powerful cooperation and stimulus to the independence movement within

India. After winning independence for its motherland the government will affiliate itself with the government of Free India and work for the welfare and prosperity of the people.

Establishment of the Provincial Government means that the independence movement outside of India is no longer fugitive decentralised sporadic movement but that it is an open well organised and consistent activity, which will continue to grow increasingly strong until freedom is own.

Mobilising Own Resources

In addition to these facts, the National Army brought out a new idea as to making the non-participation more effective. It is the idea of saying and using India's resources and manpower for her own independence. England is struggling desperately to improve her position in the war by mobilising the wealth and fighting population of India. By using the same old promise of post-war independence the promise which she used during the First World War, and which she broke after the war she is demanding that India surrender all her wealth and ablebodied population for England to use.

To yield to that demand is to prolong the days and horrors of slavery for India. As it can be seen in her past action, England has no intention of liberating India

What, then, should India do ? Should she prolong her days of servitude by offering her wealth and blood to England, or should she continue her passive resistance despite persecution and death?

It is this question which the Indian National Army answered, by openly hoisting its battle flag against England and by proving ; the fact that; India's effort to liberate herself will have support of all the right thinking nations, it; called for the patriotic Indians to use their resources and ; manpower on the way of Independence. Why make sacrifices to prolong the days of servitude? Let our sacrifice be the cause of our liberation. That is the thought the National Army inspired on the day of its review.

These facts must be most encouraging to the valiant sons and daughters of India, as they bring to them the thrilling realisation that independence is no longer a dangerous dream and that the time Destiny selected for India to strike for freedom is here. It is certain that this realisation will inspire all the Indians to respond to the call of ; the National Army, and starts fighting , and continue fighting, until they win the glorious diadem of absolute and everlasting independence.

32

Addressing the INA Soldiers as Supreme Commander, Bose Reminds them about their Duties and Responsibility in the War Against the British for the Liberation of India

25 July, 1943

Brother Officers! It is my wish that we should be familiar among ourselves, and all of us should know what is our object; what are our duties and responsibilities and how to discharge these duties and responsibilities satisfactorily.

First of all, I will myself tell you something about me. Because, I wish to let you know what is my individuality and what is my individual life, as, in future, we shall have to work together and tread the same path.

After the university career, I entered the political world. The most important question at the time was this: What Indians did during the last war? What was the result and what were the experience and lessons we got for the future? In India and in England it was our experience that the policy of our leaders was wrong. Of course, we were depending upon our leaders for action. But we young men and students were thoroughly disappointed. In our minds there was only one idea, that the mistake committed by our leaders in the last war should not be committed again. We thought, if we get an opportunity in future, we will not make such mistakes.

There was another big question. In Europe, after the war, in the year 1918 and 1919, there were many changes; new governments were coming into existence, which had not existed before the war. The Czechs ceased to be a part of the Austro-Hungarian Empire. Another race, the Poles, formed their own government. When I went to Europe, I had the opportunity of meeting two or three Indian leaders there. They all advised me that if we want to do anything for our Motherland we should study the history of

1. *Nippon Times*, 27 July 1943.

the war and the experiences of the such history should be utilized for our fight against Britain. We began to learn the understand things. We came to know how some leaders of Czechs went out of their country for doing propaganda and getting help from the enemies of Austria and Hungary. They joined hand with Britain and France against Austria, Hungary and Germany.

The Poles, too formed an army of 30,000 and took part in the war. It was their fortune that Germany and her allies were defeated, and after the war, they were able to form their own government.

There is no reason why we should not also go by the same path, and taking advantage of the international situation, we should fight shoulder to shoulder with the enemies of Britain, to get complete freedom.

The people of Ireland also took advantage of the war. They openly revolted under the Sinn Fein Party against the British. In the City of Dublin, the Sinn Fein Party had an army of 3,000 only. They had also an army of 10,000 strong in the country. Something went wrong with their plans and the rebellion that started in Dublin did not spread to the countryside. Anyhow they kept the City of Dublin under their control for eight days. The revolution occurred during Easter, and so the revolution is called the Easter Revolution. Though the revolt did not materialise in 1916, it again broke out in the year 1919, just after the war. They had only 5,000 volunteers. This time is was different. War was over. From England troops could be brought to suppress the rebellion. Even then this army of volunteers numbering 5,000 carried on their fight and in the end the British were brought to their knees.

In 1921, we began working in India with all the experience that we had from the study of the history of the last war. At that time as you know, Mahatma Gandhi had launched the Non-Co-operation Movement enthusiastically with the specific idea in mind that when an opportunity offers itself, we should take up arms against the British. We knew also that Germany would try to take revenge and then would come our opportunity as well.

We joined the Congress in 1921 under Mahatma Gandhi, because there was no other way to carry on our fight to keep up the honour of the nation in the face of terrible British oppression. Hindus and Muslim were united. But we knew definitely that the Civil Disobedience Campaign in India would not be completely free. Of course the movement did create the political consciousness among the prepared the people for armed struggle. From 1921 onward we were waiting for an opportunity to take up arms, and that opportunity was a war in Europe.

This is not my individual view but it is the view of many young men who came under Mahatma Gandhi in 1921. Certainly there were a few young men who believed in non-violence, but many of them were strong supporters of violence and they were awaiting the proper time to strike.

I went to Europe in 1933 and remained up to 1936. My idea in going to Europe was to study the situation and to know what was going to happen next. During the stay in Europe I visited Berlin and made acquaintance with certain Government officials and met Fuehrer Hitler. I plainly asked them when they were going to strike at British so that we might also take up arms simultaneously against the British. They replied that they were not at all going to fight Britain and they hoped that all their demands would be fulfilled by Britain. They were for a compromise with Britain. However, they expressed their sympathy for Indian freedom. I argued with them about the British hypocrisy and their cunning policy as Indians know best about that by personal experience, and warned them that, when Britain thought that the German power was getting stronger, she would openly come into conflict with Germany. In the end I told them: "Britain is our traditional enemy. We will fight her, whether you support us or not". But I had no doubt that war would start in Europe soon. Anybody could understand this, by having a look at the preparations that were going on in Germany. When I went to Europe this time, I reminded them of what I said in the year 1936.

My idea in saying this is that I came back from Europe with a strong conviction of what was going to happen. The new party that came in power in Germany was always for a fight. I clearly understood that the German demands would not be accepted by the British and if the British found the Germans growing a bit strong, they would fight the Nazis. In 1938 when I went to Europe I noticed some changes. Germany was beginning to understand that the British would never fully accept their proposals. In September 1938, when the Germans put forward the case of Sudetan Germans, Mr Chamberlain rushed to Munich to come to an agreement with Herr Hitler. There was a time when all parleys of international value generally used to take place in London. But when I saw the British Prime Minister, Mr. Chamberlain going to Germany, leaving his own country and when he accepted the German demands, I realized the secret. It was the first time in the history of the British that a Prime Minister of England relegating the usual custom, proceeded to a foreign country to accept the demands of another nation.

Then I started propaganda in India that a war in Europe was inevitable and it was the duty of Indians to be alert and to try to force Britain to accept our demands, and if they did not, to prepare ourselves for a fight. I was noticing the reaction of the public to my propaganda, and I was convinced that the full support of the general public was with me. But our leaders were thinking in a different way, particularly Mahatma Gandhi whose policy was to wait and see. But we young men were not deterred by this policy. We redoubled our propaganda. We were asking the people of India to take advantage of the golden opportunity that would be presented to them in the near future.

In the annual session of the Indian National Congress at Tripuri in March 1939, I tabled one resolution demanding freedom for India within six months and such an ultimatum to be sent to the Government. In case this demand was not conceded in that period, we should prepare the people for a fight against Britain with whatever might we possess. It was, of course, in the nature of an ultimatum and resolution was introduced, keeping in view the tense international situation and knowing full well that a conflagration would begin in Europe within six months.

When the war actually started in September 1939, the public began to realize that what I said in March was correct. It was our duty at that time to unite all the Nationalist forces and bring pressure on the British Government to concede to our demand, and if unsuccessful, to fight for it. But our leaders were thinking and acting in a different way. They were under the impression that Britain would become weak in the course of the war and to get the Indian help, they would come to an honourable agreement with the Congress. I tried to point out the absurdity of such a notion and told them whatever might be the weakness of Britain during the war they would never allow to rid themselves of the power in India. The weaker they grew the more powerful would become their grip on India. Without India they would not be able to prosecute the war successfully. They would begin looting and plundering the country's resources as they got weaker and weaker.

In March 1940 when the Congress Session was in progress, we expected a forward step. But Gandhiji had his own way. He was to wait and see. We began to lose our minds, come what may, to start our own movement. An Anti-war movement was started throughout the country. It became somewhat serious; many people courted imprisonment. Meanwhile I got information that Gandhiji himself would launch a civil disobedience movement in November as the Government did nothing. I heaved a sigh of relief that if Gandhiji starts a movement, it will have world-wide repercussions. The whole world will come to know that Indians are fighting for freedom. All the nations will think that Indians deserve freedom. We will surely get the sympathy of the world to have saved our honour.

But I thought that by the weapon of Civil Disobedience alone we will not achieve freedom. The movement would surely bring pressure on the Government and hamper its war effort, but the government would never consider our demand. That was my idea. We were thinking what to do. What new method should be adopted. Young men were doing their bit and bombs and revolvers. We got into touch with these young revolutionaries. I knew their strength. They were real revolutionaries with high spirits. But their strength and sacrifice were not enough to achieve complete independence for our Motherland.

It was then we began scanning the pages of history and found many an example and learned many a lesson. The American example was before us. I began to realise, and even came to the conclusion, that without outside help the Indian revolution would not be successful. The United States got a lot of help from France. Even General were despatched from France. In the history of the world, it is not a new thing to get assistance from other nations for winning freedom for one's country.

The news we got in India were twisted and more of a propaganda nature. It was natural that Britain should do so. But to understand the real situation of the world by remaining inside India was not possible. What would be the result of the war and how the war would end and who would win in the end? What were the ideas of Indians abroad, how they were thinking about India's fight for freedom, how to get help from them for thinking about India's fight for freedom, how to get help from them for India's independence and whether it was possible to get material help from the enemies of Britain? These were the questions which made us think that somebody should be sent outside India. I thought of sending some persons to foreign countries. Certainly it was a most difficult task, strictly restricted as our movements were. I thought also that such a person should leave India as the British really "understand" and as the India people seriously take. At last I decided myself to get out of India.

I was in jail at that time. To get out of the jail was a difficult problem. To slip away from jail would make it difficult for me to leave the country in view of the British C.I.D. At last I decided to go on hunger-strike. This decision was taken after steeling my heart, that I would either die or get out of the jail. When my decision was made known to the Government it created a stir in the official circles as they never wanted to see me die in the jail. The Superintendent of the jail came and entreated me not to undertake hunger-strike. He argued that if all the prisoners went on hunger-strike the King's Government would come to a stand-still, and warned me that if I died in the jail it would be my own responsibility. My hunger-strike went on for six days. They tried to forcibly feed me but I was determined to die the way of Jatindra Nath Das. After seven days, a secret conference took place at Government House. They wanted to do something as the medical report about my condition was serious. They set me free with the idea of rearresting me after a month. I got information of this in good time. Meanwhile some arrangements could be made for my escape from India and I left my country.

Experiences I had a lot, after leaving my homeland. I was listening in to both the radios. I had the privilege from the German authorities to hear the enemy radio and propaganda. I had the opportunity of visiting all the fortifications and other defences all over Europe. After these personal experiences, I have no doubt what will be the result of the war. As I said in your prade the other day, the war will be a prolonged one but there will surely be one result, that is, the collapse of Britain, and her empire.

Now the question is this. What is the position of India under these circumstances? The destruction of the British Empire is certain, and the whole map of the world will be changed. What will be the position of India in the new map? The British will be driven out of India, and what should be our position then? We should think about this. There are three alternatives;

One is to keep away from the war and to have a neutral attitude. Second is to go and beg for freedom from the new invader and the third is to take part in the war with the enemies of Britain and qualify ourselves for freedom.

I know what alternative you prefer. For us there is but one alternative that is, to fight hand in hand with the enemies of Britain and contribute our share in the destruction of British Empire.

The internal situation in India is very grave. It is our duty to encourage and support the forces that are in India doing, their bit against Britain. What is the internal situation in India to-day? The whole population is against the British Government.

People are carrying on the fight without arms. To suppose millions of unarmed people, a small army of thousands equipped with the all modern arms is enough. When I had the privilege of meeting Herr Hitler, I took the liberty of asking this question of India and sought his advice as to what path we should tread. The Chancellor of Germany, who is himself an experienced revolutionary, giving his opinion, said that a well-equipped army of a few thousands would be able to control millions of unarmed revolutionaries. He added that so long as an external power did not knock at the frontier no change could be expected in the internal situation. We should form part of this external power. We hear so much nowadays of a second front. It is we, who should create a second front in India. It would have been possible for them to face us in both the fronts, had not the Axis Powers crippled and maimed them. The Axis power had made our work easier. We are thankful to them for doing this, but at the same time, it is incumbent upon us to do our duty towards our motherland. To do this work an army of 50,000 is enough, but we should be prepared to raise an army of 300,000.

The question now is this: What are the duties of this army? There are two duties which this army will have to perform. The first and important duty is, of course, to fight the enemy and free our motherland; the second one is also no less important. It is to form such a powerfull army in India that will free any nations put together and to defend India forever against foreign invasion. Our sisters and brother in India are facing even bigger ordeals with cheer and enthusiasm. For the Indian Independence and for India's welfare, there is no greater work than this.

While in Europe, I tried and I was successful in forming a small National Army. I have brought photos of the army. In Berlin and Rome Indians are thinking and doing things as you are thinking and doing here. Everywhere in the world, wherever there are Indians, a new spirit, a new awakening has come among Indians.

33

Speech of Bose on the Occasion of Independence to Burma Granted by the Japanese, Reminds them that the Liberation cannot be Complete until India is Free

1 August, 1943

Countrymen and Friends! Today is the first of August, 1943. Today an event of great historical importance has taken place. Right in the midst of a World War, an Independent. State has come into being. Burma—our neighbour has achieved her Independence and she has now her own national Independent Government. Long Live Free Burma!

You all know that when the war in East Asia broke out in December, 1941, the people Burma decided to utilise the opportunity for recovering their lost liberty. Instead of co-operating with the British Government, the vast majority of Burmans did their best to help in expelling the British from the country, and the result is that today, not only has Burma been liberated from the British altogether, but she has actually realised her long cherished goal of Independence.

The Independence of Burma in this momentous crisis in world history, has a two-fold significance for us. It shows, in the first place, what a nation can achieve, if it knows how to seize an opportunity which history has offered. Secondly, just as the conquest of India supplied the British with a jumping-off ground for their attack on Burma in the nineteenth century—similarly, the emancipation of Burma has supplied the Indians Independence Movement in East Asia with a spring board, for its attack on Britain's army of occupation in India, during the twentieth century.

Burma was deprived of her liberty long after India was. Nevertheless Burma has stolen a march over us and has attained her liberty, while we are still passing through the throes of revolution. On behalf of the India people and of myself, I offer my warmest congratulations to the people of Burma

1. K.S. Giani, *op.cit*, pp. 46-47.

on the achievement and I heartily wish them increasing progress and prosperity in the days to come. I offer also my hearty felicitation to His Excellency Dr. Ba Maw, the head of the New and Independent state of Burma and I wish him all success in the discharge of the manifold responsibilities which have now devolved on him. It is a source of great pleasure and gratification for me that so soon after meeting Dr Ba Maw in Syonan, during the first week of July, I can offer him my greeting and congratulations as the head of the new and Independent State of Burma.

Friends, you are aware of the many promises which the British Government has given to the Indian people during the course of the their rule in India—promise which have always proved to be mere scraps of paper. You are aware also that these promises have been repeated since the outbreak of the present war and all sorts of silly excuses have been put forward to show that in the midst of a war, transference of power from British to Indian hands cannot take place. As against this example, we now see that right in the midst of the war, the promise of liberty made by the Prime Minister of Japan. His Excellency General Tojo, on behalf of his Government and nation, has been fully redeemed. Where there is a will there is a way and this statesmanship and generosity on the part of Japan, will bring into bold relief the hypocrisy of British politicians—while they will demonstrate the real character of Japan's state policy.

The Independence of Burma will, I am sure, be soon followed by the Independence of the Philippines. Asia is now on the threshold of a new era in her history. This is a unique opportunity for all the suppressed nations of Asia to rise and effect their emancipation. It is above all the sacred duty of the Indian people to seize the present golden opportunity and fulfil their age-long aspirations.

The liberation of Asia cannot be complete until India is free. The Indian people must, therefore, rise and liberate themselves and thereby help the emancipation of other Asiatic nations. Above all, India must seize the hand of friendship which Japan has offered to India and to other suppressed nations of Asia. Confronted by a common foe, the people of India must march shoulder to shoulder with the brave Nipponese nation, till the enemy is overthrown and India recovers her lost liberty.

Inquilab Zindabad! Azad hind Zindabda!

34

Statement by Japanese Board of Information Reiterating Support to Indians for Ending Anglo-Saxon Domination in India[1]

8 August, 1943

"A year ago today, Mahatma Gandhi was imprisoned for no other reason than for having proposed a resolution demanding the immediate withdrawal of British influence from India—a resolution which was unanimously passed by the Indian National Congress party. It was a just and legitimate demand arising from the age-long aspiration of the people of India for freedom, Independence and the right to govern themselves.

"Ignoring the wishes, the desires and the human longings of the Indian people without as much as a show sympathy and consideration and conscious only for the preservation and promotion of her own selfish interests. Britain, for the last twelve months has intensified more than ever before the pressure on the Indian masses to make them submit to her tyranny.

Since the imprisonment of the Mahatma on August 9, last year, 60,229 Indian patriots were arrested of whom 26,000 were pronounced guilty and 18,000 held under detention up to the end of the year, according to the statement of Reginald Maxwell, Home Secretary of the Viceroy's Council, on February 12. According to the same office, on August 3, 11,717 political prisoners were in prison as of June 1, and from the outbreak of the war in Europe to June 3 this year 76,646 Indians have been sentenced to hard labour throughout the whole country. This actual figures may be expected to be much larger, for we would not expect a British official to tell the whole truth.

---

1. The above statement was issued by Japanese Board of Informatioin, *Nippon Times* 9 August 1943.

"Arrests and imprisonments have not been the only instruments of oppression used by the British. They have driven Indian men into uniforms by compulsory conscription, creating an army known under the false name of Indian Volunteer Army which, according to General Auchinleck, numbers 2,000,000 men. They have gone further to press civilians into auxillary and other war services by large scale mobilization. To supply and feed the Allied armies, the British authorities are forcing the Indian farmers, by compulsory measures, to report their yearly crops which they are requisitioning for the armed forces. Nothing is done to ensure the equitable distribution of food-stuffs among the Indian people. The consequence has been serious food shortages and widespread famine, raising prices and mounting tensions in daily life.

"British policy in India, however, is neither strange nor surprising. To quote, for example, from the figures of British Empire the casualties announced my Deputy Prime Minister Clement Atlee to the House of Commons last June. India with 101,197 casualties, has sacrified as many men in Canada, Australia, New Zealand, South Africa and other British colonies combined. This alone attests the fact that India is being made to give her blood to the British cause without getting anything but oppression in return.

"Who does not know that what the British call defence of India is nothing more than the defense of Britain's imperialistic interests? Who does not know that the British policy in India today is to defend British interest against the Indian people themselves? Who does not know that the real defense of India, if necessary, can be ensured only by the full independence of India?

"India's hour of destiny is fast approaching. As British oppression has intensified and as British policy has revealed its naked self. So during the past year has the passive resistance of the Indian people grown and intensified into active resistance. India's saintly leader Mahatma Gandhi, has already issued the battle cry, "This is a fight to the finish".

"The activist leader, Subhas Chandra Bose, has called the British hand by declaring, Indian should ever cherish the illusion that one day England will be inducted to recognize India's independence. Our independence admits of no compromise. The hour has struck and every patriotic Indian must advance toward the field of battle. When the blood of freedom-loving Indians begins to flow India will attain her freedom... Now or never is our opportunity, now or never is India's chance of freedom'.

"The independence of Burma, once a province of India, has encouraged and inspired the Indian people to fight for the attainment of the same goal. And close to the borders of India there stands today a massive army force composed of volunteers, the Indian National Army, under the command of Subhas Chandra Bose, ready to go into action when the hour strikes.

"The activities of Chandra Bose and his call to arms as the only means of redeeming India has produced far-reaching effects on the Independence movement both within and without India. All the peoples of Asia stand united and ready to support the people of India in their fight for freedom, for in their freedom lies the hope of real all-inclusive Greater East Asia.

35

Special Order by Bose on Taking Over Direct Command of the I.N.A.

25 August, 1943

In the interests of the Indian Independence Movement and of the Azad Hind Fauj I have taken over the direct command of our army from this day.

This is for me a matter of joy and pride-because for an Indian, there can be no greater honour than to be a Commander of India's Army of Liberation. But I am conscious of the magnitude of the task that I have undertaken and I feel weighed down with a sense of responsibility. I pray that God may give me the necessary strength to fulfil my duty to India under all circumstances, however difficult or trying they may be.

I regard myself as the servant of thirty-eight crores of my countrymen who profess different religious faiths. I am determined to discharge my duties in such a manner that the interests of these thirty-eight crores may be safe in my hands, and that very single Indian will have reason to put complete trust in me. It is only on the basis of undiluted nationalism and of perfect justice and impartiality that India's Army of Liberation can be built up.

In the coming struggle for the emancipation of our Motherland, for the establishment of a Government of Free India, based on the goodwill of thirty-eight crores of Indians and for the creation of a permanent army which will guarantee Indian independence for all time, the Azad Hind Fauj has a vital role to play. To fulfil this role, we must weld ourselves into an army that will have only one goal—namely, the freedom of India—and only one will namely to do or die in the cause of India's freedom. When we stand, the Azad Hind Fauj has to be like a wall of granite: when we march, the Azad Hind Fauj has to be like a steam-roller.

---

1. *Malai Sinpo*, 30 August 1943.

Our task is not an easy one: the war will be long and hard, but I have complete faith in the justice and the invincibility of our cause. Thirty-eight crores of human beings, who form about one-fifth of the human race, have a right to be free and they are now prepared to pay the price of freedom. There is consequently no power on earth that can deprive us of our birthright of liberty any longer.

Comrades, Officers and men! With your unstinted support and unflinching loyalty, the Azad Hind Fauj will become the instrument of India's liberation. Ultimate victory will certainly be ours, I assure you.

Our work has already begun. With the slogan 'Onward to Delhi!' on our lips, let us continue to labour and fight till our National Flag flies over the Viceroy's House in New Delhi, and the Azad Hind Fauj holds its victory parade inside the ancient Red Fortress[2] of India's metropolis.

Subhash Chandra Bose
Supreme Commander

2. Subhas wanted to march through Manipur with the I.N.A. and to hoist the Indian National Flag at Red Fort. His slogan of "March on to Delhi" was a battle cry for the I.N.A. However, it was not Subhas, but Nehru who hoisted the National Flag at Red Fort on 16 August, 1947, where the old guards of the I.N.A. rallied to redeem the unfulfilled pledge.

36

Speech of Bose at Kaula Lumpur; Thanks Indians in Malaya for Financial Help and Requests the Young People to Join the INA.

5 September, 1943

Friends! I want to thank you most heartily for the purse you have presented to me this evening. It is a handsome purse, but I shall call it handsome, only if you regard it as a first installment. Considering, what other town are paying and within a very short time; considering also what Ipoh has paid as a first installment. I am sure that Indians in Kuala Lumpur will be anxious to see that this contribution is multiplied atleast five times and if you cannot do that, I am afraid, you will be doing a great disservice to your country. You are very proud of your city and rightly too. It is the second city in this part of the world and if you enjoy the prestige, you must fulfil the responsibilities that follow from that distinction and prestige.

I will now tell you that what we want in cash is only a part of our total requirements. The time has come when we have to give our all in the service of our mother-land. The days of minimum sacrifice are over. The time has come, when each and everyone of us has to think of the maximum sacrifice, which he or she is able to offer, and that sacrifice has to be in human life, in money, in other resources, which are necessary in order to equip a modern army for its marches. I am glad to know that you citizens of Kaula Lumpur and Selangor state are anxious to do your duty in every respect and my only remark and request to you is to expedite your collections as soon as possible so that our army may be equipped sooner than many expect and be ready to march to the field of action.

From my experience. I am convinced that so long as the Indian people remain unarmed, so long as the British Government has a modern army under its control and so long as we do not take up arms for our struggle for

1. K.S. Giani, *op.cit.* pp. 56-59.

freedom, we shall not be able to achieve independence for India. I do not know of one instance—of one single instance—in the whole history of mankind where a nation has been able to achieve full independence without resorting to arms, but apart from history, our natural experience in the course of several decades has convinced us that we have to take up arms in the final stage of our struggle if we want full independence and not a diluted form of it. So long as peace reigned all over the world it was practically impossible for the Indian people to get arms and fight with arms. It was impossible for the people inside India. It was also impossible for people outside India, but thanks to this war, what was impossible four or five years ago has today become possible. If you want arms you can get them not inside but outside India. You could not do it even if you wanted to. That is why I say this war has been a God-sent opportunity to us. It has given us a unique opportunity for achieving not Dominion Status or Colonial self-government, but full and complete independence.

The only question I would like to put to you as Indians is whether you really want full and complete independence. If you do so you must pay the price. You must organise a complete modern army and march with that army to India.

To-day the British have one front—the Indian national front, you might call it—inside India. The British with their army are able to cope with this Indian national front. If you can put up a second front—not a bogus second front, but a real second front then it will be imposible for the British to maintain their position in the country. I am convinced when the Indian National Army appears on the frontier of India its very appearance will be a clarion call to the people in general and also to the Indian army to rally round the banner of Indian revolution. This is not a wishful dream on my part. I know the people at home are fully aware of our activities in East Asia and the British too are aware, but we do not care. The time has come when we could openly proclaim to the whole world what we have been doing, what we are doing and what we are going to do in the future. Our brethern in the Indian Army who today are standing under the Union Jack and anxiously waiting for the Indian National Army on the continent of India. That is the position at home without any exaggeration. It is therefore our duty to hurry with our work and see that the National Army goes to the aid of India as soon as possible.

Ever since the existence of the Indian National Army was announced to the world and its intention of marching to Delhi, you will be surprised to learn that there has been a complete change in the tactics of British propaganda. Up to recently British propagandists have been saying that to-day Nippon has become the enemy of India and that its army intends to march into India, but ever since they realised that the Indian National Army had been formed and is getting ready to march into India, there has been a complete change in the attitude and also in the tactics of British propagandists and now they are anxiously trying to work up the Indian people to take a stand against the Indian National Army. The British Government knows, as much as we do, what the attitude of the Indian people and the Indian Army will be when our army appears on the frontier of India, and that is why they are anxious to do their best to win over the Indian people to their side so that they may take a stand against the Indian National Army.

But the most unexpected surprise came to me when I was told that British propagandists on the occasion of a Hindu Festival and appealed to the Hindus of India to get ready to fight their brothers who are going to march in from outside. The British propagandists even went so far as to say that the good old days have come back again!

Friends! The Anglo-Americans have found out now a new Napoleon. According to the Anglo-Americans, Lord Louis Mountbatten is amphibious. He is a master in land and sea operations. Well, what is the career of this amphibious monster? He is the hero of Dieppe. Dieppe was an attempt by the British army to land in France and expel the Germans from that part. Within 24 hours they were completely wiped out and there ended all the heroic exploits of Lord Louis Mountbatten. Because of his achievement at Dieppe he had been made commander-in-chief of the South East Asia command. I challenge you to show me one country in the world today where promotions are made not for success, not for victories, but for defeats. It is a unique achievement of the British army and its government in this war. I can assure Lord Louis Mountbatten that a much bigger and greater Dieppe is waiting for him in East Asia.

Perhaps, there are some people living in East Asia, and even in Malai, who are still hoping and dreaming that the British will come back. We have heard of them. There are a few such men in Syonan also. I can only pity them. You know what Syonan was and is today. The British—I do not say it, I only repeat it—took twenty years to build Singapore and how many days to get out? Seven days. This is an achievement and still there are people who believe they will come back! The biggest bulwark of the British Empire is now the biggest graveyard of that Empire and it shall be a graveyard. The days of the British Empire are over. If you have any doubt turn over the pages of history. Every Empire has had its glory and also its decline. The British Empire had its glory during the last war and since then its decline has become very rapid and we have witnessed with our own eyes the last phase of the decline.

I have always said that the last war brought about the disappearance of the two Empires—the Ottoman Empire of the Turks and the Austro-Hungarian Empire. This war will see the end of the British Empire and out of the ashes of that Empire will rise a free India. The two things are identical—the defeat and dismemberment of the British Empire and the creation of an independent India. If you want India to be free you have to work and fight for the overthrow and dismemberment of the British Empire.

British propaganda of late has adopted new tactics and that is to utilise to the best advantage the small success they have achieved in Africa and Sicily. If you were to listen to the propaganda that British agents have been carrying on all over the world you would think that with the occupation of Sicily they have already won the war. I know something of Europe, not only of peace-time Europe but war-time Europe, and I know all these places where fighting has taken place. I know also the strength and weakness of the Axis powers in Europe and from experience I want to assure you that whatever may happen in Europe has no bearing on the situation either in India or East Asia. Whatever may happen in Europe, Indians will be ready if only we put forward the required effort. Therefore, do not hesitate for one moment by any propaganda the enemy may carry on to-day or tomorrow and be firm in your belief and faith that it has become possible for Indian people to achieve independence.

First of all is it a very big effort that we have to bring an army of 200,000 to 300,000 to India? Look at the millions and millions of people fighting on all fronts in different parts of the world. For the salvation of 38 crores an army of 300,000 or even 400,000 is nothing at all and it is possible for the people of East Asia to contribute enough men for this army. It is possible also for the people in East Asia to contribute money and every material for the equipment of the army. Therefore, let us concentrate all our energy on the one task of organizing an army and bringing it to perfection as soon as possible.

Friends, our tasks to-day is to bring perfection as soon as possible to the army that exist to-day, along with it we have to expand our army because the war is going to be a long and hard one. We want more and more young men to come in and get training. I congratulate you that you have in the heart of Kuala Lumpur one of our camps where Indian young men are trained for the coming fight for freedom. Well, it is not only in

Syonan and Kuala Lumpur that they are being trained to-day. Malai is dotted with camps and many of these camps were formerly camps of the British army. They have been turned over to us for our use. That reminds me that when we go to India we shall also find ready-made barracks for our national army. We won't have to build new barracks. From Calcutta to Bombay and from Rawalpindi to Madras, there are splendid barracks not for the Indian army but for the British Tommy, but these splendid barracks are going to be taken for our Indian National Army and I promise to give the British in return all the prisons for their use.

Friends! to defeat Britain we shall need help from outside. The enemy is asking for help all over the world. The almighty British Empire, over which the sun never sets, that mighty British Empire is going round the world with the begging bowl. It is not merely at Washington that they are asking for help but all over the world, even the poor Indian people, the slaved Indian people, are not spared. Even Indian people have to do their share in men, money, munitions and war materials. They are begging even Indian people to help them in their hour of need. We have to fight today not merely the might of Britain but the combined might of Britain and her allies—a most powerful combination. If we are to fight and win we shall need help and take help when the time comes, but there will be no humiliation in accepting or asking for help when we have first done our duty.

At this juncture, the duty of the people of East Asia is to put forward the maximum effort. Remember you have an opportunity of doing something which your countrymen is other parts of the world cannot do. What can Indians in Europe, Africa, America or even in England do? They are helpless. I know many of them are dying to serve and fight for their country's freedom but it is impossible for them to do so. They are unable to organise an army or join the National Army but all that is within your reach, if you only make it your mission you can join the National Army and work for its success. Therefore, when the call of sacrifice reaches your ears do not flinch. Thank Providence that He has given you of all Indians in the world a unique opportunity to serve your country and fight for your country's independence.

37

Speech of Dr. Lakshmi, Commander Rani of Jhansi Regiment; Requests Women to Join the Movement for India's Liberation[1]

25 September, 1943

"We Indians have only two way open. Either we have to work for the liberation of our country or we have to be British agents. Which do you prefer?." asked Dr. Lakshmi, leader of the Rani of Jhanshi Regiment, in a spirited address to the Indian women of Selangor on Thursday.

The meeting was held on the Lawn in front of the Indian Independence League office, Mrs. Lukshumeyah, Member in charge of the women's section of the local League, was at home to Dr. Lakshmi on the occasion of her visit to Kuala Lumpur from the headquarters of the League in Syonan. Indian women in large numbers provided a picturesque appearance in saris of variegated colours. Conspicous among them was Dr. Lakshmi in smart military dress. Introduced by Mrs. Lukshumeyah to the gathering. Dr. Lakshmi speaking in Tamil said: "Friends! English is the language of our enemy and I am determined not to use it at our public functions. We have to eschew that as far as possible in our life and that is a prerequisite to the achievement of national independence.

"I have a lot of friends here as well as in India. But those who do not subscribe to our national cause, who do not believe in the righteousness of the Independence movement, are not my friends, I have decided to devote my undivided attention to the liberation of our motherland. That is my mission and I am determind to pursue it unmindful of difficulties and

1. *Malai Sinpo*, 25 September 1943, Dr. Lakshmi Swaminathan, was born in Madras on 24 October, 1914. After studying at Queen Mary College, went to England to get her medical degree; went to Singapore in 1940 and after the fall of Singapore joined the Indian Independence League. Bose asked her to organise Rani of Jhansi Regiment, became Minister for Women affairs in the Provisional Government of India. After Independence married Prem Kumar Sahgal, who was convicted in the Red Fort Trials.

obstructions in the way.

"The independence we want for India is not for men alone. It is for the whole country composed of men and women. So if men are doing their share, I ask you what have you to offer? If your mother is sick will you leave it to your brother alone to nurse her to health and normalcy? Will you not shoulder your part of the burden? Well, that is the condition of Mother India today. She is sick and enslaved. She wants the help of everyone of you.

"Let not posterity look down upon you that you let down such an opportunity. Opportunity comes but once whether in the case of a nation or an individual. Let not the daughters of Mother India be found wanting at the crucial hour. "Look back at the history of India. You will find that women have never been behind their men in any branch of life. I am sure you women of Selangor are not going to be behind men, providence has given an opportunity to the Indian women of East Asia. Will you let it slip and repent for it later? Will you allow the curse of posterity to fall upon your heads?

"Think of the great reaction in India when we, women, fight shoulder to shoulder with our men. I am not here to force you and you are not without patriotism to be torrid. There may be many among you who, due to various reasons, are unable to contribute to the movement by active participation in the Rani of Jhansi Regiment. To such of you I say let your hearts be with the movement. And if your heart and spirit are with the movement I know you can contribute a lot in various forms. It is a full fledged faith in the movement that I ask of you.

"Many of you may think it is only men who will have to fight at the front. Do not for a moment think so. Our army is unlike other armies of the world in this respect. If anybody had told me a few years ago of women fighting of war fronts, of women handling rifles and braving bombs. I would have scoffed at the idea and dismissed him for a knave or fool. But what was a dream. What was impossible, has became possible today. We shall fight our adversaries with modern arms right on the battlefield.

"Ever since I joined this movement I have felt a new strength, a strength born of the righteousness of our mission. I know everyone of you will realise it in your own person when you understand the true significance of this movement.

"Here lies an opportunity to live and work for a good cause, and I am sure my sister's of Selangor will rise to the occassion. I have heard some Indians, men and women, say that they are madrasis, Punjabis, and so on. Discard this parochial spirit and say. 'I am an Indian. I come from India. India is my mother country. This spirit should permeate among you.

"Friends! whatever happens India is going to be free at the end of this war. But are you going to bring upon yourself the dishonour that you were inactive and indifferent at a time when India stood at the cross roads? The British empire is doomed and in its doom is the birth of a true and independent India. We Indians have only two ways open. Either we have to work for the liberation of our country or we have to be British agents. I ask which do you prefer?

"The British are our enemies and as such we want to fight them. We shall never allow ourselves to be taken prisoner. We shall handle the rifle and kill a few Britishers before we die. What I want in you is that iron determination not to flinch from the path we have chosen. We must drive the Britishers, our enemies, out of the country. Driving them out of that holy land should be the prime aim of our life.

"Friends! Therefore, it is better that you learn to use the rifle. Women who join the regiment should be prepared for all kinds of work and they will be treated alike in the camp. What we lack is unity, and here is a golden opportunity for you to forget your caste, creed and social standing.

"I appeal to you to have absolute faith in our Netaji. His is a life devoted to the cause of Mother India. He has travelled all over the world, studied political and military conditions in every country and knows the relative strength and weakness of each. There is none either in India or outside better suited than he to lead a movement like this. Implicit obedience to him is what I require of you.

"There may be people among you who say the British will come back within six months. If you come back within six months. If you come across one ask his whether he is better informed than our Netaji. Do not for a moment believe such nonsense.

"Unless we are prepared to sacrifice our utmost, in property and in blood, we are not going to have Swaraj. Those of you who are not in a position to join the regiment can help our movement in other ways. A relief camp is being run in Kuala Lumpur and many of you can spend an hour a day assisting in the work there. You may propagate Hindustani our *lingua franca*. You can collect old clothes to dress wounded soldiers. Many ways are open to you".

38

Speech Delivered at the Chamber of Princes's Secret Session by Lt. Col. K. Himmat Singh, Briefing them about the Japanese Intentions Towards India and the Steps taken by the Government to Counter the Propaganda of S.C. Bose, Who was Collaborating with them

15 October, 1943

Your Highnesses,

There is no need for me to say that I consider it is a great honour and privilege to be given this opportunity of addressing your Highnesses today.

I most humbly wish to explain at the outset that I am not lecturing today because of my relationship with His Highness the Chancellor, nor am I here as a propagandist. I am addressing you because I have some knowledge of Japan and the Japanese, and of their aims and policies. I was Assistant Military Attache in the British Embassy, Tokyo, from 1926 – 1928 when I became a qualified Japanese interpreter. Again for nearly two years before the outbreak of the war with the Japan, I was first Secretary in the British Embassy. At the beginning of hostilities. I was interned for nearly eight months with the rest of the Embassy Staff, about ninety in number. During this time we were treated more as convicts than as diplomats, and had to do labour like any coolie. For instance, I had to work as a porter and scrub floors for the first four months. In the latter four months, my duties included gardening, removing rubbish, cutting wood and looking after children; the last was really quite pleasant work which I did not mind in the least. In some ways these occupations served a useful purpose in that they kept us busy and did not allow us much time for worrying.

As a result of my experience, and from my knowledge of Japan and the Japanese, I am convinced that Japan is a menace to our country. Her

1. Foreign and Political Department, F. No. 83-X/1944. N.A.I.

policy of the 'New order in Asia' and of the so-called 'co-prosperity Sphere' is nothing but a desire on her part for the subjection and enslavement of certain Asiatic countries, including India in the West. Australia in the South, Hawaii in the East and the Maritime provinces of Siberia in the North. Believe me when I say that if the Japanese ever came to our country, which God forbid, they will completely destroy our culture and religion, and all our cherished customs and institutions.

The subject of my lecture to Your Highnesses may be described as 'the Japanese' conspiracy against India.

Before going into the details of this conspiracy, it will not be out of place to give you a short history of Japan, which will serve as a background for what I shall have to say later. Japan, as Your Highness know, is a very young country, whose records go back only as far as twelve hundred years. However, the Japanese have recently been faking their history to show that its records can be traced as far back as two thousand six hundred years, so that they may be able to claim to be the oldest empire in the world, which, of course, is nothing but a lie. The only people who believe in this are the Japanese themselves, who have been so taught from their childhood.

In fact, Japan was not known to the outside world earlier than a hundred years ago. It was a backward country then and was ruled by a feudal system of overlords called DAIMYO, the head of which was the SHOGON or Commander-in-Chief, called TOKUGAWA. There was an emperor, but he was merely a puppet, and was kept shut up in his palace in KYOTO. The commander-in-Chief was so jealous of his power that he would not allow anyone from the outside world to enter the country, nor was any of the inhabitants allowed to leave. Even the making of boats was a criminal offence, and the punishment for it was death.

About eighty years ago an American fleet commanded by Admiral Perry, an American officer, was on a cruise in Far Eastern waters, and it put in at Yokohama. The Japanese had never seen a battleship before, and you can well imagine their surprise at seeing these huge vessels. The only name they could devise for these ships to them so queer in appearance was 'Black Ships'. They opposed a landing party with their double-edged swords, but without success. However, they were clever enough to realise the danger to their country if the fleet remained there for a long period. Accordingly they accepted without delay whatever terms were offered them, in order to be rid of the unwelcome visitors as quickly as possible. One result of this visit was that the Japanese soon realised that their segregation and the TOKUGAWA rule had prevented them from making any progress compared with other countries in the world. There was discontent in Japan, which eventually led to a civil war of three years duration. At the end of the civil war the emperor was restored to his rightful place as head of the state, and this first act on assuming power was to remove his capital to the present city of Tokyo.

Soon afterwards, a number of scholars were sent to England and other European countries, to study their constitutions. On their return, these scholars recommended the adoption of the Prussian model as best suited to Japan; accordingly a constitution very much like the Prussian was adopted. There is a Lower House known as the Diet, and an Upper House or House of Peers. It is interesting to note that an Englishman, Sir Francis Piggott, assisted in drafting the Japanese constitution. His son, Major-General Piggott, R. E., served as Military Attache of the British Embassy in Tokyo for about fifteen years.

The first foreign Embassy to be established in Japan was the British, and it was the British Embassy and its staff who acted as advisers to the Japanese nation until the end of the last Great War. The Japanese Navy also has been trained by the British on more or less British lines. It is well known that in the Russo-Japanese War, some Japanese naval vessels had British Naval Officers abroad as advisers. In short, the point I wish to make is that the Japanese have cunningly and cleverly utilised the British to attain their present position; and they realised that their planned object of ruling Asia could only be achieved at the expense of England and America. In order to carry out their plan, they made up their minds twenty years ago to go to war with us, and since then they have been secretly preparing to that end. Meanwhile, England and America who had been trying their best to make a settlement with Japan, were being cleverly deceived by the Japanese into believing that she had no intention of resorting to war for the solution of grievance outstanding between them.

We must give the devil his due, and we must give the Japanese credit for being a shrewd people. They appreciated the world situation as follows:–

In 1935 Japan had calculated that in about 1939 or 1940 the European War was likely to break out. She also appreciated that by about 1942 the Axis would be winning the war, and that therefore it would be to her advantage to join the war against us; and strike us in the back to gain her object. This is where she made her mistake. We also unfortunately made several blunders; for example, when Japan attacked China, in 1937, we believed as a neutral, and both America and ourselves sold to Japan various war materials such as petrol, iron, etc. We thought that Japan would use them for her normal purposes but she cleverly deceived us, using China as a training ground for her troops, and hoarding most of the stores and materials for future use against us. She also increased her navy, army, and air force several fold during those years. Meanwhile we all the time were trying to pacify her, and reach a permanent settlement. Your Highnesses probably remember the negotiations that went on in Washington for a month before the outbreak of war with Japan. They were on the point of breakdown when Japan cunningly bluffed and deceived us by sending a special envoy, Kusru, who said that he had special instructions to make a permanent settlement. While the negotiations were still going on in Washington, they made their treacherous attack on Pearl Harbour, Hong Kong and North Malaya on December 8, 1941. However, this did more good than harm, because it brought America into the war from the beginning—which otherwise might not have happened for some time.

Often on my tours the Indian troops asked me the question, 'Are the Japanese superior, that they had all these successes?' I can assure Your Highnesses that the Japanese are not superior to any British or Indian troops. The reason for their initial successes is that they had been preparing for the last twenty years, whereas we had been making no preparations. That we must admit; and that is the cause of the initial setbacks. I can assure Your Highnesses that things will be different in the near future, and the Japanese realise this better than anyone else.

Now, reverting to the main subject of my talk, namely the Japanese conspiracy against India, I will begin with the early days. Your Highnesses may be aware that Japan's interest in India as a target for attack and eventual annexation is no new development. Even when she was Britain's active ally in 1914-1918 against the Central European Powers, our counter- espionage service discovered Japanese intelligence activities in India. some of them carried on by government officials acting under the cover of diplomatic privilege. But Japan was active not only in her use of agents in India, but in her sedulous cultivation of Indian subversive elements in the Far East; the use to which these elements have since been put leaves no doubt as to Japanese intentions from the start. As early as 1915, Rash Behari Bose, having fled from India after his unsuccessful attack on the life of Lord Hardinge, found asylum in Japan. He was made the protege of Toyama Mitsuru, an arch schemer whose name has figured frequently in the history of Japan's underground plottings. Bose married a Japanese wife, by whom he has had several children, adopted Japanese nationality and to a large extent the Japanese way of life, and has identified himself with the interests of his new country. The Japanese, for their part, have generally accepted him as their fellow countryman and have made use of him both for internal propaganda—for he is reputed to write and speak Japanese excellently—and in their approach to the Indian community in Japan.

Rash Behari's headquarters have for many years been in Tokyo, and his influence in Indian circles there has been very great. He became in fact the doyen of the Indian community of merchants, students and a few masters who had found a niche there. The Japanese assisted the development of his influence by judicious means: for instance, after a time it became difficult if not impossible, for an Indian student to get himself accepted for one of the technical universities without being guaranteed by Bose. While he consolidated his position locally. Bose did not make the mistake of forgetting to maintain his connection with revolutionary and nationalists circles in India, with which he kept up a regular correspondence. Bose has always been a terrorist, and he has made no secret of the fact that he considers non-violence a mawkish and ineffective creed for the winning of Indian independence. He did not therefore identify himself whole-heartedly with the Indian National Congress; at a time when Congress associations abroad could still be affiliated to the parent body, he ran his own nationalist society in Tokyo with the title of the Indian Independence League. This did not, however, prevent him from keeping in touch with a number of important individual political leaders in this country.

In 1923 a Bihari named Anand Mohan Sahay went to Japan as a student. He had previously been private secretary to Babu Rajendra Prasad, whom he has always affected to consider as his Guru. It was not long before he went over to the Japanese possibly ambitious to emulate Bose, and by similiar means he became the political leader of the Indians in Kobe and its neighbourhood. He too increased his influence with Japanese assistance, and Indians of all kinds found him useful as a go-between in dealings with the Japanese authorities. In October 1932, he made himself president of the Indian National Congress committee in Kobe, and when all foreign Congress bodies were disaffiliated by order of the parent body, in March 1936, he kept the association going as a purely local body of nationalist-minded Indians, under the name of the Indian Nationalist Association of Japan.

R.B. Bose and A.M. Sahay, both ambitious and both sold to a nation which, as they must have realised in their secret hearts, intended little good towards India, have always been more or less rivals for power and the favour of the Japanese. The latter, however, succeeded in making good use of both of them, each in his particular sphere of influence and while Bose has apparently always been trusted by the Japanese, and has been the bigger figure for propaganda purposes. A.M. Sahay was used not only in Kobe but to develop subversive activities among Indians in other parts of the Far East. The Germans also had a hand in Sahay's work, but that is not relevant to the subject of this talk.

In Shanghai in Canton and in Bangkok, there existed besides the law-abiding Indian merchant community (most of whom were however trained to some degree with what they called "nationalist" stentiments) a number of Indian renegades and malcontents of the worst type. Some of these were fugitives from British justice, and all were given over to sedition and traitorous activities. In 1940 Sahay was sent to organise these seditious elements in Shanghai as well as to encourage nationalist opinions. The open result of his work was the formation of an 'Indian National Association of China'. Likewise, a lieutenant of Sahay was sent to Bangkok, where a nationalist body called the 'Indian National Council' was formed under the presidency of an ex-Bengal revolutionary who went in Siam by the name of Swami Satyanand Puri. Simultaneously with these activities the Japanese in Canton were engaged in efforts to suborn the Indian troops in Hong Kong, and in 1941 Indian agents were despatched from this area to perform the same task among the Indian troops in North Malaya, but were exposed and caught before they had achieved anything useful. These efforts, however, did bear some fruit, as was shown during the fighting in Malaya, where Indian fifth columnists organised and trained by traitors in Bangkok were sent down to create confusion among the Indian troops in the front line and to go to work without delay in an effort to suborn those who were made prisoner.

The local subversive elements outlined above achieved little in the first months after the Japanese victories in the Far East as a result of the personal ambition and jealousies of the leaders and the total lacks of discipline in their followers' ranks. Realising this, Japan attempted to improve matters by forming an organisation which would place all these subversive elements under one control and would at the same time establish itself as the controlling influence in the lives of all Indians in the Far East—the intention being of course to mobilise all possible resources which could eventually be used against India itself. A preliminary conference of the better known traitors was held in Tokyo at the end of March, 1942, and a fulldress convocation was held at Bangkok in June of that year. Delegates from the Indian communities in most of the countries of the Far East were present and everything possible was done to ensure that the conference should come to the previously approved conclusions which the Japanese desired.

This result, Your Highnesses, was achieved—but not without some opposition on the part of some of the delegates, who, though they might be nationalists were not traitors. In the end, however it was agreed that an organisation known as the 'Indian Independence League' was to be the only recognised association for Indians in the Far East; that it was to assist the Japanese with military forces which were referred to by the high sounding but false title of the 'Indian National Army' in the war against the allies; and that it would not only organise fifth column activities in India, but would accept all enemy assistance necessary to defeat the British and drive them out of the country. It was at this time that the name of Subhash Chandra Bose was first importantly associated with Japanese sponsored acitivities among Indians in the Far East, for he was declared to be the patron of the Indian Independence League. By the end of 1942, but not without considerable difficulty due to jealousy among the erstwhile leaders of local national associations in various parts of the Far East, these bodies were merged into the newly formed League or driven out of existence. It was on this foundation, Your Highnesses, that the Japanese proceeded to build their fifth column offensive against India.

With regard to the civilians in Occupied Territories, the Japanese lost little time in making it clear to them that, whether they desired it or not. Indians were to assist in furthering the Japanese aim of a Greater East Asian Co-prosperity Sphere under Japanese domination. Although there has been little indication that Indian civilian themselves have been subjected to the ruthless treatment meted out to others immediately following the Japanese occupation, the treatment given to the Chinese, who were tortured, raped or butchered in thousands, was carried out openly without any attempt at concealment, thus indication without a shadow of doubt what Indian civilians could expect if they attempted in any way to hinder or oppose the Japanese plans.

This first phase, the creation of fear in the minds of Indian civilians, was soon followed by Japan's virtual recognition of branches of the so-called Indian Independence League inaugurated at Bangkok. This League, whose leading members are disgruntled anti-British and Pro-Japanese

Indians, was given what amounted to the power of life and death in regard to the control of all Indians, in that civilians who did not enrol were deprived of the right to obtain rationed food and to do business. Although on the face of it the League was an authority independent of the Japanese, it was in reality, whether always voluntarily or not we cannot say, taking its orders from the Japanese and dancing to the tune piped by them.

Once this regimentation of Indian civilian had been started, the League was used by the Japanese for the purpose of stirring up hatred against the British, by means of intensive propaganda and false war news. In the propaganda field, much play was made of the Japanese intention to free India for the Indians, while false war news was intended to suggest that the defeat of Britain and her allies was inevitable, that the Japanese were to become the rulers of the Far East for all time, and that for these reasons it was obvious that it would greatly benefit Indians if they co-operated with the Japanese and assisted in the setting-up of a free India within the co-prosperity sphere.

Indian military personnel on the other hand, were obviously intended to be put to more important use by the Japanese, which is the reason perhaps for the treatment accorded to them after capture. There is an abundance of irrefutable evidence to show that in an attempt to break down their morale, and so their loyalty to the Crown, Indian military personnel were subjected to torture, such as the refusal of food and drink, flogging and extremely hard labour for long periods under the most trying weather conditions; while there were numerous instances in which soldiers who refused to allow their loyalty to be shaken were put to a cruel death in front of their brother officers and men. At the same time, as in the case of civilians, disgruntled Indians were later brought in to disseminate propaganda which, *inter alia,* indicated that if the soldiers would serve the cause of Japan they would be accorded good treatment and be comparatively free again.

This propaganda aimed not only at persuading soldiers to join an Indian Traitor Army, which the Japanese proposed to use against the Allied forces in a possible invasion of India or alternatively for the purpose of opposing any Allied attempt to advance into Burma or other Japanese-occupied territory further south; it also aimed at persuading them that unless they did so join they could expect no amelioration of the intolerable conditions in which they lived.

In these circumstances it is not surprising that a considerable number of military personnel did outwardly profess their willingness to serve in the traitor army, after their powers of endurance and resistence to propaganda and their physical discomfort had reached a very low ebb. How much reliance the Japanese will be able to place in any army raised on these lines, however, is another question, there are indication that a very great majority of these suborned troops will revert to their true loyalty immediately a suitable opportunity presents itself.

In order to create a fifth column weapon in India, which could sabotage the Allied war effort, perform espionage, suborn the Indian Army, and create a state of public opinion favourable to their intentions, the Japanese began sending their agents into India early in 1942.

In the first three months of their campaign, the Japanese used only prisoners of war who had been suborned in the ways that I have described. After a full of three months during the monsoon, they relaunced this offensive in September, 1942, this time employing Indian civilians as well as prisoners; most of the agents had been trained for fifth column work at one of the ageneies set up by the Japanese for schooling agents in this type of warfare. The greatest number of agents arrived in October, and then the numbers began to fall until they ceased in January of this year.

After two months of inactivity, March saw the arrival of new agents, and this time prisoner of war who had captured in the recent Arakan campaign were among those apprehended. The peak figure was reached in April; since then agents have been arriving in decreasing numbers. All of them have been given a variety of tasks to perform in India, including sabotage, espionage and propaganda. They have been supplied with money and many have been equipped with weapons that they have been taught to use.

The total number of agents despatched to India since the initiation of this campaign cannot be disclosed for reasons of security. We are confident however that these agents have not paid a dividend. This is partly due to the excellent security measures in operation, partly to the poor type of Indian who volunteers for this type of work, and partly to the increasingly favourable position of the Allies on all fronts. Whatever new steps the Japanese attempt in this direction, we shall meet them confidently.

Realising possibly that they cannot hope to achieve any results in their territorial designs against India unless the Indian Army which has resisted them so fiercely in the past has been corrupted through subversive activities, the Japanese have devoted considerable attention to suborning Indian Army personnel. In the forward areas they have attempted in various ways to cause panic and confusion in front-line troops and by distributing anti-British literature. Against units and regiments centres within India, the Japanese have tried to suborn Indian troops through the medium of prisoners of war who have been told to rejoin their units and there to spread anti-British propaganda. They have also been told to instruct men whom they could suborn to kill their officers and to desert with their arms during operations.

Turning their attention to the general public, Japan's first object was to dispel the feeling of mistrust from the minds of Indians. Their agents have been ordered to attempt to win over the Indian public by impressing upon them Japan's peaceful intentions towards India, and her desire to see an independent India on the lines of Burma. The Japanese have tried to bolster up these impressions with propaganda stories of the invincibility of the Axis powers. The latter line must need revising! Their propagandists and fifth column organisers have also turned their attention to Government servants, to certain committees, and to political parties notably the Congress Party. S. C. Bose at present their chief propaganda weapon. These attempts on the morale of the general public have not been as well received as Japan might have expected, since a feeling of distrust for the Japanese still exists in the minds of many Indians.

Your Highnesses will know that the Japanese have not confined themselves to the use of agents and broadcasts in the attempt to further their aims. They have produced papers and pamphlets printed in various Indian languages, which have been scattered among front-line troops and also dropped by air in India. In the forward areas, they have also coerced the local inhabitants into distributing much of their propagandists literature. Japanese efforts continue, but so far we have fought them successfully and shall go on fighting successfully any attempts to create a fifth column organisation within India which has its object the paving of the way for a Japanese army intent on the aggrandisement of Japan and the humiliation of India.

It would be wrong to lose sight of the part played by the arch-traitor Subhas Chandra Bose in this nefarious campaign against India. The Japanese realising that they were not attaining the desired result, asked the Germans for the loan of this renegade, in the belief that an ex-President of Congress would be a figure capable of restoring new life into a decaying movement. S. C. Bose arrived in Japan from Berlin at about the beginning of June; soon afterwards, he moved to Singapore where be was proclaimed supreme Commander-in-Chief of what is commonly known as the JIF Army, (i.e., Japanese Inspired Fifth Column Army) whose existence was at this time formally announced. The Japanese at last had found a willing tool, notorious enough to feature prominently in their Indian broadcasts.

Subhas Chandra Bose now stands (in the place once so confidently occupied by Rash Behari) as supreme head of the Indian Traitor Organisation established by the Japanese, and is co-operating whole-heartedly with enemy by coercing Indians into furthering Japanese designs on India. Bose's past condemnations of Japan's brutal attack on China have been temporarily and conveniently forgotten by his masters.

Since his assumption of office as C-in-C of the Traitor Army, he has devoted much of his subject matter in his broadcasts to the supposedly increasing strength of his army, and to the opening of training camps. He has also threatened an invasion of this mothercountry by these traitor forces; but the successive dates so unwisely announced by him for this coup have passed harmlessly by, and have brought him only scorn in his listeners' eyes and a reputation as a vain boaster. Even now he must be pondering the unhappy fate when the Japanese find their fifth column weapon to be unwiedly and futile, when their armies are being annihilated, their ships lying on the sea bed and their aircraft obliterated from the skies.

But, Your Highnesses, we are not waiting till that day comes to combat this threat to India. At this moment vigorous counter measures are in hand. One of them is the direction of propaganda against the enemy himself and against the peoples of the territory he has occupied. Responsibility for this propaganda is divided between various departments interested in the Far East, and it is carried out by means of broadcasts and of leaflets dropped from the air.

G. H. Q. is particularly interested in the preparation of broadcasts addressed to Japanese troops and in both broadcasts and leaflets for Indians in occupied territories. Large numbers of these Indians are of course, prisoners of war, and we hope that some of our news gets through to them. Some of you have already been asked, and have graciously agreed, to broadcasts messages of encouragement to these prisoners. In fact, several speeches by Princes have already gone over on the air.

It is an unfortunate fact that most people in India are, or were until recently extremely ignorant about the Far East and about Japan especially. The Japanese had been carrying on propaganda all over Asia for some years, so that people who had no direct knowledge gained a vague impression that the Japs were perhaps quite nice people. Naturally they are trying to keep up this impression in the occupied territories by intensive propaganda and it is the task of a special section in G. H. Q. to expose their real character and intention. Working on this job there are a number of people who have a good knowledge of Japan, and, of course, we are able to make use of a certain amount of the information that reaches us from the occupied territories. I cannot give you many details about the subjects covered in these broadcasts, as it would take too long but our main objects are to refute the lies told by the Japs, to show how their smooth words cover the most barbaric acts, to describe the sufferings they have caused by their aggression, to expose their intentions of ravaging India, and to show that for all their boasting, they cannot hope to win against the Allies.

There are, I am sorry to say, a few Indians who have turned traitor and are attempting to help the enemy. As you can imagine, our propaganda does not neglect these men and we have, I hope, left them in no doubt as to India's opinion of them and the punishment they can expect after the war. We have been able to show that Subhash Chandra Bose's talk about invading India is nothing but a bluff and a propaganda stunt, and that he himself is an ambitious self-seeker.

We have reason to believe that our propaganda is being successful to some extent since the Japanese controlled station go to a good deal of trouble to answer us back and Bose himself has declared that one of his main objects is to combat propaganda from Delhi.

Another of our counter measures which is applied to the Indian Army has been the setting-up of a Central Group, consisting of a number of officers themselves apprised of all the relevant facts, who give the truth regarding the Japanese—not as propaganda but as information—direct to a group of Indian other ranks in each unit. These informed troops then pass on the matter to their fellow soldiers of all ranks. It can be compared with the system existing in some of the territories governed by Your Highnesses, where news is sent through the Station House Officer who passes it on to villages through the daily Chowkidar parade.

Its effect has been to enlighten the Indian sepoy about his enemy in an idiom which he can understand fully. As Your Highnesses will realise, a man is seldom apprehensive about things that he knows and understands. The theme of Central Group is 'KNOW YOUR ENEMY'.

The setting up of these contacts, called 'Josh Groups' in each unit has had a valuable result in establishing a quick and very direct channel of communication which can manifestly be used for constructive purposes, apart from merely combation the J.I.F.C.

Now for a few words about Security. Broadly speaking, you can divide military intelligence into two parts. One: Information, or finding out about the enemy's plans; Two: Security, or preventing the enemy finding out about your plans. This general security of plans can itself be divided into three branches of Security, namely: Security of Information, of Personnel, and of Material.

First, Security of Information. This, as the form implies, deals with preventing the enemy learning about such concrete facts as our operational movements, the relative strength of our forces and so on. 'Security of Personnel,on the other hand, deals with the less tangible factor of troops' or it may be civilians, morale: and its object will be to prevent the enemy getting at our minds through defeatist propaganda, subversive appeal, and so forth. The third branch, Security of Material, is meant to prevent the enemy getting at our physical resources, such as arms and ammunition, shipping and other transport, aircraft and airfields, all of whose destruction would vitally interfere with the success of our operations.

Much has been said in this war of the danger from the Fifth Column, but it is only one aspect of the 'Security problem, namely the existence of enemy agents in one's own country. Officials and other persons in positions of responsibility must, of course, know of the implications of the fifth column, but there is a good deal to be said for the idea that talk in public about the fifth column should be discouraged as it, tends to create a feeling of uneasiness and distrust which is very demaging to public morale. And this very damage to morale is in fact an aid to the enemy. No, Your Highnesses, all this mystery which surrounds the subject of the fifth column and of Security generally, really does more harm than good. Security is just one factor of Intelligence , and Intelligence is just one factor in military strategy or tactics. They both have the same end in view as has the operational side of planning and should thus be based on co-operation and regarded as integral parts of the same general scheme. There should be no room for that attitude summed up in the early days of the war by a security officer who complained that he was asked either, 'Why the hell are you snooping around?' or (when things went wrong) "Why the hell didn't you snoop round?"

Nevertheless though the Fifth Column can be given undue notoriety, the danger of the indirect attack has assumed an importance in this war considerably greater than ever before, and it is to combat this that the Field Security Service was formed and embodied in the Intelligence Corps. Its duties are, broadly speaking, to combat the triple menace of Espionage, Propaganda, and Subotage directed against the armed forces of the Crown; that is to say, to help in preserving the Security of Information, Personnel and Material. It does this mainly by instilling into the armed forces a sense of what we call 'Security-mindedness and touches them to adopt such

Security measures that the enemy agent will get no information, the saboteur be kept at arm's length and the propaganda fall on deaf ears.'

Field Security Sections are attached to formations in the field, located on important lines of communications at bases and in ports. Their duties, for which they are specially trained are primarily to advise and supervise in Security matter; but in operational and protected areas they are largely engaged on Security Controls to prevent any hindrance to military operations and to ensure their secrecy. May personnel are linguists and they often undertake the duty of interpreter, help in the control of prisoners, seize abandoned enemy documents and material, and undertake a multitude of other duties to safeguard the operations in progress.

The sections in ports, in conjunctions with the police and civil authorities assist in the maintenance of Security of port installations and shipping, the secrecy of troop movements and of shipping inforamations. They also help to control the merchant seamen and passengers using the port. Airport sections, composed of R.A.F. personnel, perform similar duties at important airfields where aircraft enter or leave India.

Our own Field Security Service has already done invaluable work in the India Command and in operations on the Eastern Frontier; with the advance of our armies it will extend its activities to S.E. Asia.

Already there is a growing interest in all measures pertaining to Security on the part of the forces and police from many States under your Highnesses control. It is felt that the Army can help Security organisation in the States of considerable extent by sharing the experiences gained throughout the war; and as the outcome of a suggestion made by the delegates attending the first States 'Security Conference at Bombay, the fighting services have undertaken to train as many States' military and police officers as they can find vacancies for , both in basic and specialised Security duties, first at the Intelligence Corps (India) Training Depot at Karachi, and afterwards by attachments to Army or R.A.F. field, seaport or airport Security Sections in accordance with the special needs of the States.

Your Highnesses, in my humble opinion the adoption of proper Security measures in the States is of the utmost importance; this is especially so if one considers the known views and policy of the Japanese regarding rulers and states. It is the aim of the Japanese to destroy the Princely Order entirely and from the root. It is indeed their aim, should they ever come to India, to destroy all the privileged classes and stable elements of the country. Before us is the example of Korea and the Northern Malay States. In Korea, the ruling family has been completely destroyed, with the exception of one prince who lives in virtual custody in Japan. His name is Prince Rio. He was forced to marry a Japanese girl, and is now three-quarters Japanese, and the only member of the Korean ruling family left in existence. Even I was treated like a prisoner before the war and during the war. I was interned, as I have told you earlier in my talk. My only crime was that I was related to an Indian Ruler and was a loyal subject of the King. However I feel that the Japanese paid me a great compliment by treating me as they did, I could describe to you at length the various episodes and example of ill treatment which I had to undergo, but this is not possible owing to limitations of time.

The Japanese aim is to destroy, in the territories they occupy, all culture and religion which is not of Japanese brand. This would happen were they to come to India. Your Highness will excuse me for reverting to the subject, but I must repeat that Security of the States is of very great importance, and it is essential that in matters concerning Security of the States should fully co-operate with, and obtain advice from, the military authorities who are in a position to advise from their past experience. Immediate steps should in my opinion be taken by the States to guard against Sabotage of ports, railways and airfields, subversive elements such as Congress, Forward Bloc and activities of other undesirable bodies, and false rumours spread by enemy agents. The States should also provide for security of information of military value and should counteract enemy radio propaganda and keep a watchful eye on the pro-Japanese elements living in States, who either had contacts with the Japanese before the war or who have been repatriated since. I cannot urge too strongly the necessity of early steps being taken to increase the security mindedness in the States by sending military and police officers for training in specialised security duties.

I apologise to Your Highnesses for taking up so much of your valuable time and I thank you for attending this talk, and beg to be forgiven for any unintentional mistake I may have made.[2]

2. Major Himmat Singh was the younger brother of Maharaja Jam Sahib of Nawanagar, was sent to Japan as Assistant Military Attache in the British Embassy. His main task was to report on the activities of the Indian Nationalists in that country and how to prevent their collaboration with the Japanese before the war.

39

British Intelligence assessment of Bose and His Activitites in East Asia after His Arrival from Germany[1]

15 October, 1943

20. Brief accounts have been furnished in previous Surveys of Subhas Bose's Movements and main activities in the Far East since the date of his arrival there from Germany sometime in June this year, but it should be remembered that the contents have all been based on information culled from Axis sources in the form of broadcasts and Domei press message, and that we therefore know neither more nor less than the Axis have been prepared to tell us. On the hypothesis, however, that what they have made known in regard to his actual movements and activities is founded on fact, a short review of the main events up to date and an attempt to appreciate the effects of his presence on the Far Eastern situation and in India may prove of interest, though the conclusions reached about reactions in occupied territory must, of necessity, be treated with reserve.

21. Soon after his arrival in Tokyo, Bose attended the 82nd Extraordinary Imperial Diet Session on the 16th June, following a conference with Premier Tojo and Foreign Minister Shigemitsu. He later interviwed the Press. This intereview gave us the first indications of the general lines on which all his subsequent utterances were to be based, namely that India could no longer expect to gain her freedom by passive resistance but must resort to the use of force; that while Indians should be prepared to accept Japan's active assistance in an outside attack on India, Indians in India must also be ready to begin the fight for freedom from within.

22. No estimate can be made of the true and immediate effect of Bose's appearance on Indians in the Far East, but within a short period the

1. War office F. No. 208/818. Public Record office.

either was loaded with eulogies, resolutions, reviews, interviews and propaganda descriptions of other ceromonies, in an attempt to indicate that this Axis move was a popular success of no mean proportion. In India, on the contrary, there was little evidence that the news was received with more than mild interest.

23. At the beginning of July Bose arrived in Singapore from Tokyo and officially assumed the Presidentship of the so-called Indian Independence League and concurrently the post of Commander-in-Chief of the JIF Army, the inauguration of which had just been officially announced; but he did not at this time do more then hint that he intended to use this army for something better than mere propaganda purposes, when in his speeches he emphasised the militarisation nature of the struggle that would be necessary in order to bring about independence. Once again he stressed the need for action within India and the necessity for all organisations whether within or without India, to transform themselves into a disciplined fighting organisation under one leader. He described the international situation at that time as favourable to this purpose.

24. It was from Singapore also that Bose announced his intention of forming a Provisional Goverment of Free India, which was to prepare Indians for an armed struggle and ultimately make room for a permanent Goverment chosen by the people.

25. Intense propaganda on these lines continued to have no very marked effect in India, though an increase in rumours was noticed, while some personal interest was evinced among nationalists and revolutionaries in regard to future developments and Bose's military pretenions in particular. As regard reactions in Malaya and elsewhere in the Far East, it is difficult to assess the degree of spontaneity in what the Axis claimed to have been an overwhelming response, but in Singapore and Bangkok, in particular, where there are a considerable number of disgruntled anti-British Indians to assist him, it is reasonable to suppose that Bose used his appeal and his knowledge of mob psychology to good effect and that the results were, perhaps within definite limits, fairly gratifying to him.

26. Towards the end of July Bose left on a visit to Bangkok, Rangoon and Saigon, returning to Singapore in August; Axis broadcasts contained no news of this until after he left Rangoon on the return

journey, in Bangkok he visited the Japanese, German and Italian embassies and conversed with the Thai Foreign Minister, and on the 27th July attended a welcome mass rally before leaving for Rangoon. In his address at this rally he made it clear that the JIF Army was to be used for the invasion of India, when he reminded his audience that their slogan was to be 'On to Delhi' and said that he felt there would not be many who would not revolt from the Indian Army when the JIF Army arrived on the frontier.

27. Bose was in Rangoon from the 29th July till the 3rd or 4th August. He attended the Burmese State Foundation Assembly meeting on the 1st August, while a visit to the Civil JIF H. Q. , an address to an Indian mass meeting and interview with the Press were the other main items on his programmes. He had little new to say, except that he suggested that the majority of Gandhi's followers would be prepared to extend even their complete physical support to the independence movement once the JIF Army had successfully penetrated India.

28. His attendance in Rangoon at the proclamation of Burma's independence was good propaganda from the 'fight for freedom' angle, particularly among Indians in Burma, who must have been considerably impressed by the standing of their leader in the new Greater East Asia, in view of the fact that Indians are generally despised and hated, and reckoned of no account, by the Burmese. In India, however, such interest as came to notice in this connection at the time was centred more in Japan's apparent generosity towards Burma than in Bose's well-timed arrival and presence at the proclamation ceremony.

29. On his return to Singapore, Bose's first engagement of any importance was a rally of 20,000 Indians, whom he addressed on August the 15th. In referring to his Rangoon visit and the inauguration ceremony he had attended, he drew a bright picture of the JIF Army's victory parade in Delhi after his conquest of India. Informing his listeners in the Army and among the civil population that the JIF Army was now on the move, he declared that it was the task of Indians to start a second front in India. He subsequently told the Press that great preparation were under way in Burma for the accommodation of the JIF army and that Burma was to be the future headquarters of the independence movement. It was at about this time also that the first

mention was made of Bose's offer to supply rice to India. Other propaganda was to the effect that Bose's agents had reported unrest in the British Indian Army an Bengal and Assam; that Indian youths all over India were forming secret military organisations and undergoing training in order to join the JIF Army when it arrived in India, and that sabotage was on the increase in Indian factories.

30. The only noticeable result of this propaganda was in connection with Bose's rice offer, for very shortly afterwards the Bengal Provincial Hindu Mahasabha passed resolution recommending that Government should consider importing rice from Burma and Siam. Though the resolution did not go so far as to suggest that Bose's offer as such should be accepted, it is clear that it wsa prompted by that offer, the motive being, however, political expediency with the intention of embarrassing the Bengal Government rather than sympathy with Bose. Apart from the action of the Hindu Mahasabha no developments have been reported, though, as was to be expected, rumour-mongers did not let the opportunity slip entirely.

31. At the end of August Bose again left Singapore for a tour of North of the Malaya and further visits to Siam and Burma. It is claimed that the tour was in connection with supervising the work of the Civil JIF organisation and the training of the JIF Army in these areas. In Bangkok he inspected the Siam committee of the Civil JIF organisation and participated in the celebrations of Mahatma Gandhi's 75th birthday, when he addressed a mass meeting. He also broadcast from the Bangkok station. In Burma, where he arrived on the 24th of September, he attended the celebrations of Burma's independence and conversed with the Premier and other leading Burmese officials. Here also he inspected the Burma committee of the Civil JIF organisation, visited training camps and gave addresses to youths undergoing training. In an apporach to Muslims, Bose visited the tomb of Bahadur Shah, the Late Mughal Emperor of India, and laid wreaths on the grave. He was "shocked to see the tomb in ruins" and asked the Burmese authorities to carry out repairs, thus demonstrating, beyond all doubt, what was called "his profound love and respect for Muslims." In a Press interview he said that the JIF army was well equipped with modern weapons and was ready to march on Delhi. Other details concerning Bose's visit to Rangoon were furnished in the last issue of this summary.

32. There are no indications as yet to the effect of Bose's recent tour, but after his return to Singapore at the beginning of October he declared himself satisfied with the progress so far made towards the goal of "total mobilisation"; the morale of both civil and military JIFs and the I.N.A. was everywhere very high, while in the case of the latter men and women were coming foward in large numbers to volunteer. At the same time a less boastful and somewhat plaintive note was to be detected in his warning that the final struggle for liberty would be hard and long and that it would take at least twelve months, or perhaps more, to liberate the whole of India. Likewise in earlier utterances during his tour in Malaya, he pointed out that manpower and materials must be contributed by Indians themselves before they turned to others for help. All this tends to suggest that Bose's claims that the JIF Army was ready to march on India have been a little premature, while there is also a hint that the Japanese have not implemented their much publicised promises of unlimited help in his plans.

33. Detailed conclusions regarding Bose's plans and the ultimate effect of his activities on behalf of the J.I.F.C. organisation as a whole must await further evidence. All that can be said at the moment is that no slackening of efforts to develop and organise the fifth column and militant potentialities of the so-called Indian Independence League and the JIF Army can be assumed while Subhas Bose remains at the helm of affairs, while it is also easy to believe that any useful role played by the JIFC in Japanese plans will be very largely due to his inspiration and leadership.

40

Address by A. Yellappa Welcoming Bose on His Second Visit to Singapore; Requests Indians to Follow Bose for Achieving Indian Independence[1]

21 October, 1943

Friends,

This is the second occasion since the arrival of Netaji Subhas Chandra Bose that the Indians in East Asia have come to attend a conference of this kind.

We met on the 4th of July this year, when Sjt. Rash Behari Bose, the pioneer of the Indian Independence Movement in East Asia, brought for us Sjt. Subhas Chandra Bose as a gift from Tokyo.

On behalf of the Syonan Indians, I welcome you all to this conference.

Many great changes have come into being in the International world since the arrival of Netaji Subhas Chandra Bose. Burma has been declared independent. Announcement of the Philippine independence has been made; and I can assure you, ladies and gentlemen, that under the leadership of Netaji, our Hindustan will be also free in the near future. Now I am asking the two million Indians in East Asia whether they wish to be free or not. If your reply is in the affirmative, then follow Netaji and obey his orders. This is not the time for political discussion. Leave all the questions for Netaji and learn to obey orders. Then and only then can Indian be free.

Delegates, Friends, Ladies and Gentlemen, I have great pleasure in once again welcoming you to this conference.

1. I.I.L. Papers, F. No. 45/3, N.A.I.

41

Proclamation of the Provisional Government of Azad Hind by S.C. Bose[1]

21 October, 1943

After their first defeat at the hands of the British in1757 in Bengal, the Indian people fought an uniterrupted series of hard and bitter battles over a stretch of one hundred years. The history of this period teems with examples of unparalleled heroism and self-sacrifice. And, in the pages of that history, the names of Sirajuddaula and Mohanlal of Bengal, Haider Ali, Tippu Sultan and Velu Tampi of South India, Appa Sahib Bhonsle and Peshwa Baji Rao of Maharashtra, the Begums of Oudh, Sardar Shyam Singh Atariwala of Punjab and last, but not least, Rani Laxmi Bai of Jhansi, Tantia Topi, Maharaja Kunwar Singh of Dumraon and Nana Sahib — among others — the names of all these warriors are for ever engraved in letters of gold. Unfortunately for us, our forefathers did not at first realise that the British constituted a grave threat to the whole of India, and they did not therefore put up a united front against the enemy. Ultimately, when the Indian people were roused to the reality of the situation, they made a concerted move — and under the flag of Bahadur Shah, in 1857, they fought their last war as free men. In spite of a series of brilliant victories in the early stages of this war, ill-luck and faulty leadership gradually brought about their final collapse and subjugation. Nevertheless, such heroes as the Rani of Jhansi, Tantia Topi, Kunwar Singh and Nana Sahib live like eternal stars in the nation's memory to inspire us to greater deeds of sacrifice and valour.

Forcibly disarmed by the British after 1857 and subjected to terror and brutality, the Indian people lay prostrate for a while — but with the birth of the Indian National Congress in 1885, there came a new awakening.

1. I.N.A. Trial Papers. The above proclamation was read in Hindustani by A.M. Sahey, in Tamil by Mr. Cidambaran, and in English by Netaji himself.

From 1885 until the end of the last World War, the Indian people, in their endeavour to recover their lost liberty, tried all possible methods—namely agitation and propaganda, boycott of British goods, terrorism and sabotage and finally armed revolution. But all these efforts failed for a time. Ultimately in 1920, when the Indian people, haunted by a sense of failure, were groping for a new method, Mahatma Gandhi came forward with the new weapon of non-co-operation and civil disobedience.

For two decades thereafter, the Indian people went through a phase of intense patriotic activity. The message of freedom was carried to every Indian home. Through personal example, people were faught to suffer, to sacrifice and to die in the cause of freedom. From the centre to the remotest villages, the people were knit together into one political organisation. Thus, the Indian people not only recovered their political consciousness but became a political entity once again. They could now speak with one voice and strive with one will for one common goal. From 1937 to 1939, through the work of the Congress Ministries in eight provinces, they gave proof of their readiness and their capacity to administer their own affairs.

Thus, on the eve of the present World War, the stage was set for the final struggle for India's liberation. During the course of this war, Germany, with the help of her allies has dealt shattering blows to our enemy in Europe while Nippon, with the help of her allies, has inflicted a knockout blow to our enemy in East Asia. Favoured by a most happy combination of circumstances, the Indian people today have a wonderful opportunity for achieving their national emancipation.

For the first time in recent history, Indians abroad have also been politically roused and united in one organisation. They are not only thinking and feeling in tune with their countryment at home, but are also marching in step with them, along the path to freedom. In East Asia, in particular, over two million Indians are now organised as one solid phalanx, inspired by the slogan of 'Total Mobilisation'. And in front of them stand the serried ranks of India's Army of Liberation, with the slogan 'Onward to Delhi', on their lips.

Having goaded Indians to desperation by its hypocrisy and having driven them to starvation and death by plunder and loot, British rule in India has forfeited the goodwill of the Indian people altogether and is now living a precarious existence. It needs but a flame to destroy the last vestige of that unhappy rule. To light that flame is the task of India's Army of Liberation. Assured of the enthusiastic support of the civil population at home and also of a large section of Britain's Indian Army, and backed by gallant and invincible allies abroad but relying in the first instance on its own strength, India's Army of Liberation is confident of fulfilling its historic role.

Now that the dawn of freedom is at hand, it is the duty of the Indian people to set up to a Provisional Government of their own, and launch the last struggle under the banner of that Government. But with all the Indian leaders in prison and the people at home totally disarmed it is not possible to set up a Provisional Government within India or to launch an armed struggle under the aegis of that government. It is, therefore, the duty of the Indian Independence League in East Asia, supported by all patriotic Indians at home and abroad, to undertake this task of setting up a Provisional Government of Azad Hind (Free India) and of conducting the last fight for freedom, with the help of the Army of Liberation, (that is, the Azad Hind Fauj or the Indian National Army) organised by the League.

Having been constituted as the Provisional Government of Azad Hind by the Indian Independence League in East Asia, we enter upon our duties with a full sense of the responsibility that has devolved on us. We pray that Providence may bless our work and our struggle for the emancipation of our Motherland. And we hereby pledge our lives and the lives of our comrades in arms to the cause of her freedom, of her welfare, and her exaltation among the nations of the world.

It will be the task of the Provisional Government to launch and to conduct the struggle that will bring about the expulsion of the British and their allies from the soil of India. It will then be the task of the Provisional Government to bring about the establishment of a permanent National Government of Azad Hind constituted in accordance with the will of the Indian people and enjoying their confidence. After the British and their allies are overthrown and until a permanent National Government of Azad Hind is set up on Indian soil, the Provisional Government will administer the affairs of the country in trust for the people.

The Provisional Government is entitled to, and hereby claims, the allegiance of every Indian. It guarantees religious liberty, as well as equal rights and equal opportunities to all its citizens. It declares its firm resolve to pursue the happiness and prosperity of the whole nation and of all its parts, cherishing all the children of the nation equally and transcending all the differences cunningly fostered by an alien government in the past.

In the name of God, in the name of by gone generations who have welded the Indian people into one nation, and in the name of the dead heroes who have bequeathed to us a tradition of heroism and self-sacrifice we call upon the Indian people to rally round our banner and strike for

India's freedom. We call upon them to launch the final struggle against the British and all their allies in India and to prosecute that struggle with valour and perseverance and full faith in final victory until the enmy is expelled from Indian soil and the Indian people are once again a Free Nation.

Signed on behalf of the Provisional Government of Azad Hind

Subhas Chandra Bose (Head of the State, Prime Minster and Minister for War and Foreign Affairs)

Captain Mrs. Lakshmi (Women's Organisation)

S.A.Ayer (Publicity and Propaganda)

Lt. Col. A.C. Chatterji (Finance)

Lt. Col. Aziz Ahmed, Lt. Col. N.S. Bhagat, Lt. Col. J.K. Bhonsle, Lt. Col. Gulzara Singh, Lt. Col. M.Z. Kiani, Lt. Col. A. D. Loganathan, Lt. Col. Ehsan Nadir, Lt. Col. Shah Nawaz, (Representatives of the Armed Forces) A. M. Sahay, Secretary (with Ministerial rank) Rash Behari Bose (Supreme adviser), Karim Ghani, Debnath Dass, D.M. Khan, A. Yellappa, D. Thivy, Sarder Ishar Sing (Advisers), A. N. Sarkar (Legal Adviser).

42

Message of the President of the Board of Information Welcoming the Formation of the Provisional Government of India and Assuring that Japan has no territorial designs on India[1]

22 October, 1943

"Valiantly shouldering the hope and trust of the peoples of East Asia, the Provisional Government of Free India, headed by Subhash Chandra Bose, has come into being on October 21."

"The independence of India has for a long period of time been the aspiration of the entire Indian people and the hope of the entire world, in East Asia, Burma, who has long been in the throes of agony under the aggression and exploitation of Britain, has become independent. The Philippines, who has been prevented from manifesting her true natural traits by the oppression of the economic imperialism of the United States, has also attained independence as a genuine East Asian country. And now we witness the establishment of the provisional Government of Free India adding a new glory in India.

"Since the beginning of the 17th century, when she extended her tentacles of aggression toward India, Britain has consistently oppressed and exploited the Indian people, and the British people have lived in luxury and comfort at the sacrifice of the Indian people. However, the people of India gradually generated a strong sentiment for resistance against British rule and in particular following the Russo-Japanese War the Indian desire for Independence became increasingly intense.

"In the last World War, the British Government utilized to the maximum extent the manpower as well as material sources of India, baiting the Indian people with the promise of self-rule after the war. However, they not only broke the promise, but, more than that, they intensified their

1. *Nippon Times*, 23 October 1943.

oppressive rule, as witness the horrible massacre of several thousand innocent Indian people at Amritsar."

"In the present great war also, the British pressure on India has been further strengthened and the Indian people have been involuntarily conscriped for military service and sent to the most dangerous front lines. According to the figures announced by the British Government in June of this year, the casualties of the British Empire forces reached 500,000 of which the Indian losses were as much as 100,000 the casualties of the British empire forced to bear an immense share of the military expenditures as well as an enormous amount of munitions of war, with the result that the whole of India is now suffering from vicious inflation and lack of commodities. Moreover, due to British mal-administration, the condition of starvation has been created in the provinces of Bengal and others with numerous people dying day after day. Reports of these miserable conditions have been spread in Britain and the United States and have become the subject of serious discussion in the newspapers of those countries even in the British parliament.

"Despite these conditions that British pressure on India instead of being relaxed, has been further intensified, especially since August of last year. In the so-called Atlantic Charter, which Britain and the United States claim to be their war aim, there is a principle of the self-determination of peoples, but its application is excepted in the case India, further exposing deceptive policy of these two countries.

"In view of these circumstances, it has come to a point where the freedom of India can never be granted merely by entreaties toward Britain and where British influence must be cast out of India with force of arms. The righteous indignation of fair minded people throughout the world has been aroused against the despotism and oppression of Britain.

"Mr. Bose has for a long time been fighting for the independence of India. When he was arrested by British authorities in India in July 1941, the Indian people protested in sympathy against Britain by engaging in hartal. Subsequently he fled from India and spent his time in Germany laying his plans for independence of India. In June of this year, he made a sudden appearance in Japan after which he went South where he has since strengthened the Indian Independence League, organized the Indian National Army and proceeded vigorously to make various preparations for independence.

"The time having ripened, the Provisional Government of Free India has been established. This government has in its hands the glorious destiny of developing in the future into a government of truly emancipated India.

"The Indian National Army under the command of this government is made up of vigorous young men who are burning with enthusiasm for Indian independence and are ready to make the supreme sacrifice for their country. When this army begins its march of liberation into India, it will be the time for the emancipation of entire India from the British Shackles wih which it has been bound for centuries.

"In pursuance of the great ideal of enabling all nations each to have its proper place and all peoples to live in peace and security, the principle underlying the founding of our empire, the Japanese Government have repeatedly in the past expressed their sympathy and their intention of extending all possible support to the independence of India. Firmly believing that the establishment of the Provisional Government of Free India is an event of profound significance to the complete realization of Indian independence, the Japanese Government have recognized that government today and have reaffirmed their policy to give every support to its efforts for the attainment of its object.

"In order to resist these developments perchance the British will adopt further oppressive measures or a policy of cajolery toward the Indian people. Whichever attitude they may take, it is clear beyond any doubt that what she will give to India is nothing but repression and suffering. We have risen to eliminate these expressions and sufferings. The Indians also have arisen. Japan and India will fight together and together will surely win through. As stated by the spokesman of the Provisional Government of Free India, Japan has no territorial or economic ambition whatever toward independent India. Her sole desire lies in the promotion of the well-being of the entire Indian people. It is our firm conviction that the day when this desire is realised will surely arrive in the near future."

43

Speech by Bose at the Opening of the Training Centres for the Rani of Jhansi Regiment[1]

22 October, 1943

Sisters and Brothers

The opening of Rani of Jhansi Regiment Training Camp is an important and significant function: it is a very important landmark in the progress of our Movement in East Asia.

To realise its importance, you should bear in mind that ours is not a merely political movement. We are on the other hand engaged in the great task of regenerating our Nation. We are in fact ushering a New Life for the Indian Nation, and it is necessary that our New Life should be built on sound foundations. Remember that ours is not a propaganda stunt; we are in fact witnessing the re-birth of India. And it is only in the fitness of things that there should be a stir of New Life among our womenfolk.

Our past has been a great and glorious one, India could not have produced a heroine like the Rani of Jhansi if she did not have a glorious tradition. The history of great women in India is as ancient as the Vedic period. The greatness of Indian womenhood had its roots in those early days when India had its Sanskrit culture.

The same India which produced great women in the past also produced the Rani of Jhansi at a grave hour in India's history. And today while we are facing the gravest hour in our History, I have confidence that Indian womanhood will not fail to rise to the occasion. If for the war of independence of Jhansi, India had to produce and it did produce a Lakshmi Bai today for the war of independence of the whole of India to liberate 38 crores of Indians India has to produce and shall produce thousands of Rani's of Jhansi.

In the same way as we have figures like Maitreyi in India's ancient days, we have the inspiring examples of Ahalyabai of Maharashtra, Rani

---

1. *Nippon Times*, 24 October 1943.

Bhawani of Bengal, Razya Begum and Noor Jehan, who were shining administrators in recent historic times prior to British rule in India, I have every confidence in the fertility of the Indian soil. I am confident that India as in the past will also produce the best flowers of Indian womanhood.

When in 1921 a new political life started in India thousands, nay lakhs of our sisters also joined the movement and came forward to make sacrifices. In those days it was great thing to go to prisons. Our Indian brothers and sisters got ready to undergo the ordeal of prison life and I remember still how in December 1921 at Calcutta the two jails were full. The Britishers built two more jails and these two were also packed in a few days.

When the Britishers found that the Indians were not restrained by fear of prison life, they changed their tactics. They resorted to the method of throwing leaders into prison and using lathis and bullets against the masses. Joining the Civil Disobedience Movement then meant willingness to face lathi charges and gun-fire and the Indians not only men but also women got ready to face lathi charges and gun-fire. I cannot forget an incident in Calcutta when we held a procession against the orders of the Government and when the police tried to break the procession by lathi charge, some of our sisters made a cordon around us (coming between us and the police) without flinching to free lathi charges. Thus I have witnessed while in India how the spirit and determination of our sisters have been growing stage by stage.

Not only in the history of the Passive Resistance Movement but in th history of the Revolutionary Party also we have the examples of our brave sisters who have played a noble part. I know of many sisters who became daring revolutionaries. If one type of courage was necessary for passive resistance another and more active courage is necessary for revolutionary efforts and in this too I found that our sisters were not wanting. In 1931 an English magistrate was shot by two girls; the age of one was 16 and the age of the other was 17. In India even ordinary men will shudder before magistrates, but these two young sisters bravely went to the house of the magistrate and fired at him. You can easily imagine what wonderful courage those young sisters might have had Such courage does not descend from the skies; it comes from the soil of India; it has its roots in the age-old traditions of India's past.

Since 1928, I have been taking interest in women's organisations in India and I found that given the opportunity our sisters could rise to any occasion. There was one Rashtra Mahila Sangh of ladies in Bengal which did splendid work. In December 1928 a volunteer corps of 500 women was formed which was not only run on sound lines but their parades and their discipline gave us great hopes and confirmed my belief in the fact that given the impetus and opportunity Indian women could perform duties entrusted to them in a befitting manner. I have also seen women organisations in India giving training in arms available in a slave country like lathis and daggers and the way our sisters were progressing was remarkable.

And so when I began to undertake the task of guiding the Indian Independence Movement I felt that our sisters should also be given the opportunity to serve India at this grave emergency. I consulted many and I was told by some that though to raise a women's regiment might be possible in India it would be an impossible task in East Asia. What they said did not affect my conviction and my determination. And today you have before your own eyes what our sisters have accomplished. Their work has started in July and only now the training Camp for them is being opened. The delay is not due to any shortcoming on their part. The delay was due to our difficulties in finding the accommodation and making the necessary arrangements. Meanwhile, I know that our sisters were getting impatient and anxious. I heard that they were intending to lead a deputation to me to ask me whether I have forgotten them. I feel happy today that the camp is ready and the camp is being opened today on the anniversary of the birthday of the Rani of Jhansi.

I may at this jucture say a few words about the Rani of Jhansi. When the Rani of Jhansi started her fight her age was only Twenty. You can easily imagine what it would have been for a girl of twenty riding a horse and wielding her sword in open battle. You can easily realise what courage and spirit she must have had. The English Commander who fought against her said that she was the best and bravest of the rebels. He made this admission because Jhansi Rani's bravery was something which he could not hide, for he himself had to fight against her. First she fought from the Jhansi Fort and when the Fort was besieged she escaped with a party to Kalpi from where she put up a fight. When she had to retreat from this battlefront she made an alliance with Tantia Topi, attached and captured Gwalior fort and using that Fort as the base continued the battle and in this last and great battle she died fighting.

Imagine what amount of courage would have been necessary to carry on the fight in spite of more than one defeat. Yet this 20 year old Rani had the courage and showed a valour which shall be a source of inspiration to Indians for generations to come.

Unfortunately Jhansi Rani was defeated; it was not her defeat. It was the defeat of India. She died but her spirit can never die, India can once again produce Jhansi Ranees and march on to Victory.

156 of our sisters are going to start their training in the Camp which is being opened today. But I hope that their number at Syonan will reach 1,000 very soon. Training Camps for women have also been started in Thailand and Burma but at Syonan we have the Central Camp and I feel that in this Central Camp we should at least have one thousand potential Ranees of Jhansi.

You have just now heard the brave words of the Commandant of the Rani of Jhansi Unit at Syonan. She expressed their determination to work ceaselessly day and night to get prepared for the onward March to Delhi. I feel joyous at hearing that slogan "On to Delhi" from our sisters as I have been hearing it from our brothers.

With these words I declare the Training Camp open. And I would appeal to all the delegates present to carry my message to their localities and to make every effort to realise the programme I have now laid before you."

44

Japanese Press Reaction to the Formation of he Provisional Government of India by Bose[1]

22 October, 1943

The Provisional Government of Free India

The formation of Provisional Government of Free India under the leadership of Subhas Chandra Bose and its declaration of war upon Britain and the United States yesterday constitute an important advance toward the goal of an independent India. To be sure, the Provisional Government is still a government without territory, but that fact does not in the least detract from its legitimacy. For it is obvious that the country of India itself is not its own but a hostage in the hands of an alien conqueror, and the Indian living within India are not free agents with the power to exercise their own will but are slaves forced to submit to the dictates of their British masters. The only free Indians are those to be found outside the territory of India and the only untrammeled expression of Indian will is to be found among these Indian refugees abroad. It is hence but a logical move, in fact an imperative move, that a real Government of India be composed of these overseas Indians who alone are in a position to represent the genuine will of their country.

That these Indians abroad have long been carrying on an active independence movement is an incontrovertible indication of what all India feels, and the fact that recently under the practical, leadership of Subhash Chandra Bose this independence movement has produced a formidable Indian National Army proves the resolute force with which the Indians are determined to carry out their will. Now the formation of a Provisional Government to back up this Army and to give its political direction demonstrates that one more tangible step has been taken in the evolution of the movement for India's

1. An Editorial from *Nippon Times*, 22 Oct. 1943.

liberation. The movement for independence has had a long history, but never before has there been a real Army and a real Government to give it practical and substantial power. The emergence of the Provisional Government is therefore one more indication, and a most momentous one, that the goal of an independent India is at last perceptibly at hand.

The declaration of war by this Provisional Government upon Britain and the United States of course means that there can never more be any talk of compromise or bargaining with the British or their American ally. That is as it should be, for past experience has shown how futile is any attempt to reason with such a predatory beast as the British Empire which can live only by feeding upon the living bodies of its victims. The infamous record of broken promises, the solemn pledge of self-rule given when Britain need India's help in the last World War only to be shamelessly retracted when the need was over, merciless beating down of even such passive and pacifistic mass movements as those inspired by Gandhi, the spurious proposals of Sir Stafford Cripps for an illusory and conditional "dominion" status to be granted at some indeterminate future time under extensive reservation and restrictions, the reactionary obstinacy of Amery and the militaristic high-handedness of Wavell, the callous indifference and criminal incompetence of the British administration toward the present frightful famine the very while the starving Indians are being pushed to the front lines of Britains war, the fact that even the most patient advocates of sweet reasoning have been rewarded by being clapped into prison—these are proofs enough of how futile it is to attempt to deal with the British with anything other than their own weapons of force. In fact, all movements for political arrangements through negotiation or peaceful methods have not only proved futile; they have proved positively harmful to India's cause, for they have only served to delay the necessary resort to the only effective method of force.

If India is to become free, as indeed justice and moral necessity demands, it must be through the efforts of the Indian people to fight and to build. No time is more opportune than now when Britain is reeling under the mortal blows of war and when strong friends like Japan are at hand to give aid to the Indian National Army; the instrument for the building of a regenerated India has now been created by the formation of the Provisional Government.

45

Recognition of the Provisional government of Azad Hind by Japan and other Foreign Power[1]

23 October, 1943

The Board of Information, Tokyo, on October 23, announced the Nippon Government's recognition of the Provisional Government of Azad Hind. The announcement was as follows :

"The Provisional Government of Free India, having been established with Mr. Subhas Chandra Bose as the Head, the Nippon Government in its firm belief that it is a great forward step toward the realization of an independent India for which the Indian people have long aspired, has recognized it as the Provisional Government of Free India and hereby declares its intention to extend every possible co-operation and support in the Provisional Government's efforts to attain its object."

The following telegram was received by Netaji Subhas Chandra Bose, from His Excellency Premier General Hideki Tojo—

"Your Excellency—I have the honour of sending you my hearty congratulations on the establishment of the Provisional Government of Azad Hind which has been Your Excellency's long cherished desire and thereby dashing forward to expel the British influence to attain the everlasting prosperity of India. The Nippon Government is firmly determined to render every possible co-operation to your Government.

"I take this opportunity to offer my best wishes for the successful and prosperous future of your Government and pray for your good health."

At the 83rd session of the Imperial Diet which met on Oct. 26, in Tokyo, Premier Gen. Hideki Tojo made the following reference to India in his speech:

"Turning to India, we find her 400,000,000 people still under Britain's ruthless heel and, with the ambition of United States recently added to

1. D.B. Das, *op.cit,* pp. 184-187.

that pressure, they are continuing to experience indescribable miseries. The cruel rule of Britain and the oiutrageous conduct of the Angol-American forces have further intesified the friction and antagonism between them and the Indian people, thus creating a profound social confusion accompanying an unprecedentedly great famine. The grave situation which is becoming aggravated day by day and month by month, is admitted even by Britain and the United States themselves.

"With many Indian patriots thrown into prison by the British and millions of innocent people thrown into agonies of starvation, the conditions is India at present are indeed tragic and the object of common grievance of all humanity. Such a situation we can by no means leave to take its own course. At this very juncture, Indians who hold their motherland close to their hearts have risen in unity under the leadership of the great patriot Mr. Subhas Chandra Bose and on the twenty-first of this month, the Provisional Government of Free India was established. Thereupon, Nippon proceeded to recognize that government on the 23rd.

"It is truly a great pleasure for us to declare to the world through this chamber that Nippon is determined to support that government consistently in the future and to put forth her utmost efforts for the independence and emancipation of India.

"The complete independence and freedom of India and the lasting prosperity of the 400,000,000 Indian people are what Nippon sincerely desires. I have not the slightest doubt that in the purpose Nippon may count not only upon the wholehearted co-operation of all Greater East Asia peoples but also meet the earnest desire of all high-minded peoples throughout the world.

"It is my strong conviction that this rising tide of the movement for India's emancipation with the active co-operation of the people of Greater East Asia will inevitably bring, in the not distant future, the glorious day of independence and prosperity to India."

In a statement on the speech by Premier General Hideki Tojo Netaji Bose declared:

"The first speech of His Excellency represents a fitting climax to a series of soul-inspiring pronouncements on the Indian question since the fall of Singapore last year. The Indian people owe a special debt of gratitude to him for the personal interest in and sympathy for Indian Independence that he has consistently cherished and demonstrated.

"I am confident that Indian people will give practical proof of the gratitude on the filed of battle."

Germany

The Reich Foreign Minister, Herr Von Ribbentrop, officially notified Netaji Subhas Chandra Bose, by telegram, that the Reich Government was extending its recognition to the newly formed Provisional Government of Azad Hind.

Burma

On 25th October information was received in Syonan that the Independent State of Burma recognised the Provisional Government of Azad Hind.

Philippines

The Philippine Republic's recognition of the Provisional Government of Azad Hind Ws conveyed to Netaji Subhas Chandra Bose, Head of the Provisional Government of Free India, by Jose P. Laurel, President of the Republic of the Philippines, in the following message :—

"The Philippine Government and people have learned with profound gratification the establishment of the Provisional Government of Free India under your leadership in the firm belief that the freedom of India is essential to a new world order based on justice. The Philippine Government is pleased to recognise your Government and sincerely hopes to see established a new free and independent India as befitting the race that has made one of the greatest contribution to human civilization."

Croatia

On October 27, the Government of Croatia extended its formal recognition to the Provisional Government of Free India.

China

It was officially announced at Nanking on Nov. 1 that the National Government of China extended recognition to the Provisional Government of Free India.

The following is the text of the telegram from the Foreign Minister of the National Government of China to Netaji Subhas Chandra Bose, recognising the Provisional Government of Azad Hind:

"Your Excellency, learning through the Nippon Embassy in Nanking that a Provisional Government has been established on October 21 under Your Excellency's leadership, I have the honour, on behalf of the National Government, to extend formal recognition and sincere congratulations on the determination of your government to participate in the war and the reconstruction of Greater East Asia, and to place the Indian people in a position of realising their long-cherished aspirations and of contributing to final victory. With assurance of my highest consideration, Tsu Min Yee, Minister of Foreign Affairs of the National Government of China."

Manchoukuo

It was officially announced on the same day in Hsinking that Manchoukuo formally recognized the Provisional Government of Free India.

Italy

The Provisional Government of Free India was formally recognized by the Fascist Republic of Italy on Nov. 9.

Thailand

The Government of Thailand officially recognised the Provisional Government of Azad Hind, it was announced over the Bangkok radio on the night of Nov. 18.

Thus the Provisional Government of Free India was recognised by Nippon, Germany, Burma, the Philippines, Croatia, the National Government of China, Manchoukuo, the fascist Republic of Italy and Thailand.

46

Addressing a Mammoth Rally Attended by More Than 50,000 Indians, Bose Exhorted the Indian to Rise as One Man to Oust the British from India; Informs Them About the Significance of the Formation of the Provisional Government of Azad Hind

24 October, 1943

When I addressed you last on October 17th, on the occasion of our meeting to congratulate the Philippines on its achievement of Independence, I told you that Burma and the Philippines had become independent and that the next would be India's turn. To-day I fell joy in informing you that the turn of India has now come and the Provisional Government of Azad Hind has been established by us and recognised by the world.

When we look back at the succession of events which had slowly but steadily led to this important landmark in the history of our independence Movement, we could clearly see that everything has been happening under the guidance and help of Providence. The will of God has been with us and if to-day the Provisional Government of Azad Hind has been established, it is a Government which has been declared to the world in the fulness of time and fitness of things.

With the beginning of the present War in Europe, our life-long enemies, the Britishers received their first blows in the West and became weakened thereby. If they had continued to receive blows in the West only, the cause of Indian Independence could not have benefitted thereby. But when the Greater East Asia War started in the East, our enemies received greater blows and became more weakened by one defeat after another. More important and significant than the losses in the East was the fact that a new door—a door undreamt of by them—was opened in the East for the emancipation of India.

The British strategists had always expected a menace to India from the North Western Frontier; little did they envisage the possibility of an

Army of Liberation marching into India from the Northern Frontier. They never dreamt of this possibility: nor were they prepared to defend an attack from this direction.

There is another interesting aspect of this question. Even supposing that the Britishers, suffering defeat after defeat in the West, had retreated up to the North Western Frontiers of India, even that would not have helped the cause of Indian Independence. Because there is Western Asia, we do not have any colony of Indians. On the other hand, Destiny had kept three millions of Indians in East Asia. And when the enemy was driven out of East Asia and the help of Asiatics was forthcoming, the material was there in these three millions of Indians for a real bid for independence.

With the Britishers driven to North East Frontiers of India—to the Indo-Burma borders—a golden opportunity thus arose for liberating India, and if the Indians in East Asia had not risen to the occasion, even that opportunity would have been lost. But the Indians in East Asia, I am glad to say, did not fail India at this great hour; they heard the call of the times and organised themselves into the Indian Independence League and started the formation of the Indian National Army. A retrospective survey of the events of the past few years clearly shows that Destiny had prepared the stage in an undreamt of way for the final war of Indian Independence. Things have happened steadily in the fulness of time and the fitness of things and who can deny when I say that the grace of God, India's Hour has come, that India's turn to be free has come.

When I came to East Asia and took up the lead of the movement, my first objective was to re-organise and strengthen the Indian Independence League, and to reform and stabilise the Indian National Army.

In my address to you on the 15th August, I told you that I am determined to set my foot on the holy soil of India before the end of this year. I always mean what I say. Mine was not an empty declaration or a mere boast. Since then, our preparation have been continuing slowly but steadily. You will remember the Military Review which took place here on this madian on July 9, and this morning you would have noticed that the Indian National Army which took part in the Review was far smaller than that of July last. I revealed in my address at the Military Review that morning that a considerable part of the Indian National Army had left Syonan already and that they were on the road to India. All our preparation have been proceeding in a satisfactory manner and recently it became necessary to take another and more important step, a decisive stop in our march towards Independence.

The question would naturally arise as to what would be the leadership under which the Indian National Army would fight. And it was right time for us to clear our position. The world in general and Indians in particular had to be told under whose leadership the Indian National army was going to fight and who would take over the territorial rights in Indian when the enemy is driven out. And so, at the right time, we established the Provisional Government of Azad Hind at the Conference of Indians in East Asia held on 21st October.

If we had formed such a Government three years ago, the world would have called it a farce; and the enemy might have called it a propaganda stunt. But the Provisional Government having now risen as a natural sequence to the oranisation of the three millions of Indians in East Asia and the establishment of the powerful Indian National Army, even our enemies would have to think twice before calling it a propaganda stunt. The present Provisional Government of Azad Hind is not a plaything; it is a solid and powerful body having as its sanetion the will of the three millions of Indians united as a granite wall by the Indian Independence League and having as its support the Indian National Army.

In forming this Government, we have made no innovations because it has always been part of the technique of revolution to declare a Provisional Government just on the eve of a final War of Independence. Many examples are available in history for the adoption of this method. We have for instance, the case of the Czechs and the Irish as well as the case of Mustapha Kemal who formed a Provisional Government of Anatolia before the Turkish War of Independence. By taking this step on the 21st October, we have not only acted at the right time but we have also adopted the fight method.

It is true that it would have been better if such a Provisional Government could have been established within the frontiers of India. But under the present circumstance it is not practical politics to have such an organisation like the Indian Independence League or such an armed force like the Indian National Army within the frontiers of India. And any Provisional Government declared within India without the proper organisation and armed strength would be a farce; it would be some thing which our enemies could suppress in no time. This being the truth, and taking all the factors into consideration, patriotic Indians cannot but come to one and only conclusion that the only practical path for the achievement of our Independence is the path which we have now chosen.

In the proclamation of the establishment of the Provisional Government of Azad Hind on the 21st October, I have clearly defined the objectives and limits of this Government. We are not a Government like the ordinary administrations established in normal times; and hence, we have not followed the normal method nor have we opened departments which are essential only for the administration of a country in normal times. The first and foremost function of this Government is to wage the war of Independence and hence our Cabinet is primarily a War Cabinet.

Secondly, this Government would undertake to administer the liberated territories during the transitionary period only. We shall continue to function till the last Englishman is driven out of India, till India becomes Independent and law, order and peace are restored in Free India and till a Permanent Government of Free India is et up according to the will of the thirty-eight crores of Indians in India. I appeal to you and to every Indian in East Asia to read the Proclamation issued by us on the 21st October and understand fully the true significance of our Provisional Government.

I would also take the opportunity to emphasie that if a few have been elected as members of the Government does not mean the vast majority are absolved of their duties or responsibilities. For the sake of administrative convenience and necessity, a few have been made members of the Government, but the responsibility of the Government lies equally on all the Indians in East Asia.

Those who have assumed functions in the new Government machinery have not assumed any grand positions; they have assumed in fact greater burdens and responsibilities. The path of the Government is not a path of roses and very soon this Government will have its trail on the battlefield. You must not think even for a moment that there has been any elevation of individual position.

If there has been any elevation of position, it has been that of India and the Indians. Who can say that by the formation of this Government and its recognition by the world, the status and position of the Indians have not increased in the eyes of the world? You must realised that this is your Movement and that this Government is you Government, and that your duties as members of the Indian Independence League have now increased ten-fold.

We have two great tasks before us. The first task is to make full and final effort with a view to crossing the frontiers and setting foot on the holy soil of India before the end of this year. The second task is to continue our work and carry on our preparations for a long war. The retreat of

Britishers from India would mean the final destruction of the British Empire and so it is only natural that the British will try to cling to India with all their might.

It is not going to be an easy affair to drive the Britishers from India, but I am confident that once we are on the Indian soil we shall get necessary help and strength from the Indians in India. The Indian in East Asia, however, should realise that their efforts must continue as ever till our final objectives are achieved.

I would once again reiterate that our programme of Total Mobilisation must be carried out with greater vigour as a sequal to the formation of our Provisional Government. I would once again repeat my appeal for Men, Money and Materials. It is the duty of the Indians in East Asia to see that there is a continuous stream of men, money and materials forthcoming till we achieve final victory.

I may say in this connection that my call for men to rally round the Colour has been receiving satisfactory response. The way young Indians in East Asia have come forward as volunteers and the way in which our sisters have responded to my call to from the Rani of Jhansi Regiment have been inspiring indeed.

And about the offer of money and materials, I may say here that the response from the poorer and middle classes has been encouraging. I have come across instances of the spirit of sacrifice among our poor brethern which would bring tears to the eyes of even a stone-hearted man. A washerman came to me and gave his "all" and further said that he hailed from Jhansi and he would like to march along with our sisters of the Rani of Jhansi Regiment as their washerman. A poor ill-clad Indian who was a barber came forward with 200 dollars which represented his saving for years and gladly offered it for the cause.

Especially moving are the sacrifices of our Gowala brethren. These brothers came, gave all the cash they had, all the cattle they possessed and offered themselves as Volunteers for the Indian National Army. The poor classes have been showing by their actions and example the meaning of Total Mobilisation. It is only the rich who want to know whether Total Mobilisation means five or ten per cent of their savings. The poor have been spontaneously coming forward with their all and their own selves.

It is high time that the rich revolutionised their outlook. They should realise that when a Volunteer joins the ranks and goes to the front he does not ask whether he should spill five per cent or ten per cent of his blood. He goes to the front tos pill every drop of his blood. The life of one such volunteers is to me more precious than millions of dollars. What I would ask the rich to understand is that if they do not want to come forward to give their lives, they should at least come forward to give their possessions.

I have heard that some of the rich people have been saying that we are a nuisance and that the nuisance would be over when we leave Syonan on our march of India, I want them to know that though we may march, the Indian Independence League would still be here carrying on our "Home Front" programme while we are engaged on the fighting front. We cannot spare the rich; we cannot spare any Indian because ours is a life and death struggle and we are determined to carry on our fight to victory by all means and at any cost.

I have also said that some of our rich friends are thinking of changing their nationality to dodge the Indian Independence League's demand for funds. To these misguided friends, I have to say that there are only two alternatives before them; either they must become true Indians and do their duty at this hour of need or they must say that they are friends of Britain and be treated as such. In East Asia, there is no room for Britishers or their friends except in jails and the time is not far off when in India also their position will be the same. I hope there will soon be a re-orientation of outlook among the few rich Indians who have not satisfactorily responded to our call.

I shall now inform you of two very important decisions of the Cabinet of the Provisional Government of Azad Hind and place them before you for your ratification.

There was a time when the Britishers in their propaganda tried to ignore or belittle our Movement in East Asia. Now they have taken it seriously and for want of any other tactics they have resorted to abusing me from their radio stations. The tactic of abuse is the last refuge of the weak, of those who are at their wit's end.

But it is significant that the enemy has realised our strength and he understands that ours is not a mere propaganda stunt. The reactions and repercussions of the establishment of our Provisional Government has been world-wide and it will be no exaggeration if I say that it has created panic both in London and Washington.

The enemy radio stations were rather quick this time in flashing out the news of the formation of our Government through their broadcasts. Meanwhile, we have received the recognition of the Imperial Government of Nippon, and this, I must say, is a historic event of tremendom importance. If this recognition was a solitary act without any precedent there could have been opportunity for people to question have bonafides or this gesture. But, fortunately, this has not come as an innovation. This has come as one of the corollaries of Nippon's Asiatic policy based on justice and equality. The world has heard of this policy; it has already heard of the independence of Burma and then of the Philippines and so the recognition of the Provisional Government of Azad Hind has come as the natural result of the policy.

The Anglo-Americans have been proclaiming from their house-tops that they were the champions of Liberty and Democracy but their actions have repeatedly given the lie to their claims. Apart from their determination to maintain their hold on India, they have enslaved independent countries like Iraq and Iran. They have been and are trying to enslave free Burma.

In contrast to this, we have the action of Nippon in recognising Independent Burma, Independent Philippines and now the Provisional Government of Independent India. Our Nippon friends have always been showing us every sympathy and now, by this recognition, they have rendered us the greatest moral assistance for which we are greatly thankful. And so, the Council of Minister of Azad Hind have unanimously passed a resolution deeply appreciating this gesture of Nippon. I place their resolution before you for your ratification.

"The Provisional Government of Azad Hind (Free India) places on record its deep appreciation of the message conveying the news of recognition by the Imperial Government of Nippon of the Provisional Government of Azad Hind. The Provisional Government of Azad Hind expresses its grateful thanks to the Imperial Government of Nippon for the generous offer of wholehearted co-operation and assistance contained in the above message."

Our thanks are due to Premier General Tojo for the great interest in Indian Independence. We have to thank also Colonel Yamamoto, the Chief of the Hikari Kikan, for his co-operation, especially in the establishment of the Provisional Government of Azad Hind.

The next Resolution which was unanimously adopted by my Council is a more important one. The Council after discussing the political, economic and military situations in India came to the unanimous conclusion that the hour has struck for the declaration of war against Britain and America by the Provisional Government of Free India.

Last Night at 12.55 a.m. we declared war through the radio and it is interesting to note that 2 a.m., the enemy radio stations also gave out the news of our Declaration of War. This shows how alert they are in watching what steps we are taking. The Britishers know me well enough during my fight against them in India and they know well enough also that I will not make a declaration without having the strength to enforce what I say. Our declaration is not again a propaganda stunt. The coming events would show that we meant what we said.

Before I place our resolution declaring war on Britain and America before you for your ratification, I would ask you to realise its implications and to give your decision after full consideration.

Our Declaration, I repeat, is not an empty threat. We are resolved to carry it out with the last drop of our blood. And when I ask you to ratify it, I do not want to have the resolution carried in a formal ceremonial way. You ratification would mean that you are as much resolved as we are to shed your last drop of blood in enforcing the Declaration. I know that I need not put this equation to the Indian National Army because I know their mind and their deep anxiety to be on the Road to Delhi. I am now asking the Civilians as to whether they are one with us in making this Declaration, because if they are one with us they should come forthwith to give the fullest effect to our Programme to Total Mobilisation.

Friends! I want you to realise that we are taking part in a meeting which is not a propaganda show; this is not a ceremonial affair. We are here at a historic meeting to decide on a life and death issue. If we succeed in the project, thirty eight crores of Indians will be free. If, on the other hand, as God forbid, we fail, for at least another century our Nation will be doomed to slavery and untold misery. I have told you at the outset how the hand of God has created this golden opportunity for us. I have shown you how we have moved from stage to stage and we have reached the right opportunity to strike at our enemy, I have told you how e now have the organisation, the army and the Provisional Government of Azad Hind recognised by the world and how we have secured every help and support. Are we going to fail India at this great hour in her history?

Realise all these things, consider deeply all the implications of a Declaration of War and if you decide to take the war path, if you feel in your heart of hearts ready to face anything and everything in the historic fight against the British, if you feel that you are ready to give body, soul and all to fight our enemy until victory is won, then rise and give your ratification to our War Declaration by your acclamation.

Friends! My joy and pride knows no bounds at having witnessed the outburst of enthusiasm and spirit of revolution in you, and your thirst for Independence. With this spirit permeating the hearts of the Indians in

East Asia there could only be one sequel to our Declaration of War. And that is a fight which cannot fail to end in victory and with this demonstration of the united will and unified spirit of the Indian Nation, it may be an easy victory over our enemies. The meeting is now over and I would appeal to you to calm yourselves and to return to your homes, resolved forthwith to make every effort to bring our war to a victorious conclusion.

I would, lastly, call upon you to give three cheers for Revolution, for Free India and for the Government of Nippon.

At the 83rd session of the Imperial Diet which met on October 26, in Tokyo, Premier Gen, Hideki Tojo made the following reference to India in his speech:

"Turning to India, we find her 400,000,000 people still under Britain's ruthless heel and, with the ambition of the United States recently added to that pressure, they are continuing to experience indescribable miseries. The cruel rule of Britain and the outrageous conduct of the Anglo-American forces have further intensified the friction and antagonism between them and the Indian people, thus creating the profound social confusion accompanying an unprecedentedly great famine. The grave situation which is becoming aggravated day by day and month by month, is admitted even by Britain and the United States themselves.

"With many Indian patriots thrown into prison by the British and millions of innocent people thrown into agonies of starvation, the conditions in India at present are indeed tragic and the object of common grievance of all humanity. Such a situation we can by no means leave to take its own course. At this very juncture, Indians who hold their motherland close to their hearts have risen in unity under the leadership of the great patriot Mr. Subhash Chandra Bose and on the twenty-first of the month, the Provisional Government of Free India was established. Thereupon Nippon proceeded to recognize that government on the 23rd.

"It is truly a great pleasure for us to declare to the world through this chamber that Nippon is determined to support that government consistently in the future and to put forth her utmost efforts for the independence and emancipation of India.

"The Complete independence and freedom of India and the lasting prosperity of the 400,000,000 Indian people are what Nippon sincerely desires. I have not the slightest doubt that in this purpose Nippon may count not only upon the wholehearted co-operation of all greater East Asia People but also meet the earnest desire of all high minded people throughout the world."

47

Bose Assessment of the Greater East Asia Conference, Anticipates Unity of Asian Nations in Future under the Leadership of Japan[1]

9 November, 1943

I arrived in Tokyo on October 31 from Shonan, alongwith my party. I had heard before my arrival that an Assembly of Representatives of Greater-East-Asia would meet in Tokyo—but I had received no details about that Assembly. I had myself been thinking for sometime past that such a conference was urgently needed, in order to mobilize the whole of East-Asia for the war-effort and also for post-war reconstruction. Consequently, the news of the conference delighted me beyond measure. I was naturally curious to meet the representatives from East-Asia and also attend the Assembly. Owing to the special situation of India and of the Provisional Government of Azad Hind (Free India), it had been decided between us—and very correctly too—that I and my party would attend the Assembly as observers. Hence, I was in a position to take a thoroughly objective view of the conference and its proceedings.

At the aerodrome, as we alighted, we were given a very hearty reception by Their Excellencies the Foreign Minister and Minister of Greater East Asiatic Affairs, the Navy Minister and Major-General Arisue, as well as other Army leaders and notable personalities. Many of them I had known before during my last visit to Tokyo and I was glad to meet them again and to be able to greet them once more. I was then driven to the residence of my host, Viscount Shibusawa, and the round of public function arranged for us, begin at once.

1. *Nippon Times*, 9 November 1943, Greater East Asia Conference. Was held in Tokyo from 5 November 1943. It was attended by the representative of asiatic nations, i.e., China, Burma, Thailand, Phillipines, Manchuko. Subhas Chandra Bose attended the conference as an observer, while General Tojo led the Japanese delegation.

The prologue to the Assembly of Greater East-Asiatic Nations took plac? on November 4 at the official residence of His Excellency, the Prime Minister, General Tojo, when the Representatives were all invited to tea. I and my party were included among the guests -though we were not among those who were to participate actively in the proceedings of the Assembly. At this tea party I found that I was personally acquainted with Representatives of Nipon, Thailand and Burma but the Representatives from Manchokuo, China and Philippines were strangers to me. Nevertheless, I found that within a short time, the atmosphere became very cordial and friendly and toward the end of the function, while talking to some members of the Nippon Government, I said that the function appeared to me like a family party. This was also the impression some other gentlemen present at the tea party, with whom I compared notes.

It was an excellent idea to arrange this function the day before the Assembly was to meet. The result was that when the Assembly gathered the next day–November 5–the participants were no longer strangers to one another. This added greatly to the cordiality of the atmosphere which prevailed at the assembly and helped to make it a success.

The keynote of the conference was given expression to in a characteristic manner by His Excellency, the Representative from Burma, Adipadi Dr. Ba Maw. He remarked in one of his speeches at the Assembly that though the representatives of the East-Asiatic Nations spoke different languages and perhaps used different forms of expression, there was one underlying thought—one objective and one will behind all their utterances. He was absolutely correct and truthful in interpreting the mind of the participating Representatives, for the atmosphere of the Assembly declared emphatically—"East Asia is one."

Though there was an underlying unity pervading the Assembly it was an intellectual treat to notice and to study among the participating representatives a difference in temperament and also in the form and manner of expression. For instance, his Excellency Prime Minister General Hideki Tojo stood out before the Assembly as the soldier— statesman— whose utterances were incisive in character and why being inspired by idealism, were remarkable for their clarity and convincing logic. His Excellency, the Prime Minister of Manchoukuo, was the type of the elderly and experienced politician, who had weathered many a strong, but had ultimately steered his ship to port. His Excellency the President of the Chinese Republic, was the seasoned politician, ripe with knowledge, who was sure of his own position and had grim but silent determination— and who did not, therefore, need gesticulation to convince his listeners. His Excellency, the President of the Philippines, had the fiery eloquence of an expert Parliamentarian who could by his sincerity and passion, brings tears to the eyes of his listeners and carry audience with him. His Royal Highness, Prince Wan of Thailand, was a perfect mannered, cultured aristocrat, conscious of the proud tradition and heritage of his country, who would be an ornament to any society in the world. And His Excellency Dr. Ba Maw was—as he himself said—like a soldier, coming from the front, who knew that his country was within the firing line and whose heart was burning with the desire to contribute in giving a knock out blow to the enemy and thereby make his contribution to the creation of a free and united East Asia.

The Assembly of Greater East-Asiatic Nations proved that East Asia was really and fundamentally one. Nevertheless, for the critical observer, it was a delight to see that the unity was manifested in a diversity of form, expression and temperament.

The Assembly of Greater East-Asiatic Nations was a complete success. There can be no doubt at all about it. It helped to consolidate firmly's the East-Asiatic Nations - for the purpose of winning the war and also for that of constructing a new order, to replace the old and worn out one. All honour to his brain that first conceived of this conference! And all credit to those who organized it made it such a striking success!

As for the Joint Declaration, unanimously and enthusiastically passed by the Assembly, it will prove to be a Charter of Liberty for the Nations of East Asia. And I may venture prophecy that the world at large will hear more of this Charter in future and will also need it when the time comes to attempt once again the formation of an internatioal society of nations.

As for the enemy, I am sure that when authentic news about the Assembly and its achievements reaches the enemy's camp, there will be a anxiety, fear and consternation.

48

Military Intelligence Assessment of the Indian National Army, after its Re-organisation by Subhash Chandra Bose; Issues Guideline for Dealing With it

10 November. 1943

General Description

1. Owing to a recent reorganization, following upon the arrival of S. C. Bose from Germany, definite information regarding the strength, organization, etc. is scanty.

2. In 1942 we estimated that about 15,000 P. W. might have been suborned, or more probably coerced, into joining the I.N.A. A revised, but very tentative estimate is 41,500; this is based on the reports of agents and escapes. The latest Axis broadcast claim a strength of 200,000. As the total number of Indian P. W. in Japanese hands is 70,000, this figure could only be attained by extensive recruitment of largely indifferent civilian material.

3. HQ and the bulk of the I.N.A. are probably still located in Singapore, but are believed to be moving to Rangoon. In February 1943 there were two camps in Singapore, and one each in Kluang, Johore, Seremban, Rangoon and Hong Kong.

4. In 1942 the I.N.A. in Malaya was believed to be organized into 3 Bdes (Guerilla Regts) and a Field Group, under a HQ organized on British lines. The new organization is unknown, but a recent addition is a regiment of women, in which lies potentialities for trouble if it goes into the field.

5. Some Light Automatics and rifles have been issued, and a few British wheeled vehicles and carriers. A standard uniform was accepted in 1942, which Bose is said to have redesigned. A number

1. War officer No 203/4756. PRO.

of training camps are known to exist, notably in Penang, which have been played up in recent Axis broadcasts. There are also several schools where JIFS (both ex P of W and civilians) are trained in espionage, sabotage, subversive propaganda and wireless before being sent to India as enemy agents with definite tasks. Some are trained in parachute dropping and about twenty four have been dropped by air to date. Of these twenty have been captured. Two parties each of five were landed by submarine and were also captured.

6. What morale and espirit de corps existed in the I.N.A. had a set back owing to temporary disbandment followed by reorganisations. There has also been evidence of communal intrigues, which resulted in the Sikh leaders being largely displaced by Hindus and Muslims. On the other hand there is no evidence of definite ill feeling amongst the communities.

7. I.N.A. personnel have hitherto been used for espionage and propaganda tasks, and in assisting the Japanese to "control" the population in forward areas. Bose has however repeatedly claimed that the I.N.A. is being trained to take the field as a fighting formation to "liberate" India. While there are, as yet, no signs of such a move, it would be in keeping with Bose's character for him to attempt a spectacular coup.

Counter Measures

8. **The Central Group.** The Central Group is a body of carefully selected officers who after preliminary training visit units and set up small cells known as Josh (enthusiasm or Verve) Groups. These cells are selected by C.Os and generally consist of one officer and Indian officers and NCOs. Their task is to expose the Japanese and their tools, includate doctrine that India must destroy the Japanese, or be destroyed by them and so prepare Indian units for possible encounter with armed JIFS in the field. 750 Josh Groups have been formed and results are most encouraging.

9. **GHQ Broadcasts.** These are directed in various languages to Japanese occupied territory. The Indian Army has, of late, been encouraged to listen to them also. Amongst other indications of the effect of this campaign, Bose stated in an interview in Singapore that one of his two main objects was to crush the enemy propaganda directed from Delhi at Indian Nationalists working abroad. An outline

of GHQ broadcasting is given in an Appendix[2]. Leaflets in vernacular languages are also dropped in enemy occupied areas encouraging JIFS to take every opportunity to return to our lines and make a clean breast of their activities. These leaflets are also designed to sow distrust in JIF leaders.

10. **Instruction Issued to Troops.** Commanders have been instructed that all troops are to be taught that I.N.A. personnel (JIFS) encountered in the field are to be treated and fought as enemies until they are killed or surrender.

Security and Legal arrangements

11. **Interrrogation.** All I.N.A. personnel on capture or surrender are passed to the nearest forward Interrogation Centre for a rapid interrogation. More detailed interrogation is carried out by similar centres in rear, selected personnel being sent to the Combined Services Detailed Interrogation Centre (C.S.D.I.C.) in Delhi. All persons whether suspected of being JIFS or not who return from enemy occupied territory also pass through this interrogating organisation which also extracts from them intelligence about the enemy.

12. **Classification.** Following upon interrogation and a cross check from records, personnel returning from enemy occupied territory are classified as White, (loyalty and morale unaffected) Grey (loyalty or morale temporarily affected) or Black (definitely dangerous). Military Whites and Greys are reconditioned at a special camp, Blacks are detained under Defence of India Rules or special ordinances or when possible brought to trial. Similar arrangements exists for civilians, but there is as yet no reconditionsing camp for them.

13. **Trials.** In the case of military persons a Standing Court Martial has been established, which is duplicated by a Central Tribunal on the civil side. Military and civil legal advisers study the cases, berif interrogaters, and advise the prosecutors. There is a special Enemy Agents Ordinance under which both military and civilian personnel may be tried in camera.

14. **Detention.** Civil Blacks are segregated in civil jails; military Blacks are sent to a separate place of detention. Both classes will be removed in due course to a special jail now under construction.

15. **Security Staffs.** A combined DMI/DIB (Director Intelligence Bureau) staff section has been set up at New Delhi to deal with all matters of

2. Not printed.

policy, intelligence, and security executive action concerning the I.N.A. (and I.I.L.). Provision has been made for this section to be represented in all major formations in operational areas. The Security corps, which is based on Calcutta, provides the staff (civil and military interrogating officers and police personnel) for Forward Interrogating Centres which ate established at various focal points in operational areas in Bengal and Assam.

49

Decision of the Liaison Conference for the Transfer of Andamans and Nicobar Island to the Provisional Government of India

10 November, 1943

Re—The Andamans and the Nicobars

1. The time to transfer the Andamans and the Nicobar to the Provisional Government of India should be decided separately and for the time being the subject is to be disposed as follows :

(a) Provisional Government staff will be allowed to stay in the area, participating in administration provided such participation will remain within the limit of smooth military campaign and its related activities will not be jeopardized.

(b) The said participation in the administration will be further extended by and by, and the desire of the Provisional Government of India will be fulfilled by and by under the leadership of Regional Supreme Commander.

(c) It is granted for the Provisional Governmnet to make use of the point that the transfer of the said area to the Provisional Government as an existing fact.

(d) Even after the transfer of the said area, it should so be arranged as all the request in connection with the defence of the area should be compiled with.

1. Ministry of Defence War History Section Proceedings of the Liasion Conference, Tokyo.

50

From Takazumo Oka, Vice-Admiral Imperial Japanes Navy to Bose; Informs him about Arrangements Made for his Visit to the Andamans

16 November, 1943

Dear Sir,

I have the honour to send you herewith the reply of the Imperial Japanese Navy to the desires expressed by your excellency in the course of our conversation on November 12th. I desire to avail myself of this opportunity to convey my sincere wishes for your excellency's continued good health and for the speedy attainment of the object of the founding of Free India.

His Excellency Mr. Subhas Chandra Bose
Head of the Provisional Government of India

Mr. Bose's visit to the Andaman and Nicobar Islands. Barring a sudden change in the military situation, arrangements will be made to have this visit made during the early part of December. Details of the trip will be communicated to Mr. Bose by the Commander-in-Chief of the Fleet stationed in Shonan. This trip is to be kept strictly secret until in its completion.

Publicity subsequent to the completion of the visit. It is desired that this publicity be undertaken along the lines formally communicated to Mr. Bose by Prime Minister Tojo on November 13th, i.e., to the effect that "We are already going ahead with preparatory measures necessary for a speedy and smooth transfer of the islands (such as .... etc.)".

1. I.N.A Trial Papers, It was at the Greater East Asia Conference, that General Tojo decided to hand over the Andaman and Nicobar Islands to the Provisional Government. These islands were under the charge of Japanese naval authorities. Bose went to Andaman towards the end of December, 1943 to decide about the appointment of an Indian Chief Commissioner and the nature of his participation in the administration alongwith the Japanese. After the visit Lt. Col. A.D. Loganadan alongwith his staff went to Andamans in February 1944.

Appointment and dispatch of a Governor. In accordance with the statement made by the Prime Minister, a Governor is to be appointed after completion of the transfer. It is to be understood that, pending completion of the transfer, an official of the Provisional Government bearing some such title as "Chief Commissioner for the Andaman and Nicobar Islands" should be dispatched to co-operate fully in the military administration of the Islands under the direction of the Naval Commandent there.

Dispatch of an army contingent by the Provisional Government. The Naval Authorities can fully appreciate the reason for the Provisional Government's wishes in this matter. But since the time and method of carrying out this measure must be made to fit in with the conditions prevailing on the Islands, an answer on this point will be given later after further consideration. There would, however, be no objection to the dispatch of two or three military liaison officers.

Dispatch of Indian engineers. Considering that the two Islands constitute an area of intensive military operations, there would be no objection to carefully selected technicians being sent after consultation with the Naval Commandant of the Islands. But in view of the conditions now prevailing there. It is to be understood that for the time being such technicians are to co-operate in undertakings connected with military operations. Attention must be called, finally, to the fact that since the transportation and communication facilities are only sufficient for our military needs, it will be difficult for the present to carry out any policy which will make any considerable demand upon ships or communication facilities.

51

Status of the Indian National Army as Decided by the Hikari Kikan; Declars I.N.A. as an ally of the Japanese Army[1]

3 December, 1943

The Indian National Army constituted by the favour of His Imperial Majesty, is the armed forces of the Indian Independence League.

The Indian National Army will be treated as the army of an ally. Do not strike its members, be not haughty and keep your temper. Give up false sense of superiority.

Contents

1. War office F. No. 208/863. P.R.O.

Chapter I

The 400 million people of India, oppressed by the British for many years, have come forward with the desire to abolish the British rule and to obtain complete independence for their Motherland. They have obtained strength from the opportunity afforded by the Great East Asia War to drive out the force of America and England for Japan. They have come forward to these steps from all quarters and abandoned their policy of non-resistance and non-violence and have advanced to obtain independence at the cost of their own blood..

The essence of this battle for independence is the Indian National Army.

To achieve the object of the war, laid down in the Imperial rescript on the declaration of war, which is the destruction of the enemies England and America, we must drive their force from India. The Indian National Army, whose object is to overthrow the British raj in India, is therefore our ally.

This booklet is to give a rough idea of how we should feel and not towards the Indian National Army.

Chapter II

The Origin of the Indian National Army

In consideration that we, the Imperial Army, under the divine guidance of His Imperial Majesty, are to overthrow the power of England and America in East Asia, the question was considered of building up an army of Indians resident in East Asia who, with an understanding of Japan and with her help, would fight England for the independence of their Motherland guided by a true spirit of patriotism. "India is not England's watch dog". The Indian National Army was formed in September 1942. After about a year of instruction and training under the Japanese Army it was reorganised and its existence was published to the world in July 1943. Thus it is an army, constituted by Imperial favour, fostered by the Imperial Army, composed of Indians who with their life-blood fight for the Independence of their Motherland, and are fighting our common enemy with a common purpose.

Chapter III

Underlying principles of the I.N.A.

1. The Indian National Army is the Indian People's own army. The purpose of the I.N.A. is to secure the independence of India by Indian and although they are fighting our common enemy with a common purpose are not by any means a "Fifth column of the

Japanese Army" nor are they a "fatigue party". They are the army of the Indian Independence League and with the dawn of the Independence of India will constitute the forces of the new state.

2. The spirit of I.N.A. officers and men. Officers and men swear an oath of loyalty to India through the Indian Independence League. Their creed is unity, fidelity and sacrifice. They are banded together with the one object of overthrowing England and achieving independence for their Motherland.

3. The principle of having picked men. Only picked men from among volunteers are used as this is preferred to large members.

4. Relation to Japanese Army. They are treated as an ally by the Japanese army. In combined operations the senior commander of the I.N.A. will receive instructions from the senior Japanese commander.

In combined operations the control by the senior Japanese commander will be exercised through the senior I.N.A. Commander.

Chapter IV. See Appendices I, II, III and IV. (Annexure X)[2]

Chapter V

Treatment of the Indian National Army

Officers and men of the I.N.A bear friendship and trust towards the Imperial Army and treat us as real allies, friends and helpers. Their hundreds of years of oppression, tyrarmy and deceit and exploitation at the hands of the British have instilled in them a perverse shrinking and lack of spirit. Owing to anti-Japanese propaganda by the British they have very wrong ideas of Japan. They are strong individualists and materialists as well as possessing many customs arising from their religious beliefs—This makes them very difficult to handle. They frequently have quick tempers especially on the battle field. We Japanese, as leaders in the building of a new world, as being comrades in the destruction of England and America, must treat them with a kindly and tolerant leniency whatever weak points they may have. The following are the chief practical points regarding our treatment of them—

1. Approach them as a real ally. As has been stated, the Indian National Army has been constituted by the favour of his Imperial Majesty; it has the praiseworthy mission of obtaining independence for its Motherland; it is fighting the same enemy and with the same object as ourselves; it's essence is Indian's patriotism. For these reasons it has

2. Not Printed.

been decided that it shall be treated as an ally. We must thoroughly understand this principle and approach them as a true ally. Owing to the cruel treatment they have received from the British over so many years they have a suspicious nature, and therefore there must be no action which might lead them to think that we have given them the name of "ally" without the status. It is necessary to handle them in such a way that they will have the same feeling as ourselves.

2. Value your fights of command. It is obvious that the rights of command of the forces of an ally are to be held in high esteem. It is only by placing a high value in these rights that the capabilities of the I.N.A. can be developed to their highest pitch. Command will be exercised and through the senior I.N.A. commander and great care must be taken that odd units who have no rights of command do not issue orders off their own bat. The HIKARI 'Kikan' is the medium through which control and co-operation of the I.N.A. is exercised smoothly so as to develop its capabilities to the best advantage.

3. Compliments will be paid as to allied army. Where there is no respect there is no confidence and no co-operation. Where there are no compliments there can be no respect. The Imperial rescript ordering punctilious saluting in the army covers also allied armies and it has been decided that military compliments will be given to the I.N.A. as to the force of a friendly country.

4. Memorize their dress, badges, pass words and signals. By memorizing their dress, badges, pass words, singles etc. difference of opinion and friction regarding saluting, intercommunication, etc, can be avoided.

5. Discard the feeling of superiority and do not look down on them. The thought that white people are a superior race and coloured people are inferior one is to be thoroughly eradicated. It is to break down this that we are waging the Great East Asia War. In the bottom of our hearts we have the mistaken pride that we Japanese are a superior people. This must be discarded and we must cease to look down on them and show respect for their official powers. It is only by such respect that they will be happy that their blood is Asiatic and will make a favourable comparison between ourselves and the English and so draw closer to us in their esteem and reliance.

6. Do not strike its members, be not haughty and keep your temper. These are the secrets in handling the I.N.A. If these are not observed, all is finished. One blow will destroy years of kindness and the ear

will not incline our way a second time; such an act will be the biggest insult in a man's life and will leave its mark which can never be expunged. For this reason striking I.N.A. personnel is strictly forbidden. Haughtiness will never bring friendliness but antipathy which cannot be eradicated. If we get angry they cannot understand us and become unhappy. We cannot then get close to them even if we try and alienation and friction result.

7. Do not tell lies. They have extremely good memories. They remember who said what and when and where and having laboured under British lies for so many years are extremely shrewd at discerning them. If we tell lies they will think that we are the same as the British, trust will be lost, suspicion increased. We must therefore get them to believe that we Japanese value the truth and we soldiers never tell a lie.

8. Assert your rights and understand their custom of not showing gratitude. They are very strong in the assertion of their rights. For instance, they think that they are entitled to a fixed ration at all time and if owing to difficulties of supply we ourselves do not get a meal but supply them theirs, they will not be happy if it is not full scale. Rather will they insist on their right to the amount deficient. In such cases anger is futile. It is equally futile to think that they will be grateful for any trouble we may take to look after them. If there is anything we do that seems to earn gratitude it is best to forget about it. If we do some kindness that may warrant some regard they will never even think of it as a kindness at all. They are quite fixed in this line of thought.

9. As far as possible respect their religious prejudices. Indians have many and various religious prejudices and are stricter in their observance of these than we Japanese imagine. Very serious problems arise if they are prevented from observing them and it behoves us to respect these prejudices as far as possible. For example :

   (a) To resist in the slaughter of cattle in front of Hindus and Sikhs and pigs in front of Mohamedans. (in the I.N.A. all religions are mixed and the consumption of beef and pork is entirely abolished).

   (b) The removing of the turban or cutting the hair of Sikhs.

   (c) Pulling the tuft of hair on a Hindu's head.

   Remember the points in the other booklet "commonsense about India".

10. It is advantageous to have someone appointed in each 'butai' as in charge of Indian troops. From the points of view that Indian troops are very awkward to deal with, a suitable person appointed to this position will be able to develop their best co-operation and will make them contented.

11. Handling of front line operative. Officers and men of the I.N.A. are not only employed in battle as the Japanese army, but are employed on various duties vis-à-vis Indian troops inside the enemy's lines. For this purpose they may wear mufti or be disguised or again in proper uniform pass through our front line troops into the enemy. They may pass to and fro between the opposing forces and in order that there may be no possibility of their being shot by mistake, our front line troops should have explained to them methods of recognition, pass word etc. At the same time we must proffer them a warm helping hand. Further when they seduce and bring over personnel from the enemy we must treat these strictly in accordance with the regulations for the treatment of prisoners of war and it is forbidden to kill or ill-treat them in the presence of the operatives who bring them in.

Chapter VI

Conclusion

The problem of India is of the greatest importance in the satisfactory prosecution of Great East Asia War. Attack on India is absolutely unavoidable but in India the British and American forces are our enemy, the 400 million Indians are not on any account the same.

But, hand in hand with these 400 million people we can destroy the British and Americans and go far towards victory in the Great East Asia war, liberate India and establish her independence.

Already the people of India have risen in war against the English. The Indian National Army is in truth their advance guard. Furthermore, they are blessed by His Imperial Majesty's favour and have limitless faith in Japan and the Imperial Army and look to us for help which we have promised them. The people of India expect much from them. We are Japan's advance guard to India and are divine soldiers of Japan the Righteous. By helping the I.N.A. without losing their trust, we together will succeed in the object of the war, to win the destruction of England and America and so carry out the will of His Imperial Majesty.

52

General Staff Branch to G.O.C. Indian Army Comments on the Subversive Activities in the Indian Army, from Abroad and its Linkage with the Indian Nationalist Inside the Country; Issues Directions to Deal with the Situation

18 December, 1943

To :

G.O.C.-in-C. N.W. Army, etc.

1. In this HQ No. DMI/4746 dated 18 March 1943[2], reference was made in paragraphs 3 and 4 to attacks on the loyalty to the Indian Army being made from within India by subversive organizations affiliated to the underground section of the Congress movement, in appendix 'A' to that letter was a copy of a document referring specifically to this attack.

2. Now attached are extracts from reports on what Jai Prakash Narain has said in the course of conversation with police officers who are dealing with him. He is the notorious underground leader of the Congress Socialist Party who was recently arrested. He is described as being in a "blustering mood", and what he says cannot all be taken at its face value. His remarks, however, confirm that efforts continue to be made to undermine the loyalty of the Indian armed forces, and that those responsible for the campaign consider that they are making some progress, especially among technical personnel and emergency commissioned officers. The reference to the "Air service" should be compared with the reference to the "technical staff of the Royal Air Force" in Appx. 'A' of our letter of 18 March 1943. Even while discounting J.P. Narain's sweeping claims, there is no doubt that the type of educated youth which the technical arms and services require is, potentially, the most receiptive medium for subversive approaches, and certaining (together with the emergency commissioned officer) the most likely I attempt to make what capital he can from his

1. Ministry of Defence, Historical Section F. No. 601/19869/H.S.
2. Document No. 7

position in the armed forces to further his own future ends, or those of the political party to which he belongs.

3. You are requested to handle the information given in the attached extracts with great care, in order to avoid compromising further interrogation and action arising therefrom.

Sd/-

For Chief of the General Staff

Extracts from the Reports on Talks with Jai Prakash Narain Recorded upto the 25th November, 1943

"I have held the office of the General Secretary of the All-India Congress Committee from January to October, 1932, during the Congress campaign of that year. Dr. Saifuddin Kitchlew, Mrs. Sarojini Naidu and C. Rajagopalchariar worked as President, one after the other, during my tenure of office. I was arrested at Madras in October 1932. I was underground and had my office in Bombay."

"I was arrested in 1940 for an objectionable speech and was released from jail in December, 1940, when I went to Calcutta to meet Subhas Chandra Bose. He was recouping health. We discussed various political problems."

"Subhas told me that Bengal was prepared for a mass movements and he was too keen that a conflict be picked up with the Government on some issue. He suggested that Holwall Monument could be utilised for the purpose. He did not mention to me about his intentions of disappearing but he did express the view which tended to show that he believed in accepting foreign help for India's emancipation. He was not very clear with me on account of Congress Session, when the C.S.P. remained neutral on Pant's resolution. There is, however, no difference between our and Forward Bloc's ideology as far as the independence of India is concerned. There is no doubt about Subhas Chandra Bose's sincerety. He is a fervent patriot. He is definitely not Japanese quisling. He advocated socialism in his presidential address at the Haripura Congress Session. He is prepared to accept foreign country's aid for liberating India from British yoke. He believes in accepting help from the Axis, but we Congress Socialists are prepared only to receive aid from a sympathetic country like China, Just as the Irish people received help from Americans. I don't believe that Axis invasion could directly help us. We can, of course, exploit an Axis invasion."

"Both Nehru and Subhas favour mass movement and are ultra anti-British, determined to end British rule in India. They differ in methods of attaining the same. Nehru does not believe in foreign aid and is anti-fascist, but Subhas holds the view that Indians do need foreign help. Athough Nehru does not believe in foreign aid, he would not lose the opportunity to exploit a foreign invasion on India to get rid of British 7yoke."

"I have not heard Subhas Bose speaking on the radio but as far as his propaganda goes, he has one million Army of Indian and I believe that to be in Burma with headquarters at Singapore. I don't think M. Ghandhi will take back Subhas in the Congress in the event of his return to India, which is only possible under a national government. His being taken back in the Congress is also not an impossibility."

"Subhas was elected Chief of the National Army set up by the Japanese and Rash Behari worked as his Deputy. There was no possibility of a Japanese invasion previously, nor is there one now. It is either Subhas's creation or this propaganda calculates to be exploitation by the Japanese. It appears that Subhas had discussed his plans with Germany when he visited that country before. It was for that reason that he first went to Germany and then after discussing plans with them he went to Japan. I don't think that he had been to Japan previously. I tried to contact Subhas Bose but could not find a suitable person to arrange that contact. I wanted to consult him to chalk out a plan for coordinating our efforts for the liberation of the country. I wanted that he should continue his activities from outside while I should carry on my work from inside the country."

"In those days (November, 1942) Benares was the storm centre of the movement and I stayed there for about a month. Here I met all my co-escapees and it was decided to work in labour, among students, in police and other Government departments and among kisans. Dislocation was one of the most important items of the programme and we paid special attention to it. The Central Directorate was already in existence, and I learnt that some I.C.S. and other Government officers helped us in this movement, but their number unfortunately is much less as compared to those who promised and then did not help. Most of those officers, who supported us, are quite safe because the Government could not afford to stir up resentment by wholesale dismissals."

"During the present underground movement we have been publishing lot of literature in Calcutta, Bombay and other places for distribution in military, police and public. In Bengal we had formed committees in all the districts. Literature was sent to these committees and they arranged further distribution. Literature was published in almost all the languages and for all Government departments. We succeeded in subverting many Government Servants through out literature. No Government servent is a member of C.S.P. but lots of Government servants and even the I.C.S officers assisted us in the present movement. We enlisted the sympathy of Government servants by propaganda. I can confidently say that we were successful in all ranks of the military but in police we could only subvert lower ranks. We had the strongest contacts in the military in Assam sometime before my arrest, but later a number of workers were arrested resulting in loss of many contacts. Now our propaganda is best in Eastern India, particularly Bombay, Ranchi and Gaya. We have found that new entrants in the Army are far more nationalist than the older people. We have got our own people enlisted in the military in order to disrupt the British Government from inside. We exploited the present famine situation and did propaganda in public through posters and pamphlets urgeing them not to dislike rats (sic) but to go to jail for national cause."

"In February 1943, when I was at Bombay, I discussed with my colleagues the present Congress campaign. I found that the present movement had been a failure in as far as that we could not maintain our hold even in those *illaquas* where we succeded in ousting British Authority. There were two phases of the Congress mass movement. The first one was the open agitation which was started by the unorganised masses and in which violence took place, but much less in comparison to the intensity of the movement. The second phase was the underground movement which was organised secretly and in which terrorist activities were resorted to. It was in the first unorganised mass movement that we were able to oust British Authority from many districts, but in view of lack of solid programme our workers could not continue the agitation successfully. My idea is that we shall have to set out plans for the next movement much ahead of inaugurating the actual movement."

"I placed a plan before my other colleagues for the formation of a military volunteer organisation. I thought that we could make use of arms and ammunition collected and manufactured during the present phase. We would be able to prepare the masses in order to produce another mass rising. A meeting was held at Bombay and violence was discussed."

"I laid the foundation of a new organization. The Central Directorate did not approve of my action, but they did not condemn it as well as it was considered that after M. Gandhi's arrest everyone was leader of himself. The new organisation was also not to be under the C.S.P. I named it 'Azad-Dastas' and later changed the name to 'Azad Sena'. It is completely to be a secret organisation. Congress Socialists, Congressmen and even non-

Congressmen are its members. After drafting its constitution, I got first part of 'ABC of Dislocation' printed at Bombay and sent messangers to all the Provinces for the organisation of the same. I took inspiration in the formation of the Azad Sena from the news of 'guerilla warfare' in China, which had also been practised in Russia, American War of Independence and other freedom struggles. I decentralised the organisation and the Azad Sena is only a Provincial and local body. It is functioning in the eastern parts of U.P., Bihar, Bengal and Assam. There may be in other provinces but I am definite that there is none in the Punjab. The object of the organisation is to prepare bands of trained political workers, who could not act as the nucleus of the future military side of the administration when the British Rule ends. They have instructions to try to make contacts with the military to make them disloyal to the British Rule. The looting of mail bags, small post offices, revenue collections, Government property is their line of work. They make up their funds by such means. They will be of much use to us in the third phase, which I am sure will come about shortly and will be of a revolutionary nature with open terrorism by using the arms and bombs collected in the second phase. The Azad Sena also believes individual terrorism to be inevitable at a certain stage. Looting of public men for political purposes is not approved. Manufacture of arms and collection of the same is part of their programme. The ones manufactured locally are no good and the best are the arms and ammunition obtained from servicemen. One object political purposes. The Azads are trained in handling of firearms which they have to use in their self-defence and also in their plan of looting etc. I am 'Pahla Azad' and all writing issued over that name are mine. The Azads are locally numbered and ten Azads form one Dasta."

"As far as the war is concerned we have never been concerned with its consequences. It was immaterial for us as to who won. Japan was not an enemy of India and if after the expulsion of the British they persisted in invading our country we could consider our plan of action. We would have negotiated with Japan. We do not care if our struggle helped the Japanese because we thought that if we could overthrow the British we could also fight the Japanese. I assured the workers that Gandhiji would not take action as usual. I assured the workers that Gandhiji would not take action as usual against those indulging in the underground activities. I further explained to the "Azads" that they should try to pick up the support of as many militarymen as possible."

"We have done lot of propaganda in the military. We were late in coming out to take control of the situation. Although the economic situation in the country helped us in fomenting an agitation yet the international situation was such that it did not let us extend our field of work. We knew that masses had spontaneously risen to the occasion in August, 1942. We hoped for another mass-rising and tried to prepare the masses for it. In order to keep in touch with the masses we sent workers in rural areas. We tried our best but failure was due to no change in the international situation. In Bihar and Assam the movement was strongest on account of the strength of the Congress organisation in these two provinces, in Bihar the Congress work was supplemented by the Congress Socialist Party and the Kisan Sabha while in Assam organisation had been started much in advance. Shanti Senas had been formed in Assam with 50,000 membership. The Congress movement has been successful only at places where organisation had been done before the starting of the movement. I.C.S. and I.P. officers also helped us in such provinces. In Bihar we had the maximum sympathy from the police and our sympathisers included I.P. offiers. In Bengal I.B. the highest officers who supported us were Deputy Superintendents.

As far as military was concerned, we never asked them to desert. We had pledges of loyalty to the Indian Republic printed which were required to be signed by militarymen offering to join us. We were contacting them with a view to make them disloyal to the British Government and to get arms through them. This was also the work and an item in the programme of the Azad Senas. We knew that military never revolted unless their masters were in crippled state. We did not feel that the present international situation was such that the Government was weak and a military revolt could have been successful. We only wanted them to be ready for action when the Government was about to collapse. The Indian military is generally dissatisfied and we were able to win over 80 per cent of the men in Air service, 50 per cent of Garhwalis, 50 per cent of Sikhs and we also succeeded in the formation of cells in all technical units stationed in Bihar and Assam. The emergency commission officers are generally more nationalist and it is too easy for us to win them over. It is an easier task to convert them than it is to get an information from the Imperial Secretariat at Delhi. During the movement I used to receive copy of a 'strictly secret' report of the Congress movement sent by the Viceroy to the Secretary of State for India.

Appendix–I

American Intelligence Report on the Activities of Indian National Army and the Working of Hikari Kikan in Burma; gives Comprehensive Account about the Emergence of the Indian Independence Movement under the Leadership of Subhas Chandra Bose (Extract)

Literally translated, Hikari Kikan means "Light Organization", but a better rendition of the phrase may be "Enlightenment Agency". The Burma branch of the Hikari Kikan is the agency of the Japanese Army which is charged with the training and use of Indians in the war against the Allies. As such, the Burma branch combines many functions, including espionage, sabotage, propaganda, combat intelligence and even military government.

Espionage constitutes one of its primary functions. The Hikari Kikan Annual Report for 1943 lists 568 men dispatched from Rangoon to forward areas. Many of these agents were destined for deep penetration into India. Some of the parties were briefed in specific subotage missions, but most ot them combined espionage sabotage tasks.

The Hikari Kikan Command includes both civilians and military Jifs (Japanese Inspired Fifth Columnists). The military Jifs are enrolled in the Indian National Army (I.N.A.), which is nominally the army of the "Provisional Government of Free India" under the leadership of Subhas Chandra Bose. The Civilian Jifs are agents directly responsible to Hikari Kikan officers.

Most of the personnel under Hikari Kikan are devoted to operational contact work rather than to deep penetration. Indians trained in Hikari

---

1. Hikari – Kikan a successor organisation to Iwakuro Kikan was established under the command of Col. Yamamoto. *Hikari* in Japanese means "Light" and Kikan means organisation. It served as a liaison agency between the I.N.A. and the Japanese Government. The note was prepared by office of the Strategic Services, U.S. Government and throw considerable light on the relations between the I.N.A. and the Japanese military authorities, Diet Library, Tokyo.

Kikan schools and camps are detached in small groups to regular Japanese Army units. Their tasks are to infiltrate behind the Allied lines for reconnasissance purposes and to attempt to suborn Indian troops by distributing leaflets or by personal contact with small isolated detachments. On occasion such infiltrating groups have been known to practice deception tactics, shouting misleading command to Indian Army units. In at least one skirmish they were able to capture a position because they were not recognized as enemy troops until it was too late for the defending forces to repel them.

The Indians under Hikari Kikan have not often been used in actual combat. Civilian Jifs are used either as interpreters or liaison men or as agents for deep penetration. The military Jifs of the "Indian National Army" have been employed largely as auxiliary details for the use of Japanese battallion and regimental commanders.

In the field of propaganda, Hikari Kikan operates both in combat and in general sphere. Radio broadcasts in Indian languages from Rangoon are under the aegis of one section of Hikari Kikan headquarters. Agents sent into India have carried leaflets and have been instructed to disseminate rumors. For combat propaganda, one I.N.A. unit carried 210,000 leaflets; another was equipped with 285,000 leaflets. A few portable printing presses have been available and have been used at the front for producing leaflets.

Certain field units of Hikari Kikan's I.N.A. are charged with the reception and indoctrination of Indian prisoners of war. A recent Japanese Army directive for the treatment of prisoners of war in Burma laid special emphasis on the way in which to deal with captured Indian troops. They were to be handled with special care, and any who demonstrated a desire to join up with Japanese controlled forces were to be enrolled in the I.N.A. After a few weeks of indoctrination and conditiong in one of the centers just behind the front, they were to be returned to combat as allies of the Japanese. This "quick release" treatment of prisoners succeeded in some measure in augmenting the I.N.A. forces, but some of the presumably indoctrinated Indian troops promptly returned to the British lines. The Japanese have had much more success with the so-called "hard-core Jifs". These are either civilians or former Indian Army soldiers, most of the latter captured in Malaya, who have become so thoroughly indoctrinated by Japanese propaganda that the Japanese can place absolute reliance on them.

Still other Hikari Kikan personnel have been trained as Civil Affairs officials and appeared during the short-lived Japanese occupation of part of the Manipur plain. Civilian Jifs wearing armbands inscribed with the letters 'A-D'[2] in white have been seen. Their role presumably was to take over the administration of conquered territories in India.

The possibilities of exploiting the Indian political situation have not been overlooked by Hikari Kikan. The use of Subhas Chandra Bose, in itself, was a brilliant though futile attempt to arouse the Indian population. Beyond that, agents have been dispatched into India to contact political leaders and thus to pave the way for a Japanese invasion.

The Japanese General Staff counted heavily on the aid their troops would supposedly receive, once the Japanese standard was planted on a bit of Indian soil, from the revolt of the people of India. Hikari Kikan was to be the instrumentality whereby the nominally independent forces of "Free India" were controlled by the Japanese Army. The authority empowering Hikari Kikan to control and coordinate all phases of the "I" offensive (the propaganda-espionage-subotage assault on India) did not come into effect until the end of 1943.

While the Japanese established espionage schools and military training camps for Indians soon after the conquest of Burma, their early efforts in the utilization of these Indians were not well organized and were generally unsuccessful. Internal dissension among the Jifs at Singapore and elsewhere was temporarily halted by the advent of Subhas Chandra Bose. In July 1943, Bose assumed leadership of the Indian Independence League (I.I.L.) and of the League's armed forces, the Indian National Army. Bose proceeded to reorganize the Jif movement. In October 1943, the Burma branch of Hikari Kikan was also reorganized, its personnel increased and its authority strengthened. By December 1943, the Burma branch numbered more than 100 Japanese, including officers, civilians and non-commissioned personnel, and was empowered to coordinate the "I" offensive.

All this authority was on paper, however. In reality as one Hikari Kikan officer complained in his diary, the Hikari Kikan has no authority to issue orders in the field. Army Unit Commanders had full power over the Jif groups attached to their commands. And, the same diarist comments, the Japanese Army generally regarded the I.N.A. as an espionage group rather than as a true national army. Hence both military and civilian Jifs seem to have been used for routine reconniassance tasks and were not employed as Hikari Kikan had planned and as Army Headquarters had ordered.

2. It stood for Azad Hind Dal.

The description of Hikari Kikan activities which follows is based on incomplete evidence which occasionally contradicts itself. The internal contradictions of the data are, however, readily understandable when we realize that the Japanese and Jifs themselves are a bit confused on the exact organizational authority of Hikari Kikan, that there are internal feuds, that there are over-lapping jurisdictions, in short, that Hikari Kikan-Burma Branch, suffers from the faults of a war agency hastily conceived and too quickly thrown together and into action.

Organisation.

As a result of the reorganization of December 1943, the Burma Branch of Hikari Kikan was divided into five sections, with headquarters in the Golden Valley Estate, Rangoon. Each of these sections is responsible for certain phases of Hikari Kikan activities and the work of every section is coordinated with that of the five Hikari Kikan outpost agencies. The outposts are supposed to act as liaison posts and as forward operating bases for agents in the field.

The chief of the Hikari Kikan is Lt. General Isoda Saburu. His Chief of Staff is Colonel Yamamoto. Early in 1944 the General Headquarters of Hikari Kikan moved from Singapore to Rangoon.

The Commanding Officer of the Burma Branch of Hikari Kikan is Lt. Colonel Kitabe, who had five officers attached to his staff in December 1943, three Lieutenant Colonels, one Major and one Medical Corps Captain.

Section One. This Section is in charge of general affairs and the intendence and prevention of espionage.

Section ("Han") One of the Headquarters staff is a secretariat section, having a strength of three officers, eight non-commissioned officers and eight civilians. It has jurisdiction over administrative affairs.

This section is also charged with maintaining security and conducts counter-espionage activities. The Annual Report of Hikari Kikan for 1943 makes special note of the organization of security and counter-espionage service. It says that attempts have been made to collect information in order to forestall enemy plans, especially these directed against the I.N.A. and the I.I.L. This was done :

(a) By keeping in close touch with the military police and similar organizations, as well as with branch political "Hans" and military "Hans".

(b) By attempting positive counter-espionage work, i.e., the exposure of the enemy intelligence system.

The security paragraphs of the Annual Report assert that the Indians themselve felt keenly the need for a counter-espionage service and one was organized within the I.I.L. and the I.N.A. in August, the object being to enable the Indian himselft to detect spies. The report notes that the general system of counter-espionage, supervised by the Hikari Agency, would be complete at the end of 1943. No details of the system are given, save that it would be under the control of the Burma Branch in all important essentials. It would seen from this that an internal network in the Gestapo style has been set up within the I.I.L. and the I.N.A. The Indians in these organizations must be well aware of this and may resent its existence.

Section Two. This section is charged with the direction of the affairs of the Indian Independence League.

The supervision of the I.I.L. and its associated Youth Training Centre is in charge of the three Japanese civilians who comprise the personnel of Section Two. This section, despite its small personnel, is one of the most important within Hikari Kikan. The I.I.L. has been conceived by the Japanese command as the means whereby millions of Indians would be rallied to the standard of the Greater East Asia Co-Prosperity Sphere. The League extends its activities to all territories in conquered Asia where Indians reside, but it is specially active in Burma where the motherland of the League's members lies just beyond the front. The Burma chapters of the I.I.L. were formerly under the direction of Bileshwar Prashad, who became President of the Burma I.I.L. in September 1942.

Prashad was succeeded by Karim Gani in March 1943. About that time Hikari Kikan took hold of the League in Burma and gave a great impetus to the League's activity. Presumably Hikari Kikan furnished whatever supplies and services the Japanese Army had to offer to further the interests of the League.

Soon after that, Subhas Chandra Bose assumed leadership. His arrival in Rangoon in July 1943 marked the opening of an intensified drive to persuade and coerce Indians in Burma to "donate" their money and services to Bose's movements. Bose raised many recruits for the I.N.A. and substantial sums of money. The "mobilization of wealth" enabled him to establish the National Bank of Azad Hind, Ltd. So affluent has Bose become of late that he recently contributed a munificient gift of Rs. 500,000 to Bu Maw's daughter on the occasion of her wedding. This sum may well be charged up to the purchase of goodwill on the books of the I.I.L.

The Japanese Government has backed up Bose. In October 1943 the Provisional Government of Free India was recognized by Japan and later by other Axis countries. At that time, Bose assumed the title of "Netaji-Fuehrer"—and the Andamans and Nicobars were nominally handed over to the Provisional Government with much ceremony and protestations of mutual esteem.

Meanwhile detachments of the I.N.A. were moving into Burma and headquarters of the I.I.L. in Burma was reinforced by many of the League's top personnel from Malaya, including a Colonel Alagappan who was Bose's Deputy. The League official toured throughout Burma, giving pop talks, persuading local Indians to cooperate and inducing them to contribute cash.

A fine flurry of meetings and celebrations took place in December 1943. The monthly report of Hikari Kikan for that month lists seven gala occasions, including a "Festival of Popular Gratitude" for the transfer of the Andaman and Nicobar Islands to be staged in January 1944, a conference of League branch leaders of lower Burma, and an entertainment for "about fifty people who have contributed over ¥ 20,000 to the Nethaji fund".

One paragraph in the same report states that Hikari Kikan will furnish every facility to the Bose government in preparation for the scheduled shift of the League headquarters to Burma. Officers of the Provisional Government were seheduled to be established in Rangoon by the end of January 1944. The "Government" officers were to be in Harbin Road. Bose himself was to live on University Avenue and his ministers on Park Road.

In the same document, Hikari Kikan officials are instructed to direct the attention of the Bose establishment to the necessity for taking defensive and counter-espionage measures. Just how the Japanese in this section of Hikari Kikan exercise their control over the I.I.L. and the Provisional Government is not clear. Nor is the exact relationship between the I.I.L. and the Provisional Government clear. However, office holders of one are very often officials in the other as well.

The League's headquarters, now in Rangoon, is divided into eight units.

Unit A.	Civilian recruitment and training. This is run by Jifs of the I.N.A.
Unit B.	Propaganda. Also managed by I.N.A. Jifs, notably Colonel Alagappan and Colonel Gilani
Unit C.	Art. This presumably has to do with posters and drawings for leaflets.
Unit D.	Field Propaganda.

Unit E. Supply.

Unit F. Accounts.

Unit G. Reconstruction.

Unit H. Women's Department.

The first four units are closely allied with I.N.A. and will be further treated in the discussion of the I.N.A. The Reconstruction department is intended to furnish plans and personnel for the government of territories to be conquered in India. This contingent of military government is known as "Azad Hind Dal". The representatives of this department were in Tamu at the end of May; there were about thirty of them, mostly Bengali civilians although they held honorary official rank in the I.N.A. Each bore an armband incribed with the letters A.H.D. in white.

The Women's Department may have something to do with the Rani of Jhansi Regiment, a regiment composed entirely of women under the command of Captain S. Lakshmi.

The League has a Youth Training Centre in Rangoon which had some 700 students in November 1943. Five classes were under training, each being groomed for specialized tasks. These were :

(1) Administration of occupied territories.

(2) Special duties (possibly this means espionage and sabotage).

(3) Field propaganda.

(4) Counter-espionage.

(5) I.N.A. Trainees.

A new class was under formation for training in wireless communications. Each class had eight instructors and auxilliary instruction was given by branch members. The Hikari Kikan report for December notes that special attention is to be given to the strengthening of training in counter-espionage. The class was to be specially indoctrinated and "all members will create an atmosphere of sincerity such as is seldom seen, by swearing a solemn oath to commit suicide of their own volition if they neglect their studies or fail in their duties."

Hikari Kikan, at the end of 1943, seemed to be greatly aware of the necessity of taking counter- espionage measures. In addition to the counter-espionage system, established within the I.I.L., and the class of 33 students then undergoing special counter-espionage training at the Youth Training Centre, still more personnel were to be selected from the Centre for the Underground Spy (Senka Teicho) Section. The first class was to be ready for its duties by the end of January.

Another paragraph in the counter-espionage section of the December report stated that preliminary investigations of the officials who hold office under the British had been carried out.

Both the Japanese and Bose were taken in by their own propaganda. The whole abortive offensive into Manipur seems to have been premised on the idea that Japanese occupation of any bit of Indian territory would be sufficient impetus for a wholesale revolution in India. The consequent decimation of three Japanese divisions will undoubtedly affect the consideration of the use of Bose and his Jif followers.

An interesting exposition of Bose's fallacy is contained in a document which was issued by Hikari Kikan on 15 January 1944 at the headquarters of the Ratsu Division. In this document the part to be played by the Forward Bloc in India is stressed. The Forward Bloc was that part of the Indian National Congress which formerly adhered to the views of Bose. While it has some members in Indian even now, its activities are by no means as dangerous to the Allies as the Hikari document would make them out to be. The document says :

"The Bloc includes a Propaganda Department and 'Secret Warfare' Department. The latter had been carrying out underground activities since the foundation of the party, and its personnel unlike those attached to the former (who have mostly been arrested), have so far escaped imprisonment. They are now preparing both to enlarge their membership and stir up a revolution. Unfortunately, however, an internal revolution will not in itself suffice to eradicate British Military Power. Accordingly, as soon as the Japanese Army strikes the first blow against the British inside India, the population will be awakened from its dream about Britain's power and a really great rising may be expected. Therefore, judging from the situation inside India, the sooner the Japanese Army attacks India the better; Should the Indians make a compromise with Britain the internal situation will suddenly turn to Britain's advantage. Furthermore, militarily speaking, she will have time to strengthen the defence of Eastern India.

"For this reason military operations need never be on a large scale; our object can be attained satisfactorily by local operations. Accordingly we should gain success by creating a situation of panic within India, using our propaganda to inflame the Indians' own will to fight."

Section Three. The section has charge of general intelligence, editing of espionage reports, translation work, general propaganda, photograhic work, printing and broadcasting.

Every Wednesday, at 1500 hours, a meeting is held in the committee room of the Broadcasting Administration Office in Rangoon. Representatives of Section Three of Hikari Kikan play an important role in these meetings at which the trend of radio propaganda during the coming week is determined. The head of the Propaganda Department of the I.I.L. is present, as are officers of the Army Propaganda Department and the Burma Broadcasting Administration. But the evidence indicates that it is the Hikari Kikan officials who actually decide what the propaganda line is to be.

Several different propaganda media come within the sphere of Section Three. In addition to radio broadcasts, the thirteen Japanese civilians of this Han supervise the production of leaflets and the publication of newspapers. All propaganda disseminated from headquarters lies within their jurisdiction. Combat propaganda, however, is the task of Section Four of Hikari Kikan.

In addition to its propaganda jobs, Section Three edits intelligence reports from the field, furnishes translation services, analyzes the flow of intelligence and disseminates intelligence summaries. It acts as a reporting board as well as the agency of propaganda control. The actual dissemination of propaganda from headquarters very often is done by the propaganda Department of the I.I.L., but it is clear that the League's propagandists take their views from Hikari Kikan officials, an American or a British soldier?" and then proceeded to write the answer. Clues of effective propaganda against the enemy may well be gleanded from the enemy's propaganda to us.

Newspaper

A large printing press of Hikari headquarters of Rangoon turns out four newspapers, all of which are nominally published by the I.I.L. Our air raids over Rangoon curtailed the output of newspapers when one of the presses was destroyed and the printers fled. The shortage of newsprint further complicates the efforts to keep these publications going. But because newspapers are considered to be of high propaganda value, their production receives high priority. In the words of one Hikari Kikan report "Education of the Indians in Burma and the inculcation of the spirit of independence in them, will be promoted by the following newspaper."

Four newspapers were being published in December 1943 :

Azad Hindustan—weekly in Hindustani—2,000 copies.

Sudandara Hindustan—twice weekly in Tamil—5,000 copies.

Sawatantara Hindustan—twice weekly in Telegu—1,500 copies.

Azad Hind—weekly in English, the successor to "New Order".

Motion Pictures—Japanese propagands films are distributed by Hikari Kikan for showing to Indian troops and civilians. Photographs of the I.N.A. are posted on bulletin boards in Japanes posts.

Intelligence Report and Summaries

Hikari Kikan intelligence summaries, by Allied standards, are sketchy but fairly accurate. Ground sources in the contatizone and boradcast monitoring seems to supply the bulk of their information. Photo reconnaissance and deep penetration information are very weak. The Japanese do not hesitate to report facts unpleasant to themselves but their deductions from these facts, and their analysis of Allied intentions are frequently very wide of the mark.

One Intelligence Summary which covers the period 16 December to 25 December 1943 contained seven parts. It bore the seal "Oura", perhaps indicating authorship by Caption Oura, Commander of Section Four of Hikari Kikan headquarters.

Part 1. "Summary"—the highlights of the periods are briefly mentioned, including intensive bombing by Allied planes, numerous reconnaissance flights over likely landing points and the completion of the new road to the front by the Allies.

Part 2. "Enemy Dispositions on the Indo-Burma Frontier"—gives Allied troop dispositions in nine areas, ranging fron Chittagong to Waikhong. The information in this part is fragmentary but definitely useful to the Japanese Command.

Part 3. "Enemy Air Situation"—is very scanty. It gives nothing more than the mention of several Allied raids and the names of a few Allied Air Commanders, the latter heard over the Delhi radio. The judge from this report, the Japanese have very little information concerning our air Order of Battle.

Part 4. "Enemy Shipping Position"—is also extremely brief and uniformative. Two bits of information are given, one concerning a convoy in the Bay of Bengal, its presence deduced from wireless interception, and te other a report of an air reconnaissance over the water south of Chittagang.

Part 5. "Military Interception"—deals, in some detail, with tours taken by Allied commanders and by officials of the Government of India. Excerpts from Allied broadcasts included President Roosevelt's declaration that American had sent 3,800,000 men abroad and that the number would be increased to 5,000,000 men in July 1944. Three excerpts from statements by King George, Lord Linlithgow and Admiral Mountbatton, respectively, say that the defeat of Japan will follow the downfall of Germany.

Part 6. "Points from Military Topography"—contains road report from the Allied combat zone. These reports are comparatively full and accurate, and, indeed, constitute the best intelligence of this summary.

Appendix A.— Lists 30 more road reports which are headed "Assam Road Reports, Based on investigations carried out by the I.I.L., the Investigation Han ("Chosa Han") and the Hikari Organization Agencies at Kalewa and Homalin, dated 13th December, 1943."

Appendix B— "Organization of SEAC and India command"—Contains little more than could be gleaned from Delhi broadcasts.

Section Four. This Section has charge of military intelligence, special operative work, and propaganda in the field.

Propaganda and intelligence are functions of this section, but the propaganda carried on by Section Four is field propaganda employed in combat situations, as contrasted with the general propaganda emnating from headquarters, which is the responsibility of Section Three. The intelligence tasks of this Section include specifically military information and the intelligence derived from the activities of deep penetration agents. The training of these agents, their staging, briefing and utilization, is apparently the job of Section Four.

Field Propaganda. Leaflet distribution and loud speaker appeals are the two main media of Hikari combat propaganda. Broadcasts of Indians in the Allied ranks are given first priority. As one Hikari documents put it, "The aim of these broadcasts being to convince them (Indian troops) of the sincerity of the Japanese Army, certain victory for the Axis and the defeat of the British." Annotating this statement, the document reveals that the encouragement of anti-British resistance and the promotion of a spirit of independence will contribute to the success of the operations of the Japanese Army.

As matters actually worked out, however, loud speaker appeals carried on by Section Four badly misfired. At Kohima, for example, both British and Indian troops were subjected to intensive Japanese propaganda, but the British troops were frequently addressed in Hindustani while the Indian troops were addressed in English. The Royal West Kents were the recipients of a grand promise that all deserters would be promoted to the rank of Jamdar.

Three mobile printing presses were posted along the Chindwin, immediately prior to the start of the offensive, to turn out spot leaflets. On 11 March, one of these presses was in operation on the East bank of the Chindwin and presumably was taken into Manipur. The leaflet campaign was no more successful than the loud speaker attempt. Comparatively few Indian troops deserted to the enemy and the effect on British units was slight.

Although Hikari Kikan, together with the Special Service Section (Tokumo Kikan) of the Japanese Army, were the chief instrumentalities whereby field propaganda was disseminated, the direction of the propaganda campaign was in the hands of the regular Army commanders. An order from 15th Army Headquarters, dated 17 January 1944 and addressed to 31 Division of the Homalin outpost of Hikari Kikan, detailed the procedure for field propaganda. It placed special emphasis on the Gurkha propaganda scheme which seems to have been a particular favorite of the Japanese command. The order, signed by General Mutaguchi Renya, commanding officer, 15th Army, stated:

"1. The Army in Burma will carry out propaganda in the field according to the Gurkha Propaganda Scheme and also the Army Propaganda Scheme. In carrying out this propaganda scheme for India, the Hikari Commander will come under the orders of the Army Commanders, in the direction of field propaganda against the Gurkhas, as this part of he scheme is of military and defensive importance.

"2. Army commanders will direct field propaganda against the Gurkhas in accordance with Hayashi Operation order B/51 and based on the Gurkha Propaganda Scheme. In this field propaganda work the local Hikari Advanced Dett. will assist.

"3. Divisional Commanders will be able to carry out this field propaganda with the aid of the local Hikari Dett. (with the exception of the Maymyo

Branch), and will also utilize their own Intelligence Tais. The main object of these scheme is to sow dissension among Gurkha troops. The local Hikari detachments will come under the orders of Divisional Infantry Commanders, in this propaganda work against Gurkhas."

The Appendix to the order was entitled "Propaganda Scheme Against Gurkha Troops".

1. **Policy**—In carrying out propaganda against India, the national character of the Gurkhas and the special conditions prevailing in Nepal should be borne in mind and utilized in the anti-British struggle. In particular we must strive to arouse dissension among Gurkha troops.

2. **Organization Orders**—The C in C of the Army in Burma and the Commander of the Hikari organization will carry out this propaganda in accordance with Appendix to Mori operation order B/34. This propaganda will take three forms.

   (i) Propaganda in the field.
   (ii) Internal propaganda.
   (iii) Establishment of communications.

"Propaganda in the field is the responsibility of the Army in Burma which will instruct Hikari organizations as to method of operation.

"In accordance with the outline of the propaganda scheme for India (Appendix to Mori Operation Order B/34) the C in C 15 Army and G.O.C. 55 Div. will direct forward detachments of Hikari organization to carry out this propaganda in the field.

"Propaganda other than that mentioned in paragraph 4 will be the responsibility of Hikari organization. Outline as follows:

"Internal propaganda to breed anti-British fooling in Nepal, to prepare for the establishment of an anti-British Government and to cause disaffection of Gurkha troops. To further this propaganda we must establish reliable means of communication between Burma and Nepal.

3. **The Meaning of Propaganda in the Field**—Our object is to sow dissension among Gurkha troops in the front line and in the rear.

4. Plan of action regarding Gurkhas is based on permission to permit against the British by making use of the special conditions prevailing in Nepal due to feuds between the Royal families and hostility of the population towards these families.

"In connection with this propaganda, Japanese political attitude towards Nepal is that when India gains complete freedom we shall also be able to grant Nepal her independence without delay.

"In our propaganda, we emphasize that at present Nepal is independent only in name and that, in diplomatic and military matters, she is completely under British control. There can be no real independence for Nepal until the British are defeated. The British hinder all economic and educational development in Nepal. We believe that the British have taken away the Gurkhas livelihood and have made him merely a solider-slave."

Deep Penetartion

Among the Hikari Kikan lists which have been taken, there is one which is entitled "Table of Spies and Liaison Personnel disciplines during the year 1943". This might have been a most valuable and information document had it been more accurate and complete. Parties of agents which were definitely known to have been dispatched into India and not listed, while some groups which apparently never were sent in are mentioned. Moreover, the 104 agents enumerated as being destined for deep penetration represent only a part of the total number of Hikari Kikan personnel available for aspionage missions. No names are given in the lists. The number of "Spice and Mission—Personnel" dispatched from Rangoon to staging areas near the front comes to a total of 568 men.

These discrepanies indicate that Hikari activities have not been so well coordinated. There is other evidence to show that the weekly directive were not always interpreted in the same way by the outposts and by Army commanders as they were at Headquarters. The organization of Hikari Kikan work, specially as it concerns deep penetration operation,, was not entirely efficient. When parties arrived at staging areas, it was frequently found that no preparations had been made to send them forward. Trail Intelligence was usually lacking and communications preparations were exceedingly crude. The Japanese, however, have been quick to recognize these defects and have steadily tried to improve all phase of Hikari Kikan work. They have given special attention to tightening up the deep penetration procedures.

Training Schools for Deep Penetration

In this attempting to lighten up their deep penetration procedures, they have changed their network of agent training schools from a haphazard set of poorly organized centers to a well integrated system with relatively fewer schools but with a much more practical curriculum. More than a dozen different training schools for Hikari Kikan personnel are known to have existed in Burma and Malaya. Most of these are defunct, but three are still carrying on.

The earlier schools, all of which are now either defunct or recognized, were small and were staffed wholly or chiefly by Indians. Both the staff and students of these earlier schools were of poor caliber for Hikari purposes. It is to be remembered that the Hikari Kikan organization did not take over full control or deep penetration operations until the latter half of 1943 after the first schools had been in operation for a year or more.

The instructors at the schools which were first established were primarily propagandists with limited technical knowledge and experience. The students were, on the whole, volunteers who were motivated by political considerations and who had no training of a military nature. The instruction given was very circumscribed. It consisted chiefly of "inspirational" lectures on the holy mission against the Allies, with some training in progaganda methods and some small arms practice. The schools which were established later and those which are now in operation are more efficient. They have larger staffs and have more Japanese Army men as instructors. The Indian instructors are men who have themselves engaged in Hikari operations. The students, too, are now selected with more care and are more suitable for the work. Rangoon and Penang have been the principle centres for the training of agents. A total of some 13 schools are known to have existed in the two places, eight in Penang and five in Rangoon, out of these 13 schools only three are still in operation, namely; the Rangoon Sawaraj Institute, Kanbe and the Swaraj Young Men's Training Institute, Thingangyun in Rangoon, and the "Sandy Croft" School in Penang.

Kanba

The Kanbe school was one of the first established and became one of the largest of the training institutes. At one time, it had over 700 students. It originated as school for volunteers from the local chapters of the Indian Independence League. For a while, it ran along in a desultory fashion with a very short course of training and few practical demostrations. About the beginning of 1943 it was changed from this amateur basis and become an important centre or the production of trained agents.

The school was first heard of in a broadcast during September 1942. It was then described as an institute for training young Indians for membership in the Independence Movement. It seems that two courses, each of which lasted about a month, were held in the last quarter of 1942. Early in 1943, a six weeks course was initiated and another one was started in April 1943.

The aims of the Kanbe school were at first somewhat confused. One of the students believed that he was destined to undertake intelligence tasks for the Japanese; others seem to have believed that they would eventually become administrators of areas in India which had been taken over from the Allies.

Recruiting for this school was first done through the district branches of the Indian Independences League, although the school itself sent out recruiting parties from time to time . The recruiting was not successful.

Special Operative Section	Wireless Communication Section	Counter Espionage Section	Gaoshala Training Camp

The same captured document records that steps were being taken in December 1943 to improve and complete the training. More instructors were to be provided and more help was to be given by Hikari Kikan members; the hours of instruction in Japanese were increased; certain reforms in the internal administration and the training were effected, the latter including long route marches, all on the Japanese model.

The Special Operative Section, Kanbe S.Y.H.T.I.

Special attention was paid to the toughening of members as the following extract from a captured document shows: "all members from this section will live in the open, in tents pitcched on the sports field of the Training Centres and will do their own cooking; they will be trained in all branches of study. Though they will be plagued by mosquitoes and suffer from the severe cold at night, these hardships will build up a spirit of hardships."

Litle is known about the training carried out inside the school, but a captured document reveals that a forced march from Rangoon to Eoulmein and back was planned. On the march students were to carry out political exercises, "directed towards the 50,000 Indians in the district". These exercises were to include practice in spreading propaganda in spying, in recruiting students, in lectures and in communication by wireless.

The reference to wireless training agrees with other information that about 60 students from this section had completed their wireless training by the end of December 1943. The same report states that an additional 22 trained W/T personnel would meet requirements " for the opening of operations" which are assumed to have been the Manipur operations which commenced in March of this year. Wireless training is not a new feature of the Kanbe curriculum, for it is known that in the middle of 1943 two parties were earmarked for such training. One of these was believed to have gone to Boundary Road, Rangoon.

The Wireless Communications Section, Kanbe S.Y.M.T.I.

This sections consisted of 10 men but nothing more is known about their training or movements. They are not to be confused with the personnel of the Special Operative Section undergoing W/T training, as mentioned in the preceding paragraph.

The Counter Espionage Section, Kanbe S.Y.M.T.I.

This Section is mentioned in the Hikari Kikan Annual Report for 1943. This report reveals that Hikari Kikan's efforts for better security before the provisional Government moved into Burna lead to the formation for this section. The document clained that 33 men were especially selected for it. These men are said to have begun training on 11 December 1943, but apparently due to Bose's interference stopped it in February 1944. This appears to have been the first real attempt to set up a defensive counter-espionage system made by Hikari Kikan, which has usually appeared to engage in offensive intelligence.

Thingangyun.

The Thingangyun school is the largest of a group of schools founded and directed by an old Indian revolutionary known as Hari Singh, alias Usman Khan. It was opened at the end of 1942 to receive students for advance training from another school which Hari Singh had founded in Penang. It also took Indians recruited by Indian Independence League in Burma. The first course lasted from January to April 1943, and included about 90 students, half of the Punjabis. Their training was supposed to be very comprehensive; instruction was given in propaganda work, espionage and sabotage, and some of the students were removed from the course to undergo specialized training as parachutists or as radio operators and a few even returned to Penang for a "submarine and boating" course. Most of the original classes were dispatched for deep penetration work and a good many of them have been apprehended.

The curriculum was varied one. There was a course in the manufacture of bombs; daily instruction was given in the handling of rifles, revolvers, and submachine-guns. There were practical monouvers to test the ability of the students to carry out sabotage tasks and they were given a good deal of practice in entering places guarded by barbed wire and other abstacles. One reports they even had instruction covering methods of injecting poison.

One of the agents dispatched from Thingangyun testified undeı interrogation that his instructions were to hamper communication by damaging railway lines, telegraph wires, post offices and other government buildings. This was the usual testimony as to the training and instruction of agents at Thingangyun, but this interrogation report also included the mission of undertaking antidemolition meansures in the event of British withdrawal. The agents were instructed to join British demolition parties and, after gaining their complete confidence, to pretend to assure responsibility for the demolition of strategic intallations. In that way they could preserve these installations intact for the use of the advancing Japanese forces.

The code work for Thingangyun seems to have beeen extremely rudimentary. One member of a contact party stated that he was taught 17 words, 11 of which are produced below. Messages of a domestic nature, deaths, marriage, arrivals and departures denoting operations are sent; the subject of the message relates to a military or naval unit and the verb is either sent in clear or denotes some opertaion activity. The words of the code are as follows :

Mangni—Army
Acheha—2 Dvisionas
O.K.—3 Divisions
Bahut Achcha—4 Divisons or 2 War Ships
Pita—Aircraft Carrier
Mata—Crusier
Larka—Destroyer
Larki—Submarine
Shadi Hogai—Army has moved off
Bimar—Ready for attack
Margay—Unsuccessful

Besides the Kanbe and Thingangyun institutes, three other Jif Training schools are known to have existed in Rangoon: (1) Biren Roy's School, (2) Baba Amar Singh's School, and (3) the Golden Valley Hikari Kikan Training Centre. All three are now defunct.

Biren Roy's School.

This school was founded and run by Biren Roy, an ex detenu of Dacca. It was opened in the latter half of 1942 and was located in Neojy Building, Sparkes Street, Rangoon. There was no regular staff except Biren

Roy himself, but N.K. Bannerjee of the Thingangyun Institute and some of the senior students also lectured occasionally. There were about 32 students, all Bengalis recruited in Burma.

The training consisted mostly of informal discussions. Fire-Arms pratices was conducted on the roof. The students were not allowed to leave the building. The school was more of an informal secret group than a regular training centre.

The students were trained with a view to deep penetration operations. It was planned that parties should infiltrate into india and there cause internal confusion. Students were instructed to resort to "money actions" when in need of funds to sabotage railway and telegraph lines and to cause strikes.

From time to time small parties were sent off for infiltration into India. They were provided with revolvers and small amounts of forged Indian notes. They were told that the arms were to be used in self- defense and, if arrested, for suicide .

Baba Amar Singh's School

This school was founded in February or March 1943 by Baba Amar Singh who was brought by the Japanese from Bangkok to Burma for the purpose of organizing intelligence activities. The school was opened in Rangoon but was later moved to Mawlaik.

The staff consisted of Baba Amar Singh himself and two of his chief recruiters, Chanda Singh and Ram Kekha.

There were about 25 students who were of poor type.

While located at Rangoon, little useful training was given. After moving to Mawlaik , some elementary instruction in bomb making and the use of small arms was given.

A member of agents from this school were sent to Manipur state to contact the ex-royal family and to engage in sabotage, espionage and propaganda against troops and government employees. As far as is known, all these agents were arrested before they had approached their tasks. One feature peculiar to this school is that the parties were provided with guides, residents of the Indo-Burma frontier areas, who had been through the same training as the agents themselves. Some of these guides were intended to provide the communications between the agents and the Japanese.

The Golden Valley Hikari Kikan Training Center

At least one course of instruction for Jifs is known to have been given at the Rangoon Headquarters of Hikari kikan at the Golden Valley Estate. This course began early in June 1943.

The instructors were either wholly, or almost wholly, Japanese. The students trained in this course were all Gurkhs, some were civilians and some military personnel, who were specially selected from the Swaraj Young Men's Training Institute, Rangoon, with a view to their special training as agents for contact work with British Burkha troops in operational areas.

The training given consisted in propaganda lectures along the same lines as those given to the Gurkhas in the Penang Training School (i.e., that Nepal was not an independent country but enslaved to the British; that the Gurkhas should therefore fight to gain independence; that the Japanese, unlike the British, had no desire to rule Asia or India, but wished merely to act as guides to all brother Asiatics), and instruction in map reading, espionage, sabotage, the theory of making and using hand grenades and bombs, and guerrilla warfare.

Despite the training in guerrilla warfare, which was probably largely, if not wholly, theoretical in character, it is quite clear from the instructions they received on being dispatched to the forward areas that they were intended at act as contact propagandists against British Gurkha troops and were not expected to infiltrate behind the lines.

Penang

During the latter half of 1942 no fewer than five Jif training schools were opened in Penang: 1. the Samraj Institute, managed by Raghavan; 2. the Penang Propaganda School, controlled by Hari Singh, alias Usman Khan; 3. The Chopra School also controlled by Hari Singh; 4. A school for Muslim prisoners of war, under Colonel Gilani; and 5. a small school for Singhalese.

Two courses were held at Raghavan's Institute, the Short Course which began early in August 1942 and lasted about six weeks, and the Long Course which began about September 1942 and continued until May 1943 when it was disbanded.

The Short Course had 32 students, all civilians, largely South Indians, who were recruited in various parts of Malaya by Raghavan himself.

The time-table allotted 10 hours a day to lectures on politics, espionage, methods of infiltration, methods of secret graphic correspondence, propaganda, Indian history and Indian geography. Students were also taught Morse code, elementary Cipher work and the use of small arms. The course officially closed at the end of August but there was an additional fortnight's training in swimming and the use of canvas and rubber boats.

The aim of the Short Course was to train parties of agents who were to proceed by Submarine to India, there to link up with other parties from the Institute who should be sent by the overland route. The agents were to collect information about the strength, composition, disposition and morale of the fighting services, about communication and transport facilites, the labor situation, workshops and factories, the state of public morale, and the attitude of the civil and military towards Japan. They were also to conduct propaganda about the impending invasion and subsequent liberation of India by Japan. They were to organize strikes and boycotts and to work in cooperation with Congress elements, urging them to commit sabotage.

In most cases exact instructions regarding areas of operation were not given, such phrases as "North West India", "the East Coast", or "Bombay and Karachi" being used. Some agents were to have roving commissions all over India, collecting all the informations they could on the wide variety of subjects mentioned above.

Two submarine parties of five agents each were landed at different points on the West Coast at the end of September 1942. Some weeks later 10 other agents attempted to cross into India from Burma in small groups. The arrangement was for the submarine agents to contact the land agents by means of posts addresses and rendezvous. Each submarinc agent was to have a land agent as his partner with whom he was to work. Information was to be collected by the submarine agents and passed to the land agents who were to send it to Burma by locally administered messengers or to take it themselves. Nothing came of this plan as all the agents concerned were arrested before they could got to work. Two of the renaining six crossed into India from Burma and were arrested.

The Long Course began before the Short Course had finished. It was originally intended to last for three months but dragged on until May 1943.

The students were mostly civilians selected by the I.I.L. in Malaya, but a certain number of prisoners of war were also included. Various estimates of the total number in the Long Course have been reported but the probable figure is approxinately 100. As in the case of the Short Course, the majority were South Indians.

The training was on much the same lines as that given in the Short Course, but more attention was paid to details. Students were divided into 3 divisions, specializing in political work, propaganda, or special operational espionage. All students were lectured in Economics, Hygiene, and First Aid; they were also taught military drill and the use of rubber boats.

One member of the Long course who has been apprchened was instructed to supervise the work of the Short Course students who had already proceeded to India, and also to prepare for Long Course submarine landings on the West Coast of India early in 1943. When the other Long Course agents arrive in India, he was to try and place them in regimental contractors institutes and was himself then to form an agency and travel around inspecting his agents. There is no information of the plan being put into practices and no use has been made of Long Course students as a whole, though some may have joined other training centers. It has been stated, however, that the Long Course was disbanded and sent home because the Japanese became suspicious of Raghavan, whom they removed and interned for a time.

With the termination of the Long Course in May 1943, the school was closed. Some of the students took up duties at various I.I.L. institutions in Malaya, while, in September, many more joined the I.N.A. Officers' Training Center in Singapore.

Hari Singh's Propaganda School. Hari Sing's Propaganda School was opened in September 1942 by Hari Singh, alias Usman Khan. The school was located at 34 Northan Road, Penang, in a building which is generally known as "Dr. Jaggat Singh's Sea-side Residence."

Hari Singh was assisted by Sukchain Nath Chopra of Gujranwalla, a former schoolmaster in the Malaya Educational Service, and Mohd. Zahir Khan, alias Moti. Later R.L. Avasti, a former wireless operator from the Andamans, became the leader of the school.

Recruiting appears to have been carried out mainly through I.I.L. though individuals or small groups may have been specially selected by Hari Singh or his own recruiters. Students have come to this training center from Shanghai, Bangkok and Malaya. Some of them have been prisoners of war. In December 1942 some 70 students were reported to be attending the course, while the total intake between November 1942 and April 1943 is reported to have been 132. In December 1942, about 70 students were sent to undergo further training at Hari Singh's Thingangyun Institute, while two other batches of over 20 were detached to join other institutions at Penang.

Training

There seems to have been no fixed syllabus. Students were, however, instructed in propaganda methods, the use of small arms, bomb making, sabotage and disguises. Special items such as the establishment of communication systems, "Submarine and boating" training, and possible parachute jumping were also included. A code was taught by which agents operating in India were intended to communicate intelligence through the All India Radio Welfare.

Early in 1943, the students of Hari Singh's School came to be known as "Avasti's party", as the name of their leader was R.L. Avasti, a former wireless operator from the Andamans. More students from Singapore joined this group and also others of Hari Singh's followers from Shanghai who had arrived in Penang in December 1942. Avasti's Party faded from the Penang picture in May 1943 when he, with 30 of this party and 10 of Sangha's group left for Burma to join the Swaraj Young Men's Institute, Thingangyun.

Penang.

The Pouning Propaganda School appears to have been largely a holding centre where prospective agents were given preliminary training while waiting to be sent to more specialized and advanced courses to other intelligence training centre.

The Chopra School.

The Chopra School was founded either towards the end of 1942 or very early in the 1943. It was originally located at 82 Northen Road, but moved in March 1943 to a more secluded area. The School was under the general direction of Hari Singh, but was under the immediate control of S.M. Chopra, former Headmaster of Batu Pahat High School. The staff consisted only of Chopra and a Japanese named Sakuna.

The original students of this school consisted of five brought back to Penang by Hari Singh from the Thingangyun Institute, Rangoon, for special training. They were joined in February 1943 by 19 others, bringing the total up to 24. Most of the students were North Indians.

The training given in the Chopra School was secret and nothing is known concerning it says that it included the usual political lectures which were given by Chopra, and small arms instruction which was given by Sakuna. "Submarine and boating" training was also probably a part of the curriculum.

In March 1943 the school moved to a more secluded area and began intensive training. This continued until September 1943 when Chopra and some of his students left the school, leaving the remainder of the shool to carry on as best they could. Its fate since that date is not definitely known, but it probably closed soon after.

Colonol Gilani's School for Prisoners of War.

The school for Muslim prisoners of war had 40 students and was under the direction of Colonel Gilani. As a result of dissension among the student's themselves, the school closed in November 1943 and the party returned to Singapore.

The Singhalese School.

Little is known of the Singhalese school except that intensive training in W/T and boating was given.

These five training schools actually achieved very little in the way of concrete results. One totally unsuccessful operation was undertaken by the students of the Short Course and it is reported that a party of agents landed in Ceylon in December 1943 which was probably composed of students from the Sinhalese Training centre. These two operations, so far as is known, constitute the sum total of results of the five schools.

Deep Penetration opertion. A number of attempts of deep penetration with India have been made by JIFSs. Defils of these attempts so far as they are know, fallons. In July 1943 a group of Patharis which have served as bodyguard to the D.M. Khan, M.R. Mulliale groups. Well recruited to return to India. They were to make contact with Muslim political circles, to organize general obstruction to the war effort, and to prepare the people for the invasion of the Jif army.

The party consisted of 12 members. Two were sent ahead in September 1942 as an advance group. They were followed in November by seven members of the group and the remaining three, including the leaders, arrived early in December 1942. All of these twelve agents, except one, passed through the British security organization. Of these, two were detained under the defense of India Rules, while eight were allowed to return to their homes in the Punjab under surveillance. They have now been re-arrested.

2. The elaborate but unsuccessful attempt of two parties of students from the Penang Short Course who landed by submarine on the West Coast of India at the end of September 1942 has already been described in connection with the account of Short Course hold in Raghavan's Swaraj Institute at Penang.

The execution of four of these agents was announced in October 1943. Two of the land agents who were to have cooperated with the agents landed by submarine, T.P. Kumaran Nair of Malabar and Ramu Thevar of the Ramnad District, Madras, both of whom were living in

Malaya at the outbreak of hostilities with Japan have also been executed.

3. At the end of April and beginning of May 1943, about 50 students of the Swaraj Young men's Training Institute, Thingangyan, left the school for deep penetration tasks in India. Fifteen of them have been apprehended and the remainder found their way to the Arakan and Chindwin fronts. It was probably planned that they should infiltrate into India, but it is likely that they eventually abandoned this plan and engaged in contact opertions.

4. In the fourth week of April 1943, seven parties of Jif parachute agents were dropped in Assam. These agents were the product of the First Parachute Course, held at Mingaladon and Penang.

   One of these parachute parties which was captured was supplied with money and equipment, including wireless transmission sets. Five members of this party, Ajaib Sing of Amritsar District, Zahir Ahmed of Sheikhpura District in the Punjab, S.L. Mazumder of Chttagong District in Bengal, Andeshwar Rai and Sham Lal Pande of Gorokhpur District in the United Provinces, have been convicted and condemned to death. The sentences of the last two, however, have commuted to transportation for life.

5. Sometime in the latter half of 1943 a number of agents trained in Baba Amar Singh's School were sent to Manipur State to contact the ex-royal Family, and to engage in sabotage, espionage and propaganda against troops and government employees. As far as is known, all the agents were arrested before they had approached their tasks.

6. In October 1943, a party of seven civilian Jifs were given money and dispatched from Kanwa to Chittagong with two Mugh guides. En route two membe of the party became separated by the remaining five, together with the two guides, went forward until they were arrested by a village defense party.

This group of seven agents was selected from a group of 24 or 25 Jifs that had been brought from a village near Akyab to Khaungdok when they had been brought to Kanwa. The Akyab group was composed of 16 civilians Jifs brought from Taungaup and 8 or 9 local civilian Jifs. The 16 Jifs from Taungup were in turn part of a party of 70 agents brought there by Maruyamn from the Rangoon Kanba Swaraj Institute.

The final instructions given to the group of 7 Jifs, all of whom were Bangalis, prior to their leaving Kanwa for Chittagong may be summarized as follows:

(a) Two of them were to proceed to the Chittagong district south of the Kamfuli River and :—

 (i) Put over the usual pro-Japanese propaganda surreptitiously, and gauge the reaction of the public.

 (ii) Try the contract local Congressmen or "patriots" with pro-Japanese inclinations and take them back to the enemy.

 (iii) Inform the public that there were 3,000,000 Indians in Burma well trained in military tactics.

 (iv) Ascertain whether Indians previously sent from Burma were carrying on similar propaganda or not.

 (v) Collect all possible information about military dispositions in the area specified.

(b) One of the agents, who is a resident of a village near Chittagong Town, was to proceed to the town and carry out the instuctions contained in (a) (1) and (5) above.

(c) The two remaining members were to proceed to the Chittagong Hill Tracts and carry out the same tasks as the two in (a) above.

7. The most recent attempt to deep penetration into India took place in March 1944 when 12 Muslim ex-prisoner of war agents were landed from a submarine on the coast of Baluchistan. These agents were members of an original party of 70 Muslims formed in September 1942 by "Lt. Col" Gilani, 1 Bahawalpur Inf. at Penang.

They received training in "Lt. Col." Gilani's School in Penang. Their training consisted of physical training, which was most unpopular, history, map reading, instruction in swimming and the handling of boats, bomb making, periodical route marches, jungle warfare training and propaganda training. Discipline was not rigid, training was badly organized and there was no fixed program. The students fired a pistol and Tommy Gun course on the range and after this weapon training was discontinued. They were taught how to make and use two types of electric bombs, a tube bomb, and four types of incendiary bomb.

Upon the arrival of Subhas Chandra Bose, training was intensified and students were primed with answers to questions he might ask about the unsuitability of Pakistan. Bose was entertained with a sea-landing display. He spoke to all the students and praised their work. But soon afterwards the school was closed and students returned to Singapore. In

December 1943 a party of 20 was selected out of the original 70 as suitable for deep penetration agents and in January 1944 left for Penang where they underwent further training in the "Sandy Craft" School in sabotage, the use of disguises, swimming, the handling of boats, propaganda and wireless telegraphy.

From these 20, twelve were alternately selected and transferred to another school for special intensive training. Here decisions regarding disguises and routes in India were made and a final landing practice carried out.

The 12 were divided into two groups of six, namely, a W/T group and a propaganda, espionage, and sabotage group. The former, with cleverly disguised wireless sets, were split up into 3 groups of two each which were to operate in the U.P., Bengal and N.W.F.P., respectively while the later group was to operate single member in the Punjab, U.P., Mohmund areas and two members in the N.W.F.P. The leader of this second group was to establish his headquarters where most convenient. Members were to contact the "Forward Bloc" and collect intelligence through that organization for transmission by stages via the N.W.F.P., U.P., and Bengal, to Burma. The party embarked on a Japanese submarine on the morning of 27 February and were landed near Pasni on the Baluchistan coast on the night of 24-25 March and immediately surrendered themselves to the local authorities. They were arrived with revolvers and grenades and carried a large sum of money in currency notes and small diamonds.

Section Five. This section is in charge of the political education and military guidance of the Indian National Army.

The Indian National Army is nominally the Army of the Provisional Government of free India, and its Commender-in-Chief is Subhas Chandra Bose who is the head of the Provisional Government. But just as the Indian Independence League and the Provisional Government of Free India although nominally autonomous bodies, are actually guided and directed by the Japanese through the agency of Section Two of Hikari Kikan, so also the Indian National Army is actually controlled, not by the Provisional Government to which it is nominally responsible, but by Section Five of Kikari Kikan. The relation between Kikari Kikan and the I.N.A. is made clear from the following quotation from a captured Japanese document:

"With regard to the command and employment of the I.N.A., its autonomy will as far as posssible be respected. On points of detail it will be guided unobtrusively by the advisory officers and N.C.O.s furnished by Kikari Kikan, but the appearance of autonomy will be preserved."

The first attempts to organize an Indian National Army were made in June 1942 after the Bangkok Indian Independence Conference when it was announced, that Captain Mohan Singh had been made General Officer Commanding the Indian National Army which was about to be formed. By November 1942, it was estimated that its approximate strength in Malaya was 24,000 concentrated in and around Singapore.

A paper organisation which may have existed, and in part at least certainly did exist, on the ground, was announced as :

(a) Three guerilla brigades (Gandhi, Nehru and Azad).

(b) A field group (brigade) consisting of a signal company, an armored unit, an ordnance unit, and a supply unit.

(c) A special service group (now known as the Bahadur Group).

(d) An Intelligence Group.

(e) A cadets training group.

(f) A provost unit and detention camp.

The training was elementary and armament and equipment were on a meager scale.

In November 1942, an advance party of the I.N.A. of 400 men, 200 of the special service (or as it is now called the Bahadur Group), and 200 picked men from the Gandhi, Nehru and Azad Brigades, was dispatched to Rangoon.

In December 1942, a quarrel occurred between the leaders of the I.N.A. and the Japanese which resulted in the disbanding of the Army. A reorganization took place about March 1943, but it was not until Bose took command in July 1943 that serious attempts were to recruit, organize and train the new Indian National Army.

The Headquarters of the reorganized I.N.A. was originally Singapore but has now been transferred to Rangoon.

The majority of the Indian National Army personnel are ex-prisoners of war from Malaya.

It is probable that all I.N.A. personnel now carry pay books and identity discs. To date the only known block of serial numbers is 54307 to 54558.

In addition to passes, paybooks and identity discs, Jifs also take use of a "secret" sign in order to establish their status as genuine Jifs. The use of this sign was reported by a captured Jif whose information referred to the 4 Corps front. He stated that if a member of the I.N.A. has difficulty in convincing a Japanese of his identity he makes a "T" sign on the ground of indicated a "T" on the palm of the hand. In some cases, I.N.A. personnel have stiched the outline of the letter "T" under the lapel of the coat or on other garments. This report is confirmed and the practice shown to be general by a documents entitled "Points are recognition of I.N.A. in the front lines "issued by a Japanese regiment commander in Arakan. An extract dealing with the recognition of I.N.A. personnel returning from behind the lines runs as follows:

"On meeting with one troops, all of them must not only proclaim them identity as Hikari Kikan or I.N.A., but also expos the letter "I" sign strtched to their cash or other garments."

Special attention was given to the topography of Burma, Assam and Bengal. Bayonet training, propaganda lectures and jungle warfare training replaced guard duties and fatigues.

About the middle of August 1943, a second company was formed. The composition of these two companies was:

(a) "A" company, commanded by Captain (Jif Major) Misra, composed of 200 Singapore prisoners of war; all well trained.

(b) "B" company, commanded by Jem. (Jif Major) Ram Sarup, composed of Singapore prisoners of war, volunteers from Boundary Road Camp, a platoon of the 1/15 Punjab Regiment, many notorious Jifs, all of whom had operated conspicuously in the forward areas and been recalled to join the Bahadur Group, and a few well known Indian Officer renegades who knew the type of work carried out in the front lines.

For a short time both companies underwent intensive training consisting of lectures on the I.N.A., the art of disguise, world history, the "national struggle for independence", and map reading. The greatest stress was, however, laid on work in the front line and on propaganda, espionage and sabotage in the rear of our troops. There was instruction in the installation of loudspeakers in the forward areas, and the use of bows and arrows to shoot propagande leaflets among our forward troops.

Early in September 1943, the "B", "C", and "D" Companies of the Bahadur Group arrived in Rangoon from Singapore.

In a captured Hikari Kikan document (undated but probably issued in December 1943) the Bahadur Group is directed to "carry out operative work in frontline areas (mainly military operative work and the pacification of local Indians").

During the period August to December 1943, sixteen parties of Bahadur Group personnel, totaling 481 men, were dispatched from Rangoon to forward areas.

The intelligence group.

This group, like the Bahadur Group which it closely resembles, is composed of intelligence agents. These agents, however, unlike those of the Bahadur Group, were intended from the first for tactical operations. The function of the intelligence group is similar to that of the Battalion Intelligence Sections of the British Army. The agents of the Intelligence Group also carry out espionage in plain clothes. In the captured Hikari Kikan documont mentioned above they are ordered to collect information in frontline areas and to infiltrate, when necessary, into the enemy rear in order to collect information there.

The Intelligence Group which Bose is reported to have described as "the eyes of the Indian National Army" was formed in Singapore about March 1943, of prisoners of war from the various prison camps there. It was located in Bidadars Camp and was under the command of"Lt. Col. S. A. Malik. Malik was assisted by a Japanese officer and an N.C.O. The Japanese officer is reported to have remained with Malik and to have eventually accompanied him to the forward areas.

Training.

The training program was fairly comprehensive. Tactical training consisted of compass work, map reading, use of cover, signalling, patrolling, methods of observation and infiltration, toughoning exercises including physical training, bayonet practice, route marches, swimming and boating. "Spiritual Lectures" were also occasionally delivered by two of Bose's Military Advisors. The rest of the training was the responsibility of platoon commanders. Small arms, but no ammunition were issued during training.

Move to Rangoon.

On 22 August 1943, the whole group, total of 350 men, left Singapore for Rangoon which they reached early in September. During the journey they were joined by Companies "B", "C", and "D". The combined groups were visited by Subhas Chandra Bose who addressed them and gave Rs. 5/- to each man. In Rangoon they were located at Hingaladon where the Advance Party of the Bahadur Group was already stationed. Training was begun inmediately on more rigorous lines than in Singapore. Forced marches and "living hard" were daily features of the training. In addition, lectures were given by "Major" Ram Sarup on the topography of the Indo-Burma frontier and the location of forward British defences.

Reorganization.

In the first week of January 1944, the original organization was changed to a H.Q. section of about 110 of all ranks and six sections each consisting of 4 officers, 5 Havildars, 10 Haiks, 10 Lt/Naiks and 11 Sepoys; total 40.

At the beginning of February 1944 it was estimated there were approximately 200 members of the intelligence group in Rangoon and 150 in forward areas. It is not unlikely that the estimate of the number in forward areas was too small.

Activities.

The work of these well trained espionage-cum-intelligence personnel in Araken has included infiltrating behind our lines in civilian dress for espionage tasks, reconnoitering positions with japanese patrols, active patrolling and distributing propaganda leaflets through local inhabitants. They were all armed and morale is said to be high.

During December 1943, five parties of Intelligence Group personnel, totaling 280 men, were sent to forward areas from Rangoon.

Reinforcement group.

This group of Jifs appears to be closely similar in character to the Bahadur and Intelligence Groups. Like them, it was formed in Singapore, it arrived in Rangoon sometime during the period September-November 1943. During December 1943, five sections of 26 to 30 men each of the Reinforcement group, totaling in all 139 men, were dispatched to forward areas.

One section of 27 men went to Akyab. The other four sections had the 15 Army front (upper chindwin) as their destination. In an order to the Chief of Staff, Area Army, these sections of the Reinforcement Group were ordered to the responsible for reinforcing the I.N.A. and for taking charge of Indians including Gurkhas who were taken prisoner or who surrendered. Mixed parties of Jifs, consisting of members of the Bahadur, Intelligence and Reinforcement Groups were operating in February 1944 in the Kalowa and Le-U areas. Early in April 1944, it was estimated that some 200 members of the Reinforcement Group were present in forward areas.

The Guerilla Brigades.

There were originally only three Guerilla Brigades or Regiments–Gandhi, Nehru and Azad. These were like the Bahadur and Intelligence

Group elements in the pro-Bose I.N.A. which were carried over into the new organisation. A fourth brigade, known as the "Bose Brigade", was forced at some period subsequent to the reorganization of the Indian National Army, in March 1943.

The advance Party of the I.N.A., which moved from Singapore to Rangoon in November 1942, had two hundred picked men from the three original brigades. The Bose Brigade arrived in Burma towards the end of 1943. Five parties of the Bose Brigade totaling 447 men, arrived in Rangoon by land between 20 and 23 December 1943. Early in 1944, the remainder of the Gandhi, Nehru and Azad Brigades arrived in Rangoon from Singapore.

All brigades are reported to be organized on similar lines, each having three battalions of five companies; an estimated strength of 3000; an approximate fire power of 100 L.M.Gs., 100 T.S.M.Gs., a number of M.M.Gs., and boyes A/Tk rifles, 20 A/Tk mines, 20 demolition mines, in addition to pistols, rifles and grenades. Each brigade has a portion of Bahadur Group attached.

All ranks of Bose Brigade wear a circular cloth disc of orange and green on the left arm, the orange upper most. This distinguish badge is in addition to the circular total tri color worn on the left breast.

In unconfirmed report from a Jif states that the following green cloth identification badges are worn on the left arm by Gandhi Brigade personnel :

Brigade Headquarters and attached Bahadur Group personnel–

No. 1 Battalion – a circle

No. 2 Battalion – a triangle

No. 3 Battalion – a square

The Azad and Nehru Brigades wear similar Badges coloured yellow and light blue respectively.

Towards the end of March, the Ist Battalion of the Bose Brigades moved up to Arakan and on 1 April were in Kabaw, 9 miles south, south-east of Kaladan. At about the same the 2nd and 3rd Battalion moved up to the Chin Hills.

Sometime in February of March 19th, the four field brigades, Gandhi, Nehru, Azad and Bose Brigades, together with the Bahadur Intelligence and Reinforement Groups were organized into what is known as the No. 1 Division of the Indian National Army. The original strength of the No. 1 Division was about 15,000.

There is a Mortar Company, armed with British 2nd and 3rd mortars, attached to the H.Q. of the No. 1 Division.

The No. 2 Company of the three Motor Transport Companies of the I.N.A. arrived in Rangoon from Singapore during the last week of November 1943. Its strength was reported to be between 250 and 300 men.

No. 1 Motor Transport Company was identified at the end of the June 19th South of Ye-U.

No. 2 Motor Transport Company was working between Ye-U and Kalowa on supply carrying duties for the Japanese in June 1944.

The L. of C. Hospital arrived in Rangoon from Singapore sometimes toward the end of 1943.

The exact date of the arrival of the No. 1 A/A Coy, in Burma is not known but it was probably in October or November 1943. One party of the No. 2 Company consisting of 21 Indians and 2 Japanese, reached Rangoon from Singapore by sea on December 1943, and a second party of the No. 2 A/A Company, composed of 30 Indians and 2 Japanese arrived in Rangoon from Singapore also by sea on 8 December 1943.

On 11 December 1943, the No. 2 A/A Company, under the command of Major Matsunaga and accompanied by five Japanese, was dispatched by railway to an up country point between Pegu and Rangoon. Since December 1943, two more A/A Companies have arrived in Burma. There are, therefore, now four A/A Companies. One is located between Pegu and Rangoon, another is in Moulmein and two are in Mingaladon.

The Rani of Jhansi Regiment.

According to radio news broadcasts from Japanese controlled station elements of this regiment are now present in forward areas in Burma. The regiment has its headquarters in Singapore where presumably the main body of the regiment is still located. It is commanded by a "Captain" S. Lakshmi who is described as having been formerly a doctor in a Singapore hospital, with a "Lieutenant." Sathyavarthy Thevar as second in command.

The language of the broadcast seems definitely intended to convey the impression that the members of this regiment will play an active military, even combatant, role which, however, seems proposterous.

No estimate of the size of the regiment nor of the members now in Burma is available. It is probably that the number in Burma is small and it seems unlikely that the Rani of Jhansi Regiment will have any save propaganda value.

Special Task Unit.

This unit is commanded by "Captain" Khurana (2nd Lt. A/8 Punjab Regiment). It was located in Bidadari Camp, Singapore, in December 1943 when its strength was about 180 mostly exprisoners of war. They are said to be undergoing parachute and Secret Service training. It was reported in June to be undergoing training in Sumatra.

Sometime between the beginning of September and the end of November 1943 a group of 223 Engineers arrived in Rangoon from Singapore. This group was dispatched by lorries on 30 November 1943 to the 15 Army.

A Bodyguard Battalion which is believed to be Bose's personal unit has now arrived in Burma. Half of this Battalion went from Rangoon to Mandlay about the end of April 1944. One company of it was allotted to "Colonel" Chatterji on his appointment as "Governor of the Liberated Areas."

The Battalion organization is :

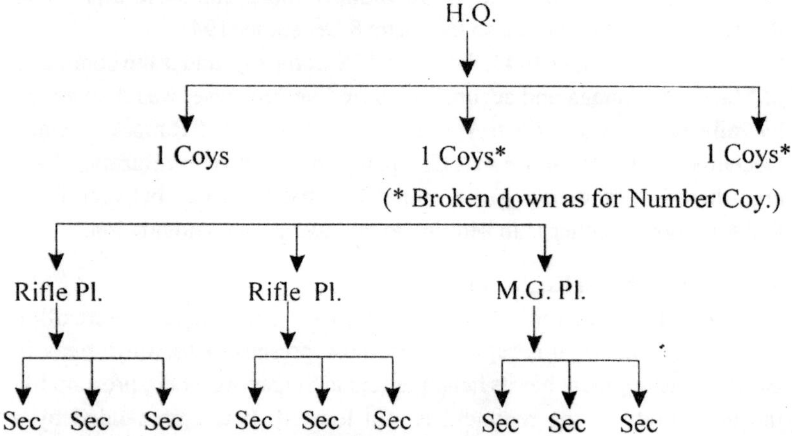

No. 1 Engineering Company was identified at morch during the second week of July, but at the end of the month it retired to Mandalay for rest and its duties were taken over by the No. 2 Engineering Company.

In December 1943, the No. 2 Division of the I.N.A. was billeted in Bidadari Camp, Singapore. The infantry Regiment of this Division was reported en route for Burma in May 1944. It is probably that all or nearly all the No. 2 Division is now in Burma.

The organization of the No. 2 Division of the I.N.A. is given in Appendix "A".[3]

The No. 3 Division is reported to consist of the 6th, 7th and 8th Guerilla Regiments.

---

3. Not Printed.

I.N.A. Training Schools

In 1943, "Lt. Col" Ehran Qadir set up Youth League Centres in Malaya for the military training of Indian Civilion youths. Two types of schools existed, one for elementary and the other advanced training, the former being styled Bharat Youth Training Centre, the latter Azad Schools, the recruits being found by the I.I.L.

The minimum age for recruitment into the Youth Training Centre is 17, and the syllabus comprises preliminary military training, discipline, spiritual and propaganda lectures. At first the staff consisted of seconded I.N.A., N.C.Os, but later was formed from trained civilians. On completion of training about 10 per cent of recruits go to the Azad Schools for advanced training, whereas the remainder go to the Azad Schools for advanced training, whereas the remainder go to the Reinforcement Group rear organization in Singapore. The selected 10 per cent of recruits sent on the Azad Schools are given further instruction in military matters, arms training and propaganda. These schools are staffed by I.N.A., N.C.Os., and the object is to produce instructions send back to the training centres. Very promising recruit from these schools may be selected for further at the O.T.S.

The training centres so far located are at Kuala Lumpur, Seletar, Seremban and Penang, and Azad Schools are not Penang and Singapore.

A similiar recruit training battalion is reported to have been opened in Rangoon for Indian civilians living in Burma. It was accommodated in what is known as Gaoshala Buildings in the neighbourhood of the Kanbe S.Y.N.T.I. It was, however, quite distinct from the S.Y.N.T.I. and concerned itself solely with the military training of recruits with a view to their eventual absorption into the I.N.A. Reinforcement group. They may also have been intended to provide first reinforcement for the I.N.A. Guerilla Regiments which were to operate in Burma this year. It is not so far clear as to whether this school and primarily organised by the I.I.L. or the I.N.A., but one Jif source who was an instructor states that it was essentially on I.N.A. organization and under district control of and responsible to "Col." Alagappan.

The first course began in October 1943 and the scheduled to last for four months. There were 500 recruits in the course, of whom three-quarters were Madrassis. They were organized into three companies which of three platoons, each of approximately 50 men. The school had an allotment of 150 rifles and bayonets, distributed on the scale of 50 per company. During training, one platoon of each company would use the rifles whilst the remainder were receiving theoretical instructions. The only weapon in which the recruits were trained were the rifle, LMG and TSMG. There was no issue of uniform and the recruits paraded in an assortment of multicolored bazaar clothing. In addition to military training recruits were given occasional propaganda lectures.

This instructors were mainly drawn from the Bahadur and the Reinforcement Groups and when the main body of these groups arrived in Burma, the instructors were withdrawn and returned to their units in order to complete their mobilization.

The Manipur Offensive.

At the beginning of the Manipur offensive in March 1944, Jif forces consisted only of composite parties of Bahadur, Intelligence and Reinforcement Groups in the Chin Hills (Kalewa), Le-U and Homal sectors under Jif sector leaders. "Lt. Col." Malik was leader in the Chin Hills sector. "Major" Maghar Singh was a leader of the Le-U group and "Captain" Ajmer Singh was in command of the Homalin forces. There were, in addition to these organized parties, several miscellaneous bodies of agents, but the part played by them was negligible. From March to June, "Lt. Col. " Malik's parties operating south of Bishenpur. Major Maghar Singh's three parties were indentified at Imphal, Palel and Kanglatongbi while "Captain" Ajmer Singh's parties were in the Kohima area.

All these groups carried out the usual Jif intelligence tests, i.e., collection of information and supplies, reconnoitering. infiltration routes to India, pacification of local inhabitants, dissemination of verbal and written propaganda, handling of Indian prisoners of war, with a view to enlisting them in the I.N.A...., decoys, suborning British Indian troops and doing fatigue duties for the Japanese. All groups were soon very much depleted and the existence of two of the groups, "Major" Maghar Singh and "Captain" Ajmer Singh surrendered in June.

In March the No. 2 and 3 Battalions of the Bose Brigade (No. 1 Guerilla Regiment) arrived in the Chin Hills. The No. 3 Batallion took over garrison duties from the Japanese in the Falan Haka area. One company was located at Falan and another at Raka, while the three remaining companies were on the line of communication east of Falan. The No. 2 Battalion of the Bose Brigade was reported to be in Tiddin area.

In April, the No. 2 Guerilla Regiment (Gandhi Brigade) arrived in the area south of Palel. This was the first Guerilla Regiment to come into action. Early in May it made an abortive attack against the Palel airfield as a result of which it suffered very heavy casualties. Notwithstanding this early set back and subsequent desertions, the Regiment continued active patrolling and skirmishing throughout May and June.The raids, however, decreased in the first half of July, probably due to the reduced strength of the Regiment which was by this time less than half the original establishment, sickness, desertions and battle casualties having taken heavy toll.

During May, the No. 3 Guerilla Regiment (Azad Brigade) arrived in the area north of the Palel Tamu Road. May and June were comparatively quiet months for the No. 3 Gueriella Regiment (Azad Brigade) though desertion to the British were daily occurrences. The Regiment became more active during the first half of duly, carrying out sporadic raids at a cost of many casualties.

Towards the end of May the No. 2 and No. 3 Battalion of the Bose Brigade (No. 1 Guerilla Regiment), with the exception of three companies which were left in the Chin Hills, one of them probably at Haka. moved from the Chin Hills to the Ukhrul Area. Events in Kohima prevented the commitment of the Regiment and the force was hastily within southwards. By the middle of July it was out of Manipur.

The 2nd and 3rd Guerilla Regiments and the 2nd and 3rd Battalion of the Guerilla Regiment were nominally under the command of the Headquarters of No. 1 Division which, by the end of May had opened up at Tamu and shortly thereafter moved forward on the Palel Tamu road.

The Nehru Brigade (4th Guerilla Regiment) was reported moving west from Mandalay in late April. A small advance, of this regiment was operating 14 miles in north–east of Tiddin early in March, but the main body of the Nehru Brigade never arrived in Manipur and little is known concerning it.

Coincident with the retreat of the Guerilla forces in the Ukhrul area, early in July, what was left of "Captain"Ajmer Singh's forces withdrew from the Kohima areas to Ukhrul. From Ukhrul they continued to retreat but whether towards Hamilin or Tamu is uncertain. Earlier reports indicated Hamalin, but a later report states they were destined for Tamu.

The Jif forces in "Lt. Col." Malik's section south of Bishonpur continued active during the early part of July, but on the 12th of that month Malik was reported to have left for Rangoon.

In the latter half of July, No. 2 and No. 3 Guerilla Regiments (Gandhi and Azad Brigades) which had respectively been south and north of the Palel Tamu Road began withdrawing. No. 2 (Gandhi) Regiment by this time was reduced to three companies. Both regiments were reported to have left for the Kalema area. No. 1 Division Headquarters was also withdrawn back from Tamu probably to Kalewa or Mandalay by the end of July.

By the end of July, most of the I.N.A. were back in Burma and reported falling back on Kalewa.

Strength of I.N.A.

At the beginning of the Manipur offensive in March 1944, the total strength of the I.N.A. in Burma was approximately 13,000. Of these, about 9,000 were Guerilla troops divided among the four guerilla regiments of No. 1 Division., the combined Bahadur, Intelligence and Reinforcement Groups personnel amounted to about 1550, distributed as follows:

Bahadur Group	:	1,000
Intelligence Group	:	350
Reinforcement Group	:	200

The remaining 2,450 I.N.A. personnel were distributed among various small units such as the Bodyguard Battalion and the Engineering, Motor Transport and Artillery Companies.

During the Manipur campaign the No. 2 Guerilla Regiment (Gandhi Brigade) suffered heavy casualties. Its original strength was about 1,900 but by the middle of June it was only 1,700 strong. Up to the 8th of July, its losses amounted to 607 (132 surrendered or captured, 278 killed and 197 wounded). It was reported that on 21 July there were only 650 of the Gandhi Brigade left in Manipur as in addition to these killed and captured there were reported to be more than a thousand sick and wounded in the Moreh Hospital.

The No. 2 Guerilla Regiment's losses were considerably smaller. Its total casualties, up to 8 July are estimated to be about 100 (captured or surrendered 44, killed 39, wounded 17).

Total Casualities

The Bahadur, Intelligence and Reinforcement Groups have also suffered fairly heavy casualties. Exact figures are not available but it seems likely that the number of their personnel does not now exceed 1,000.

Apart, therefore, from reinforcements brought in from Malaya, the I.N.A. forces in Burma number about 11,000.

According to a former I.N.A. officer the No. 2 Bahadur Group and the Infantry Regiment of No. 2 Division was en route to Burma in April or May 1944. They are therefore, probably new in Burma. Indeed, it is likely that the whole of No. 2 Division has reached Burma by this time. If this is the case, then there are about 19,000 I.N.A. troops now in Burma.

Upon the assumption that No. 2 Division started moving forward from Malaya to Burma in September 1944 when its training was scheduled to be complete there will be some 28,000 of the I.N.A. in Burma by the end of 1944, of whom about 21,000 will be guerilla or equivalent troops.

The Future of the I.N.A.

What use, if any, the Japanese will make of the I.N.A. troops now, or yet to arrive, in Burma is uncertain. One Hikari Kikan sources is reported to have said that the I.N.A. would be withdrawn and not used again. Another report has it that all I.N.A. personnel were to be recalled to Rangoon and the senior officers sent to Tokyo. On the other hand, reports believed to be reliable state that reinforcements were arriving in Burma from Malaya.

The Japanese are doubtless disappointed in the I.N.A. Nevertheless, it appears unlikely that they will make no use of the nineteen to twenty-eight thousand well trained Indian troops. Should the Japanese launch a new offensive in Burma, the I.N.A. will probably be called upon to play its part and should no new offensive be undertaken, they will doubtless be utilized in holding and delaying activities.

Outposts of Hikari Kikan.

The five branch agencies of Hikari Kikan were located at (1) Akyab, (2) Kalewa, (3) Homalin, (4) Hyitkyina and (5) Mayayo.

Akyab Branch.

The Akyab Branch of Hikari Kikan was in charge of Jif activities in Arakan. Captain Hatteri who was head of this branch was in command of several officers and civilians.

Early in 1943, six officers, seven N. C. O.s, four senior civilians, five junior civilians and two subordinate employee were dispatched from Hikari Kikan Headquarters in Rangoon to Akyab and Mayayo. After receiving its share of these reinforcements, the Akyab Agency Outpost was reorganized to form an Akyab Operative Group. The Branch was organised into three sections as follows:

(1) Military Affairs and the Prevention of Espionage

(2) Intelligence

(3) Special Military Affairs

The object of this organisation was stated to be to develop the various activities of the branch including the guidance of the Indian National Army and the Indian Independence League.

The Arakan Front

At the end of August 1943, 70 civilian Jifs, students of the Kanbe Institute were dispatched from Rangoon to Arakan. The first elements of the Bahadur Group moved up to Arakan in September 1943 and a further contingent in October 1943. "Major" Mishra, who commanded the company of the Bahadur Group in Rangoon, left on 14 October with a detachment of 33 men and established his headquarters at Buthidaung. The duties of the Bahadur group personnel were mainly military espionage in forward areas.

Towards the end of 1943, there was indication of an intensification of the "I" offensive in Arakan.

The number of Jifs in Arakan in December 1943 was estimated to be not less than 300. The bulk of them were concentrated in camps at Buthidaung and neighbouring villages. There were lesser concentrations in Mangdaw and the coastal area opposite Teknaf where Jifs were responsible for the organization and supervision of local volunteers for coast watching at the mouth of the Haf River. The volunteer patrols were allotted definite areas. Their tasks were to prevent British agents from crossing the Haf River, and to watch the movement of British patrols. The patrolmen carried lathis and the Jif patrol leaders Versy pistols.

The 300 or more Jifs in Arakan at the end of 1943 were partly civilians trained in the Rangoon Swaraj Training Schools, Kanbe, and other training schools and partly military non-combatant Jifs of the Bahadur Group. The exact proportion of each is not known, but it is likely that the two groups were roughly equal. Forward of Akyab Island firm identification indicated 44 military personnel and 54 civilians.

Although Jif positions altered from time to time in conformity with the tactical situation and Japanese troop movements, nevertheless certain parts of Arakan were more or less permanently manned. Thus, up to the time of his reported relief, Jagat Singh,who was controller of Jif in Arakan, had his headquarters either in Buthidaung or just south of it in Kanbyin. Towards the end of October 1943 he was reported to have moved to Nalpannya. Although the Japanese officer supervising the Jif activities in forward Arakan was reported to have had his headquarters in Maungdaw, it is nevertheless thought that in December 1943 the forward group headquarters still remained at Buthidaung, with subordinate headquarters at Maugandar (HQ controlling the coasts watching on the Naf) Kyankataw and/or Arakan. There were also other Jif posts chiefly around Buthidaung and Maungdaw.

Towards the end of 1943, Jagat Singh, who had previously been in command of the Jifs in the Arakan, was relieved, at least temporarily, by "Major" Mehr Dass.

Prior to the arrival of a contingent of the Guerilla Brigade on 10 February 1944, all the Jifs in Arakan were divisible into three categories.

(a) Commanders

(b) Tactical intelligence agents

(c) Strategical intelligence agents.

Commanders.

Previous to the relief of Jagat Singh by "Major" Mehr Dass, towards the end of 1943, commanders appear to have been selected by Jagat Singh himself or his immediate assistants, but therefore it would appear that Hikari Kikan began to tighten its control. The commanders were allotted to Jif posts, working on their own or under orders of the Japanese. Their functions were generally:

1. Mediating between the Japanese and the local population. Mediating included beating and blacklisting persons unsympathetic to the Japanese.

2. Helping the Japanese to administer Arakan.

3. Disarming the locals as well as coercing them into carrying out intellingence tasks for the Japanese.

These Jif commanders moved about freely and had considerable authority.

Tactical Agents.

These were hard core Jifs whose work took two forms:

1. Quasi-Military, e.g., those who with local volunteers were responsible for patrolling the left band of the Naf.

2. Purely intelligence, i.e., propaganda activities directed against our frontline troops, espionage in forward areas, and the training of local volunteers to become intelligence agents, chiefly for espionage work.

The making of propaganda broadcasts, tapping in all telephone conversations, distribution of propaganda leaflets, and oral approach to our troops, are all examples of the type of work that was carried out by these Jifs.

Strategical Agents.

These agents were, in a sense, merely guests of the Jif commanders in the forward areas and had already received their orders prior to leaving for the forward areas. They received their training and orders before leaving their training school. Having reached the forward Jif posts, arrangements, were or at least were supposed to be, made for them to proceed on their ways: arms, money, route instructions, and in some cases guides were given them.

In addition to the Jifs themselves, a considerable use was made of local inhabitants in "I" operations in Arakan. The Japanese placed considerable reliance on these agents who usually were much better fitted for frontline espionage tasks and as guides to infiltration parties than are Jifs themselves.

Until towards the end of 1943, the Jifs in Arakan were not organised in any detail by Hikari Kikan and matters were left very much to the discretion of local leaders. At about that time, however, Hikari Kikan tightened its control and attempted to make the organization more efficient. The paybooks and safe-conduct passes issued to Jifs, the equipment issued to tactical agents, e.g., tapping in equipment, and the system of coast watching, introduced at this time, are indications of the general attempt to step up efficiency which coincided with the improvement of the training schools.

On 10 February 1944, "Major" Misra and Captain Hattori were joined by the No. 3 Section of the Intelligence Group, consisting of 70 men and 110 men of the Field Force. Personnel of both forces were lightly armed. On 11 February this composite force, together with a detachment of the "A" Company of the Bahadur Group and about 50 Japanese, moved south-east of Taung Bazaar and dug in. From there mixed patrols of Japanese and I.N.A. were sent out.

The work of the Intelligence Group personnel in Arakan included infiltrating behind our lines in civilian dress for espionage work, reconnoitering positions with Japanese patrols, active patrolling and distributing propaganda leaflets through local inhabitants.

Around the middle of February 1944, it was estimated that the total number of Jifs in Arakan was still about the same as it had been in December 1943, i.e., between three and four hundred. The number in forward areas was thought to have increased to about 150, most of whom were military Jifs. These estimates were probably too low.

Jif strengths forward of Akyab in the latter half of February were supposed to be approximately:

Bahadur Group	70
Intelligence Group	70
Field Force	110
Kanbe S.T.K. students	50
Others	110

But as this enumeration omits the five to six hundred Indian soldiers reported at Poikthayat Village and Taung Bazaar, it is as best correct only with respect to the groups mentioned and must not be taken to be a complete estimate of Jif strength in Arakan at the end of February 1944.

Whereas in December 1943 it was reported that Jif forward operators were unarmed except in a few cases with rifles, and in the case of leaders with revolvers, in February 1944 it was reported that military Jifs who then constituted the bulk of the forward operations were armed with rifles, pistols and grenades on the same scale as the Japanese soldiers. While it is probable that even in December there were Jifs better armed than they were supposed to be, it should nevertheless seem that Jif armament was increased during that period. This is an harmony with the general tendency during that period towards a stricter and more military organisation. Somewhat later, probably in February or March 1944, the organisation of the military Jife was still further tightened up by the formation of the No. I Division of the Indian National Army.

On 16 December 1943, the "A" Battalion consisting of 67 men of the Intelligence Group, and 27 men of the Reinforcement Group were dispatched from Rangoon to Akyab.

Operations in the Taung Bazaar area around the middle of February provided the first known instance of Jifs being used in a fighting role. A captured document shows that a general warning was issued to all Jifs in the area to concentrate east of the Mayu Range for an important operation. In the early stages of this operation, part of the enemy's infiltration is reported to have been covered by Jifs. They also attempted to cause confusion among our troops by shouting in English and Urdu. They carried out espionage tasks and acted as messengers. About 30 Jifs were also included in a raiding party which was active in arranging communication on the road from Bawli Bazaar to Maungdaw after 6 February.

At the end of February 1944, a captured Jif stated that there were about 110 agents of the Bahadur Group alone operating on the Arakan frontline.

Quick Return Tactics.

A number of I.O.R.'s captured after February 4, 1944 were set back to our areas Japanese after a week or ten days, with instructions to contact Indian and spread discontent and arouse enthusiasm for and interest in the I.N.A. and its cause. Pamphlets were also used at this time for the same end.

During the March operations in Arakan four groups of Jifs were active. Two of these were composed entirely of ex-prisoners of war. The tactics employed by these groups were:

(a) "Semi-guerilla."

(b) Intelligence.

In their role as semi-guerillas, Jifs, always in concert with Japanese troops, raided camps, interrupted telephone communications, demolished one or two bridges, and in one operation acted as a screen for an outflanking movement. During raids they shouted to our troops with the object of causing confusion among them.

Their intelligence work consisted of reconnoitering positions, preparation of sketches, collection of information about our troops, and distribution of propaganda leaflets in forward zones and behind our lines.

Their miscellancous duties included interrogation of and guarding Indian prisoners of war and attempts to suborn them and acting as porters for Japanese troops. Some were I.N.A. uniform, others adopted local dress.

Some time prior to the middle of March the remainder of the "A" and "E" Companies of the Bahadur Group, under the command of "Ram Sarup, who had been in command of the "E" Company in Rangoon, moved up from Rangoon into Arakan.

Towards the end of March the No. 1 Battalion of the Bose Brigagde arrived in the Kaladan area. On its arrival in this area it is reported to have had an ambitious plan for independent action against the rear of our troops east of Kaladan. On 31 March and 1 April, I.N.A. forces of platoon and company strength, acting independently for the first time, clashed with our troops. On 31 March one platoon attacked our position 6 milessouth-south-east of Kaladan. On 1 April our troops engaged a company of Jifs with some Japanese and inflicted several casualties in hand to hand fighting. It was reported by a captured Jif Havildar that the No. 1 Battalion of the Bose Bridage was located in the Khabaw (9 miles south-south east of Kaladan) area. After these encounters the plan for independent action appears to have been abandoned as no further attempts at independent action were made.

The increase in Jif activities expected in the Kaladan area after the arrival of the No. 1 Battalion of the Bose Brigade at the end of March did not materialize and a portion of the battalion moved northwards with the Japanese troops. On 26 April our patrols estimated a company of the I.N.A. in the area of Amte, 16 miles north-north-west of Paletwa, and on 29 April our troops engaged an estimated force of one company of I.N.A. and two companies of Japanese.

Kalewa Branch.

The Kalewa outpost of Hikari Kikan was established in August 1942. This outpost was used as a base for the collection of information and special operative work. It was in particular charged with making efforts to undermine the loyalty and morale of British Indian troops in forward areas. In February 1943, Lt. Yamada took charge and the personnel of the outpost was increased by the addition of seven men. It was also allotted twelve non from the 33rd Division. Lt. Yamada's chief assistant was a civilians named Sudo, but he also had several other assistants, both military and civilian.

Toward the end of August, or early in September 1943, a party of the Bahadur Group made up of personnel from "A" and "E" Companies was dispatched from Rangoon to Kalewa. This party was later reinforced by seven prisoners of war from the Wingate expedition and six old renegade prisoners of war. Eventually sixteen were selected for forward work and subdivided into four groups each containing (a) one hardened renegade (b) one Bahadur Group man, (v) one Wingate prisoner of war, and (d) one renegade of the 1/15 Punjab Regiment. Those groups moved first to Hake, and then the Tauk to report on troop dispositions, distribute leaflets, and to try to suborn Indian troops. Each party was given Rs. 1000 and each man had a rifle, 30 rounds of ammunition, and three grenades. In the middle of October 1943 this group of sixteen Jifts stated from Kindat for Falam. They arrived near Falam at the end of October and a party of three including one Gurkha from Wingate's expedition and one renegade from 1/15 Punjab Regiment were given Rs. 1,000 and instructed :—

(a) To distribute Jif propaganda pamphlets in English, Roman Urdu Gurkhali on routes used by British troops.

(b) To contact and suborn Indian troops.

(c) To collect information concerning British dispositions.

(d) To report back to intelligence headquarters at or near Falam.

The Kalewa branch received further reinforcements in December 1943 when 33 men from the "A" and "E" companies of the Bahadur Group and for composite parties of Jifs from the Bahadur, Intelligence and Reinforcement groups were sent forward from Rangoon to northern fronts. The total strength of the four composite groups amounted to 600 men.

Of the 33 Bahadur personnel, 7 were designated to Kalewa and 10 to Kaka. Just how many of the 600 men of the composite parties were sent to Kalewa is not definitely known, but it is safe to assume that at least one-fourth went to the Kalewa region.

Jifs in the Kalewa area (including the Chin Hills) fell into the sanic three categories as these in Arakan, namely, (1) leaders, (2) tactical operative for local use and (3) strategically operative for deep penetration. Jif leaders in this area seem not to have exercised the same authority as their counterparts in Arakan. Here the Japanese generally handled the agents themselves. The lesser leaders, i.e., the hardened ex-prisoner of war renegades were directly under the control of the Japanese and their activities consisted cheifly of controlling in turn the rank and file tactical agents and carrying out frontline contact work themselves. There is no evidence that they were used to mediate between the Japanese and the local civil population as their counterparts did in Arakan.

Among the Jif leaders of this area were "Lt. Col." Malik, "Major" Haghar Singh, Baba Amar Singh, Schail Khan and Wazir Mohd. Khan. The three latter arrived with their own parties from Hong Kong. In the latter part of 1943 Jif activities increased, an increase which coincided with the arrival of new trainees from the Rangoon Kanbe Training Institute. These new Jifs assisted in such tasks as frontline espionage, subversion of forward troops, and the distribution of propaganda literature. In December 1943 W/T operators were very active in attempting to intrude on British W/T links with the primary object of extracting information regarding British order of battle.

Towards the end of December 1943, armed Jifs began occasionally to be encountered by British patrols indicating that the tendency of the Japanese to arm their intelligence agents had increased. Deep penetration agents were generally issued with arms before they left India.

At the end of December there had been some strategical operators in forward areas for a considerable time but up to that time they had confined their efforts to assisting tactical agents in their work except for some attempts to infiltrate through the Falam area.

As in Arakan the Japanese began, toward the end of 1943, to make increasing use of local inhabitants as guides for contact parties, and also for further espionage tasks, but these local agents were seldom armed, or trained for special intelligence work. In December 1943 Yamada was apparently concentrating on maintaining contacts with the local inhabitants of Manipur.

In February 1944, there was a composite force of Bahadur, intelligence and Reinforcement Group personnel, under the command of "Lt. Col." Malik, east of the Chindwin, near Kalewa. This forces was divided into five aprties, one of which was under the immediate command of "Lt. Col" Malik. Three of thee, including Malik's own party, worked in the Tiddin and Tonzang areads and later moved north to the Bishenpur area where they were seen about the middle of April in a very depleted condition. Despite their losses they were active during the early part of July but on 12 July, Malik was reported to have left the Rangoon. A fourth party was sent to the Fort White area and a fifth operated at first in the Minthame area and later on the Tanu Road, in concert with a party from Mawlaik.

The work of these parties consisted in the collection of information about British dispositions in the front line, and in the two cases, in Silchar and Mymensingh, sabotage behind the British lines, interrogation and attempts to suborn Indian prisoners of war, spreading of propaganda literature in forward areas and among the local population and the usual fatigues for Japanese troops. Malik himself was a prominent propagandist among Indian prisoners of war in the Tonzang area. During a night attack of 16-17 March on Tiddin Road some confusion was caused by Jifs shouting contradictory orders.

By February, Major Maghar Singh had collected, at Le-U, a force similar to Malik's and about the 10th of March it crossed the Chindwin at Paungbyin and was distributed in the Tamu ara and north of it. Members also operated at Ukhrul, and Maghar Singh and a Jif party reached MS 105 on the road Imphal-Kohima with about 500 Japanese on 4 April. On 7 April they were at work near Kanglatongbi. Some of this party looted a British ordnance dump and were later seen wearing the new-style battle dress which gave some of them access to British positions without suspicion.

The tasks of the Le-U Group were generally the same as Malik's Chin Hills Group. A moire definite indication of the role of this group is revealed by a captured document according to which one of Maghar Singh's parties was to cooperate with a raiding group and was responsible for reconnsitering the route in addition to enlisting guides.

Homalin Branch

The Homalin Branch of Hikari Kikan was the last of the five outpost to be established. The need for an agency in this locality was not felt by the Japanese until June 1943 when it was considered that an intelligence base was necessary. On 8 June 1943, Lt. Yomamara and two men were sent to Homalin where they established a Hikari Kikan Outpost.

The Officer commanding this Outpost in December 1943, was Lt. Kanako who was assisted by a staff of two non-commissioned officers and two civilians.

The Jif forces in the Homalin sector were under the command of "Captain" Ajmar Singh, an ex-prisoner of war who, prior to his capture by the Japanese, was a 2nd Lt. of the 6/1 Punjab Regiment. Ajmar Singh arrived in Rangoon with the Advance Party of the I.N.A. in 1942. He left Rangoon in December 1943 in charge of a force consisting of Bahadur, Intelligence and Reinforcement Group personnel. Upon reaching Homalin he took over command of all Jifs in that sector.

"Captain" Ajmar Sing's group was divided into three parties. One party crossed the Chindwin north of Homalin on 15 March 1944 and was attached to a Japanese battalion during its march to the Kohima area via Layshi and Jessami. On 15 April 1944, this party withdraw from its position north of Kohima and closed up with party No. 3 under Ajmar Singh cast of Kohima.

The second party reached the Chindwin south of Homalin where six numbers were attached to a Japanese unit proceeding to Sangshak while the rest were distributed over the Ukhral area. Here a detachment was formed and left for the road Map-Kohmima. Later four numbers were sent on an espionage and propaganda task to the road Dinapur-Imphal. The remainder of the party followed and were last identified 500 yards cast of Aradure, south-cost of Kohima.

The third party under Ajmar Singh at Chodima was reported cast of Kohima together with party No. 1 on 6 June 1944, "Caption" Ajmer Singh surrendered to British troops south-cast of Kohima.

Personnel from the Homalin group were present in operations around Ukhrul and Sangabak where they shouted to British troops to lay down their arms and surrender. At Sangshak a negaphone was used. These efforts had no success. They later attempted to suborn Indian prisoners of war captured in those areas. A Jif reported that in Ukhrul area a few armed Jifs were attached to every Japanese formation. The task entrusted to one party operating near Kohima was to report the British withdrawal from Kohima by lighting a fire by night or by haisting on I.N.A. flag by day.

In December 1943, the Homalin Branch of Hikari Kikan was conducting its activities in cooperation with Nishi Kikan whose branch in that area was at that time staffed by five Japanese.

Nishi Kikan—Nishi Kikan is a frontier intelligence organization in Burma working through the indigamous peoples of the Chin Hills area. The work of Nishi Kikan is similar to that of Hikari Kikan, but its contact are different.

Conclusion

Hikari Kiran "I" offensive in India has, judged in terms of its ultimate objective , so far proved a failure. India remains securely in Allied hands, and parts of Burma formerly held by the Japanese have been recaptured by Allied forces. But if the "I" offensive has failed, the blame cannot be laid wholly upon Hikari Kikan. The "I" offensive is but a part of the whole offensive against India, The Japanese made the fatal mistake of supposing that as soon as India was invaded, there would be a nationalist revolution which would completely neutralize British and American military strength in India, thereby leaving the field open for Subhas Chandra Bose's puppet forces. The Japanese did not count on having to fight for India. Rather they expected, once the borders were well crossed, to be received with open arms by the Indian masses, Bose assured them that this would happen and the Japanese predisposed thereto by the recollection of their successes in French Indo-China, Thailand and Burma believed him. The Japanese invasion of Manipur did not, however, produce the expected revolution. The Japanese met serious opposition which they had not expected and had to fight a campaign for which they were not prepared. In consequence they were defeated.

Hikari Kikan's failure to realize the falsity of Bose's claims makes them in a measure responsible for the failure of the offensive against India, but this responsibility they share with the whole Japanese command for it is clear that it was not Hikari Kikan alone that was taken in by Bose's claims.

It will be fairer to Hikari Kikan to judge it by its measure of success in the performance of its own special tasks.

Hikari Kikan's deep penetration operations have, so far as our evidence goes, been completely unsuccessful; but in operational contact work its agents have done better. Jif guerillas have achieved some success in a nuisence role, and espionage in formal areas has been moderately successful as is evidenced, by the Japenese knowledge of road and rail conditions and Allied battle order. Propaganda in the field has mostly been inept and has achieved little. The effects of newspapers and radio broadcasts are hard to estimate, but there is no doubt that Japanese controlled broadcasts to India have had considerable effect on Indian morale. The task of guiding the I.N.A. has not been without its difficulties, but on the whole Hikari Kikan seems to have done fairly well. It is noteworthy that comparatively few Jifs have deserted to the British.

Despite the unfavourable conditions of the Japanese in Burma a Japanese counter offensive may be confidently expected unless some large scale Allied operations forestall it. It is doubtful if the Japanese any longer entertain hopes of conquering India, but it seems probable that they will make as large use as possibile of Indian and Burmese puppet forces in an effort to recoup their losses in Burma and to maintain their hold on that country.

Appendix–II

Marching to Delhi a Poem by Yone Noguchi a Japanese Poet; brings out the Essence of S.C. Bose's Slogan "Chalo Delhi" Meant for the Indian National Army[1]

MARCHING TO DELHI

By Yone Noguchi

(Translated by himself from Japanese)

I

"Delhi, Delhi, to Delhi!"
The war-cry replies to a storm of cannon-balls,
And praises the might of powder and smoke.
Leap over the terror that trenches command,
And entrust your bones to a hill of the mother-land!
In a blazing sand your palm grasps,
You will find all the rewards that Death bestows.
And the hunger you suffered from hundreds of years
Can's be filled till an Independence feast is spread.

II

"Delhi, Delhi, to Delhi!"
The fighting array beats its wings;
The bugles begin to cry.
The war wagons grown wild;
The cannons send up their sacrifice fire,
Oh, the heroes, the crusaders to win liberty, they go to the front!
They know a night feast of victory is waiting behind,

---

1. The above poem was translated from the japanese by the author and was published in *Greater Asia*, Dated 2.12.1943. Bose had earlier given the clarion call of "Chalo Delhi" to the Indian National Army. Yone Noguchi, a Japanese poet, was very much interested in Indian Independence. A friend of Rabindra Nath Tagore, but they parted company when Japan marched into China. Tagore did not like the Japanese aggressive policy in China

And their hunger will be filled at last;
They know their own history has now to begin.

III

"Delhi, Delhi, to Delhi!"
Krishna bids them to burn in love of the mother-land,
Putting a holy fire on their own souls.
The glory of many thousand years comes to life again,
And will create over the Ganges a rainbow-bridge.
Lo, the snowy citadel of Himalayan peaks
Drives back law-breakers, forbids them not to invade again
The depthless waters of the Bengal gulf.
Gets graves ready and waits for their coming.

IV

"Delhi, Delhi, to Delhi!"
The war-cry rings through India's whole land;
People's blood boils and seethes.
Making an arched squall of anger,
That will never fail to ruin the enemy's camp.
Lo, the anti-British war-men go in majestic line,
The crusaders to take liberty by force are they!
Ah, what enemy can defy Heaven's will ?

Appendix–III

British Intelligence Report on Spy Schools set up by I.I.L. for Training Civilians in South-East Asia[1]

1. AZAD SCHOOLS AND YOUTH'S LEAGUE TRAINING CENTRE— Early in 1943 Capt. (Lt. Col) Ehshan Qadir, a Military member of the Indian Provisional Government and Director of the Training Centre in East Aisa, set up the following different kinds of I.N.A. Training institutions for training civilians for the I.N.A.

   (a) Bharat Youth's Training Centres—Meant for elementary military training of civilian recruits. Age limit for recruitment in these centres was 17, and duration of course was 3 months. The recruits were given preliminary military training, taught discipline and given spiritual and propaganda lectures. At the termination of the course 10% of the recruits were selected and sent for advance training in Azad Schools while the remainder were absorbed into the I.N.A. through the reinforcement group. These centres were originally staffed by I.N.A. instructors who were later replaced by trained civilians. Outstanding studens may be selected to be trained as Officers in the O.T.S.'s. Those training centres were opened at Kuala Lumpur, Seletar, Seregam and Penang.

   (b) AZAD Schools— These schools were meant for further training of recruits selected from the above training centres in order to turn them into instructors. Instructions included weapon training etc., while propaganda schools were opened at Penang and Singapore.

   (c) The following details about Kuala Lumpar Bharat Youth's Training Centre are available, and it is believed that they apply to the other centres as well—

1. F. No. 601/7378/H.S.

(i) Recruitment—As a result of propaganda carried out by the I.I.L. through notices in the papers and visits of recruiting parties, civilians in E.O.T. volunteered and were recruited. All classes of Indians in occupied torritory were accepted.

(ii) Rations—Rations were good and were supplied by local rich members of the I.I.L. in turn as a part of their war effort.

(iii) Dress—Recruits were issued with khaki shirts and shorts, boots, puttoos, socks, hosetops, and used to wear I.N.A. cap and breast badges.

(iv) Pay—Recruits were paid at the rate of $8, while Havs, Nks and L/Nks get $27, 16 and 14 respectively.

(v) Training—For the first two months, training consisted of P.T. and feet drill. In the last month rifle drill was introduced. No one ever fired a rifle during training and weapon training consisted of naming the various parts of the rifle. No other arms were taught, over theoritically. Various kinds of patrols were taught in theory, but no exercises were done except a few jungle marches.

(vi) Organisation—The centre was divided into 5 Coys, called Azad, Gandhi, Boss, Ghaffar and Nehru. Each Coy had 4 Pls each of three Sections each of about 15 men. Total strength of the course being 800/1000. Company staff consisted of an Officer Company Commander and a Hav. Major, Four Pl. Havs., 4 Nks and 12 L/Nks.

(vii) Displine—Platoon Havildars were authorised to give corporal punishment, which was the most common way of dealing with various offences. The number of strokes varied with the nature of the offence.

(viii) Morale—Student being volunteers, co-operated in training and disciplines, and there were no cases of desertion. The officers and staff were not considered cruel or exacting.

2. Goashala Training School—

(a) In October 1943 a school similar to the BHARAT Youth's Training Centre was started in Goashala building near Karbe

(Rangoon). Its object was to train civilians with a view to their eventual absorption into the I.N.A. and perhaps to provide reinforcements for **Guerilla Brigades** which were to operate in Burma in 1944. The first course started in October 1943, and was scheduled to last for four months.

(i) Organisation—There were about 500 recruits on the first course (about 75% Madrassis) and they were organised into 3 Coys each of 3 platoons, each of about 50 men.

(ii) TRAINING—The school had a total of 150 rifles and bayonets which were distributed amongst Coys at 50 per Coy. Platoons took it in turn to use rifles. Rifle, L.M.G. and T.S.M.G. were the only weapons taught.

(iii) DRESS—No uniform were issued to recruits, who paraded in bazaar-bought multi-coloured clothes.

3. Officers' Training School.

There are two I.N.A. O.T.S.' in existance, one in Singapore and the other one in Rangoon. Details as far as known, are as follows :—

(a) O.T.S. Neesoon—Although this O.T.S. existed on paper it did not actually start functioning as such until April 1943. With the reorganisation of the I.N.A., the O.T.S. was overhauled and arrangements were made to start the first course in April 1943. 60 students attended the course, 5 of whom were civilians. The course lasted till the end of July 1943. All except 4 cadets passed out, and were posted to various units of the I.N.A. as officers. A second course was started on 1st August 1943, and consisted of 75 civilians and 125 military personnel. Experience during the first course had shown that civilian cadets could not keep pace with the Army cadets, so at this course the civilians were kept separate and underwent 6 months' tranining. The first three months of their course were devoted to elementary training, after which they were to be incorporated into the military wing of the 3rd course, which started in November 1943.

Selection—Candidates for O.T.S.' were selected by the unit commanders and were interviewed by Brigade Selection Boards. If recommended, they went before the Final Selection Board at I.N.A. HQ which was the deciding authority.

Organisation—The Military wing was organised into two Coys, i.e., Delhi Coy and Meerut Coy. Each Coy had two Pls, which were commanded by cadets in turn.

Training—Syllabus covered the following subjects :—

(i) **Weapon Training**—Rifle, Pistol, TSMG, LMG, 3 inch mortar, Vickers MG, A/Tk rifle and hand granades.

(ii) **Field Work**—Trenches, wiring, mines and rafting.

(iii) **Geography**—India and neighbouring countries on the Indo-Burma border. Connection of India with East Asia with special reference to Japan. Land route between India and Burma.

(iv) **Tactics**—Advance, rear and flank guards, outposts, patrolling, field craft, street fighting. Passage of water obstacles, attack, defence, field signals, night work, jungle warfare and schemes on both sand models and the ground.

Note—No training was given in, and no reference was ever made to, withdrawal tactics.

(v) **Map Reading.**

(vi) **Spiritual training**—Lectures on propaganda and morals.

(vii) **General Knowledge**—World War, etc.

(viii) **Discipline**—I.N.A. Act and Pl Commander's power of punishment.

(ix) P.T. and Drill.

(x) **Demonstrations** of the type of Artillery and its use.

Note—At the end of the courses; cadets were taken to visit the Japanese N.G.O.'s training school at Port Dickson, where they saw demonstration of bayonet fighting, line discipline, camouflage, use of folding boats, field craft and crawling. Cadets were specially taught Japanese methods of bayonet fighting.

Text Books—Roman Urdu editions of Indian Army M.T.P.'s and S.A.T. volumes were the only text book used. Books were hold by instructors only, and students took notes.

Awards—The best cadets at the end of each course were awarded the Sword of Honour, and the next best cadet a watch.

4. **Mayangon O.T.S. (Rangoon)**—In April 1944 an O.T.S. was opened in Mayangon (Rangoon) to serve the I.N.A. troops in Burma. The course were scheduled to last 3 months, and there were 50 candidates for the first course. From other details it is believed to be similar to Neesoon O.T.S.

5. **Bangkok Training School**—An I.N.A. Training school for the civilian recruits was reported to have been opend in Bangkok in Nov. 1943 by Major Rashid, who was then appointed Chief Recuiting Officer of Siam. No details about the schools are available, except that it was situated on the coast about 40 miles from Bangkok.

6. **Shanghai Training School**—It is reported that towards the end of 1943 the I.I.L. proposed to open a training school at Shanghai in order to train Indian civilians there, with a view to their final absorption into the I.N.A. The I.N.A. was asked to produce the Instructional staff for the above institution. A party of 3 officers and 8 N.G.O.s left Singapore for Shahghai about February 1944, under Capt. B. Narain Das, who was selected as Commandant of the School. No further information is available.

7. **Zeyawaddy Youths's Training Centre**—This is a small scale Bharat Youth's Training Centre, and is typical of various similar centres started by the I.I.L. in Burma. These miniature centres are commanded by a subaltern from the I.N.A. assisted by I.N.A. N.G.O. instructors.

   It is not known whether these are meant to give preliminary instructions to recruits prior to their joining one of the main training centres of recruits are drafted straight into the I.N.A. units from here.

8. **I.N.A. N.G.O's Training Schools**—An N.G.O.'s Training School were started under the Military Bureau at Johore Bahru. The course were of six weeks duration, and each course was attended by about 100 students. The syllabus followed the training given at S.A.T. school, Pachmarhi, with emphasis of Map Reading. Jungle warfare was also taught.

9. **Batches to Japan**—It is reported that a batch of Indian students went to Japan in August 1943 for study, and were to be trained in the Japanese Academy. Early in 1944 another similar batch was reported to have been selected to proceed to Japan to undergo 3 years' training there. No further details are available.

10. **I.N.A. Staff College**—It was proposed to open an I.N.A. Staff College, but the idea was dropped in view of the Burma operation where the maximum number of officers were required for operational duties.

Appendix–IV

Copies of Platoon Lectures.[1]

DEPARTMENT OF ENLIGHTENMENT AND CULTURE

D.M.B. I.N.A.

PLATOON LECTURE

UNITY OF INDIA, PAST AND PRESENT

Unity, Faith and SacrificeN OUR MOTTO
Purna Swaraj For IndiaN OUR GOAL

---

1. Platoon Lectures. The enlarged Military Bureau organised by Rash Behari also included a new department namely the Department of Enlightment and Culture. This department did very useful job of organising the platoon lectures in Hindustani and English. The object of the lectures was to broaden the outlook of the soldiers of the Indian National Army and to create in them a sense of patriotism. These lectures were published by the Military Bureau in the form of Booklets which were distributed to the soldiers. These are copies of lecture which were given to I.N.A. soldiers during Training. All the copies of these lectures which included one on "Bushido" are available at the India Officer Library of Record, London in printed collection. M.SS. European No A. 73.

Appendix-IV

Unity of India, Past and Present

My Brothers,

Today, I want to talk to you about the Unity of India. As you know, most of the European people think that India is not one united country and that Indians cannot form one united nation. The British ruler of India and the people of Britain are mainly responsible for this evil talk; they do so because, they want to rule our country, BHARAT MATA or HINDUSTAN, for ever. Without our help and without all the nice things that our country producces, the British Empire cannot exist. If India becomes independent, the wealth of India will not be sent to England. So, England wants to keep India under her control for all time to come. That is why, the people in Britain tell the whole world that India is not one united country and that Indians are not a nation. This is one of their main reasons, for keeping Hindustan as a subject colony, under their power.

What are the reasons given by the British people for this opinion? They say that India is a very vast country with different kinds of people living in it. The people of India, they say, have many languages, and many religions, and many castes and sub-castes,.They also argue that the habits and customs of the Indians, living in different parts of India are different. A Madrasi, according to them, is not like a Punjabi and a Hindu not like a Muslim. Thus they tell every one that some other outside power, like themselves, should stay in India; in order to control the people of India. They want the world to believe that the Britishers are staying in Hindustan only for the benefit of the Indians themselves. But, they are robbing the country right and left. Their loot and plunder of our country has resulted in abject poverty of our people in Hindustan. Nearly thirty six crores out of 40 crores of our brothers and sisters in Hindustan are not able to find even one square meal a day. In the last census, more than ten lakhs of our people were officially shown as beggars. This extreme poverty of our people is one of the many results of British rule in India for the last 200 years.

Now, let us see if the reasons given by the British people against the unity of India are correct. What are the facts? To know the truth, we will have to go back, to the time of old days, about five thousands years ago; and study the real history of India. The British history of India is not correct. The British did not educate us in the proper way. They taught us in such a way, as to suit their purpose. Their whole object was to keep us under their thumb.

About 5,000 years ago, we, Indians, had a great culture, when the people in the other parts of the world were still very primitive, not knowing even how to clothe themselves. Our ancient culture was called Indo-Aryan civilisation. We had various schools and universities. Our ancestors knew various arts and sciences, like Physics, Chemistry, Botany, Astronomy, Mathematics, etc., which were not known to the rest of the world. They were also very clever in music, poetry, painting, sculpture. engineering, architecture, etc. Our ancestors, out of all this learning and knowledge, developed various social customs and manners which were of benefit to themselves, their country and their rulers.

During the last 1,500 years, India has had several foriegn invasions, including that of the British invasion. India's wealth attracted these foreign invaders to our country. Our ancestors had a very flourishing shipping industry in those days, extending from China in the east of Egypt and Rome in the west. All these foreign invaders brought with them their own languages, customs and manners. They all tried to introduce their habits into our country and get our people to practice them. But, have any one of these foreign invaders, succeeded in their attempts to any extent? Most certainly not! In spite of all these foreign invasions, our culture, our greatness, our habits and social customs, and our unity of thought and behaviour have all remained the same as in days gone by. Which-ever part of India we may visit, our food is the same, our daily mode of life is the same, our family relations are the time, our individual behaviour to the community at large is identical throughout the country; and our social conduct among our neighbours and friends, being one of the mutual help and toleration, has embraced us all into one united nation.

How have we reacted to all these foreign invasions to our country during the last 1,500 years? How is it that our ancient culture has remained unaltered to a great extent, in spite of our coming in contact with so many different types of foreign people! The Jews and the Portuguese came first, over a thousand years ago. Then came the Islamic people, as the Turkey, the Tartars, the Moghuls, the Afghans, etc. Then came nearly all the people from Europe, as the French, the Dutch, the Danes the Belgians, the Germans, and last but not least, the English people.

Nearly all these invaders were attracted to India only by our wealth. Very few of them wanted to annex territory or found a kingdom, unlike the British. The chief among the original invaders were the Islamic nations. Their rule in India lasted from 12,00 to 17,00 for nearly 500 years. The Capital of the First Islamic Empire was founded in Delhi in 1207. When the Moghul rulers settled in India, they did not know any other homeland except that of India. Hindustan was their Motherland and Delhi was their capital.

The happiness of India and the Indian people were their happiness; and the rulers of India at the time shared the sorrows and adversities of the people. The name of Akbar, the great Moghal Emperor, and his wonderful principles of Empire building, based on love of the people of India, are well known.

No doubt, the Islamic nations brought with them their Persian art and culture, the Urdu script, their music, painting and poetry, their methods of architecture and sculpture. But they did not displace the existing Indo-Aryan civilisation of the country. The culture of the Indians present at the time was so great, so noble and so tolerant that it absorbed and assimilated the foreign Islamic culture that came into the country without much difficulty: On the part of the newcomers, there was a keen desire to settle down in India and fuse with the people of our land at the time. And the Indians, then absorbed the newcomers, once the later had conquered them and founded an Empire. Any resistance that was offered to the foreign invasion at the time, was before and during occupation.

Once the Moghul rule was established, Hindu and Muslims lived as brothers. There was a happy fusion of languages, ideas, social habits and customs, and their methods of earning their livelihood was the same. These common ideas and habits are found among Hindus and Muslims throughout Hindustan today. We have produced a common language, Hindustani, out of the blending of Hindi and Urdu. This language, Hindustani, is spoken by more than half of our people in Hindustan. More than half of its words are from Sanskrit. This language may be written either in Hindi script or the Persian Urdu script. The original Dravidian languages of South India are no doubt different, but they also have half of their words from Sanskrit.

There have been several attempts in the past to unite our religions of Hindus and Muslims. The names of Guru Nanak, Kabir, etc. are famous in this connection. The great Sikh Faith is a result of union of Hindu and Muslim religious ideas. Besides the religion of the Sikhs we have had several other religions in India, like Buddhism, Jainism, Christianity, Zorastrianism or the religions of the Parsis, etc. We have had no trouble or dispute among ourselves at all, at any time. Whenever we disputed for our rights for more food, for more freedom the British called all these troubles, as religious disturbances. The real cause of all mill strikes, hartals, etc., was the extreme poverty of India, and the cry was for "more food, more clothing, more wages and other essentials of life." The British gave the name of religious disturbances for these economic troubles.

But now, all our people know the real cause of their troubles, their sufferings and their poverty, as being due to the British rule of India, producing this abject poverty, disease, famine, starvation, etc. Our people, all over India, are now united in their poverty and adversity, and they know the cause of their present state, is being due to British rule. They are therefore, united in their desire for getting rid of the British rule from India, and obtaining Purna Swaraj for India.

Mahatma Gandhi has been very largely responsible for such united effort of the masses of India. The Indian National Congress has effected this wonderful union of our people, under the guidance of Mahatmaji by efficient organisation and discipline of the masses. The All Indian Peasant Association (Kishan Sabha) has united all our peasants and small land holders. The All India Trade Union Congress has absorbed all our labouring classes, factory workers, mill labourers, miners, estate labourers and all others, employed in any particular trade, industry, or other walk of life. The organisation and discipline of this class of people is of a very high order indeed. The All India Spinners Association and the All India Village Industries Association are similar associations, for absorbing our people, in order to deal with their economic troubles. Their discipline is high, their strength is enormous, their organisation is efficient, their national consciousness is supreme and their will and determination to get rid of the British rule is very strong. Such is the mass mentality of India to day.

In the old days, Emperor Asoka achieved political Unity of India, without Railways or other communications, and his Empire was much bigger than that of Britain today, as it included Afghanistan and Central Asia. There was no trouble in his Empire, because he united the people and ruled over them, by dint of his love for them. Not so the British, who are ruling India today by repression, oppression and force. With the aid of modern science, the British, introduced Railways, etc., into India. But it was all really to enable them to take our wealth from our country to their own homes in England, and to control India and hold India under their power. If there was trouble in any part of India, the British could use the Railways to send troops, to that locality. That is how they control India.

So, it is wrong to say that India is not a United Country and that Indians do not form a nation. Even English writers have admitted that, among all the various religions, languages, castes and sub-castes in India, there is a fundamental unity among all the manners and customs of the people in India, from very old times. Our original culture has remained unchanged. Our systems of pilgrimage for religious functions in the different parts in India have preserved the unity of our faiths and principles. Our languages and dialects show evidence of unification. Our village social system and the methods of earning their livelihood of our masses, have remained unaltered in so far as the main principles are concerned.

The British conquered our country by force of arms and wars; and then united our country by Railways, etc. But all these were done for their own benefit.

The British increased our differences and promoted fights among ourselves, in order to continue their robbery and plunder of India. There is no such thing as the Hindu-Muslim problem in India. The Muslim do not differ from the Hindus in their blood. Both Hindus and Muslims belong to the same race or same mixture of races. So, they must form a united nation. The great majority of Hindus and Muslims are peasants or small traders or minor craftsmen. A few educated classes, among them, who are job hunters, help the British to promote the so called Hindu-Muslim differences, for their own personal benefit.The policy of the British is to "Divide and Rule." The Hindus and Muslims have been united before, and are united now, in their determination to drive the British away from India.

What is our lesson today? We, officers and men of the Indian National Army in East Asia should have no difference among ourselves and should form one common blood brotherhood, for the achievement of Purna Swaraj for India. We must bear our Common Indian National Tricolour Flag in mind always and contribute our all, for our common cause.

DEPARTMENT OF ENLIGHTENMENT AND CULTURE

D.M.B.—I.I.L.

PLATOON LECTURE

Requisite Characteristics For Attainment Of Our Object

Character is the Mainspring of Man's Action.
Displine Improves Character and Efficiency

Appendix-V

Requisite Characteristics for Attainment of Our Object.

My Brothers,

From the lectures that have been delivered to you under now we should all be quite clear in your mind what our movement in East Asia stands for, and what spec'al purpose is intended to be served by our policy, aims and objects. I would once again repeat to you that our final goal is Purna Swaraj for India, unfettered by even a vestige of Imperialistic foreign domination of any description, and that our immediate objective is to help in the present revolution of India. Such a statement could authoritatively be made now, because we know from current events that a state of revolution at present exists in India. Our object is not to guide India, not to determine India's future constitution or anything like that..Decisions regarding these items should be left entirley in the hands of Indians in India. We in East Asia, are only a drop in the ocean as compared to the strength of Indians in our mothercountry; and it would be presumptuous on our part to decide the fate of India for the future. Even the very idea of it is so ridiculous that it is useless and unpardonable to waste any time on this aspect of the question.

For the achievement of our object and fulfilment of our policy we depend entirely on our inner strength in India, which consist of the grim determination of our leaders in India, who have been devoting their entire life's career for the success of our mission on the one hand and of the conscious national awakening of forty crores of our masses in India who are seething with a revolutionary spirit of resistance to Anglo-American Imperialism at the present moment on the other. Our movement in East Asia is part of such movement in India, our policy here is the policy of the Indian National Congress, their representative organ which has also been voicing the feelings and remedying the sufferings of Indians abroad. Our flag in East Asia is the Indian National Tricolour flag adopted by our nation at home in India. It is just but right that the Indians in East Asia should help in our cause and in our mission for Purna Swaraj for India, as the whole outlook is identical without even a shadow of difference or doubt.

In this connection, the help of Axis Powers, particularly by Japan, willingly offered by them, is a matter of very great appreciation by the Indians in East Asia and at home. Premier General Hideki Tojo has repeatedly expressed his sympathy towards the cause of Indian Independence and promised every assistance that is necessary for the attainment of Purna Swaraj for India. The Axis Powers have realised fully well that a subject anywhere in this world is not an asset, but a liability to the world. Because their production solely for the benefit of dominating, imperialistic nations is bound to be much less than otherwise. Their economic and cultural sufferings and ignonimity due to their lower political status are bound to jar on the happiness of independent neighbouring nations. Further, as long as one nation is subject to the domination of another, as long as the idea of Empire building the Imperialism persists, there can never be any real peace in the world. That explains the change in outlook of the Axis Nations. That is the difference between the old order and the new. We should, therefore welcome their most valuable and sympathetic assistance which has been particularly offered to us by Japan for the success of our mission.

At the same time, we should not forget that it is primarily our cause, our mission and our country's Independence that we are fighting for; and it is, therefore absolutely vital that we should play the leading role in the matter of service and sacrifice for the success of our mission. It is our sacred duty to contribute our all towards our cause and accordingly we have most solemnly pledged to do so.

We should now consider in detail the essential characteristics we should possess in the Indian National Army for the success of our mission. At this stage of our national awakening it is needless for me to stress our motto 'Unity, Faith and Sacrifice', which principles are signified by our National Tricolour Flag. There is no doubt whatsoever that without full faith and confidence in our mission it is difficult to develop a keen desire for what we want. Once we evince a keen desire to achieve an object, we are bound to work hard for the same. And the obstacle which might come across our projects would all easily melt away. That is our experience in everyday life.The stronger we desire to obtain something the easier it will be for us to fulfil our heart's desire. Because, all the time we are working as hard as ever for the same and we are eagerly looking forward to final results. So it is essential that all of us should develop a very strong desire to achieve our mission and work very hard for the same, putting our heart and soul and our wholehearted zeal and energy and our entire resources into it. Our cause is a colossal one and our individual capacity may seem very limited and insignificant when compared to our immense undertaking. But there is no reason whatsoever to be despondent. Because, it is our collective strength and our joint united front, equivalent to forty crores of our countrymen, that is bound to assert itself before long for the fulfilment of our long cherished wish, the freedom of India.

It is needless to stress the necessity for complete unity to the Indian National Army, forming one common Indian brotherhood, without giving way to sectarianism. I would implore one and all of you not to think of yourselves in future on any lines other than that of Indians, first and last. Any other consideration should not take precedence over our primary object which is Purna Swaraj for India. United we stand and divided we fall. This should be our guiding principle, unlike the British policy of Divide et Impera.

It is unnecessary to emphasis the necessity of our preparedness to sacrifice at this stage of our training and experience except to draw your attention to the fact that there should be faltering on your part at any time when you may be put to the acid test. Our first thoughts should be always our country first and our national Tricolour Flag first above everything else even including our lives.

How are we going to live up to the noble principles of our motto? What are the characteristics we should develop and how should we train ourselves for the same in the I.N.A.?

First and foremost, I would place our character at the very top of the list as it really brings out the inner man and exposes the individual in his or her true colour. Character is stated to be the main spring of a man's action. Without character we can never achieve our ambitions. Human beings possess the extra faculty of thinking and acting for themselves, besides being capable of doing things in an automatic way as animal do. Our mind or conscience tells us what is right and what is wrong in any special procedure. We are in a position to judge which is correct and which is not correct. We have got the power to decide correctly and formulate our actions accordingly. We should develop our power of judgement and discrimination in our everyday life. The results of some of our actions, supposedly based on our judgment, may go wrong. But, as long as we abide by the dictates of our conscience, no harm can accrue to anyone. After all, there is not much difference between conscience and commonsense in plain language.

What is actually wanted is honesty of purpose and truthfulness. There is no harm in committing a mistake unintentionally. After all, most of us learn only by committing mistakes. Otherwise, there is little room for improvement with regard to some of us. But we must be able to prove to ourselves and to the world that our intention was good. We must be able to lay our hand on our heart and say that we made an honest effort in all our actions and we did not intentionally go wrong. A guilty conscience is the worst punishment we could have; and contrariwise a clear and satisfied conscience is the highest form of reward we could ever expect to have.........Our character is after all our mental makeup with regard to our decisions and our actions in everyday life. That is why they say that we are all judged by our character. If we want to hold up our heads in this world we should possess character. We came into this world with a clear conscience. We should, therefore abide by that clear conscience during the periods of existence in this world until we clear out of this world with the same conscience.

The least that we could do to any particular individual or cause is not to be harmful if we cannot be helpful. But the Indian National Army expects a lot of more than this passive attitude of non-interference. Our cause is so colossal and immense that there is not only ample room but also vital need for all of us in the Indian National Army and several thousands more to come, to put forth all our brains and resources for the success of our cause. Some of us are inclined to do only six annas worth of work, because our pay is only six annas. This kind of attitude will not do so. The idea of doing so much work equivalent to so much pay received is to ridiculous to be discussed. There is no doubt that we must put forth our maximum efforts. Being strict revolutionaries we should consider ourselves as being on subsistance basis. Today we may have ample, comforts by way of rations, pocket money, clothing, accommodation, etc. Tomorrow we may be deprived of all these items and we may not be in a position to obtain even the minimum essentials to preserve life. We may have to go without food for days in jungle warfare. That is where sacrifice would come in. Are we going to give up our cause under those trying conditions? What is our answer to this question? Our straightforward answer, of course, is 'No'. We shall not give up our mission under any conditions of personal discomfort or sufferings. We shall carry on until we drop down dead. Not until then shall we cease fighting. We shall carry on our struggle to the bitter end of our destiny. We shall continue our onward march until complete freedom has been won for our mothercountry. Our only glory consists in devoting our entire life's career for the success of our cause and our only reward is Purna Swaraj for India. We have no other expectations in this world! That should be our grim determination. If we are destined to die in our attempts we cannot escape it and we cannot avoid it. So many of us should have been killed outright several times over during the last Malayan Campaign. Still, some of us have yet been spared in order to fulfil some of specific purpose in this world. None of us can foretell the future. We do not know what is awaiting us. So, why should we worry? As long as we have the courage of our convictions that our cause is right we should carry on wholeheartedly until life and energy are still left in us, for the success of our mission, until Purna Swaraj has been assured for India.

Having once come into the movement it is absolutely vital for us to recognise competent authority and maintain Discipline in the strict sense. All orders and instructions issued by competent authority must be implicitly carried out in the spirit they are intended to be observed. This, however, does not preclude discussion on relevant points in the interests of our cause though the final discussion on all such matters should be left entirely in the hands of the issuing authority. Once the final orders have been issued they must be carried out wholeheartedly by all concerned without question and without challenge. All ranks may rest well assured that; whatever orders and instructions have been issued the Indian National Army in its present form, they have been done so after mature consideration in due regard to the exigencies of our cause. All personal interests would be safeguarded as far as exigencies permit and as far as facilities are available. But, as regards fundamental policy it will always be on the line of our first consideration and our first attention always for our cause. So, all of us in the I. N.A. should realise that personal consideration should be waived in préference to the cause.

It should further be pointed out that there should be no room for any doubt in our minds as regards fundamental issues. Should there be any doubt on any particular matter it should be at once cleard by reference to senior officers, etc., in the chain of command. A word of caution has to be mentioned against gossip and alarmist reports. Gossiping shows improper use of time, laziness and lack of discipline. As such, it should be discarded and discouraged by all concerned. Alarmist reports are dangerous to the cause. Officers and other ranks in the I.N.A. who are known to be spreading false rumours and alarmist reports will very soon be spotted. They are bound to be considered Pro-British and treated as enemy spies. Let them not complain if strict disciplinary action is taken in regard to their false and alarmist rumours. If anyone in the I.N.A. should hear of such rumours he should report forthwith in detail to his senior officer and get the information corrected or confirmed as the case may be. Such individuals should find no place in the I.N.A. and they would do well to leave the I.N.A. without further delay in their own interests. Fortunately, the great majority of us in the I.N.A. are thinking correctly and acting in the right direction now-a-days. The sooner we spot these cankers and get rid of them the better it would be for our movement.

SUMMARY OF TODAY'S LESSON

1. Our policy in East Asia is to help in the Revolution of India. Future of India to be left in the hands of Indians at home in India.
2. The inner strength of India, our real strength.
3. Help of Japan and other Axis Powers is welcome. But we should bear the brunt of our work.
4. Our Motto—UNITY, FAITH AND SACRIFICE.
5. Character is stated to be the mainshpring of man's action.
6. Honesty of purpose, Truthfulness, Conscience and Commonsense.
7. If we cannot be helpful, we should not at least be harmful.
8. Readiness for sacrifice, even at risk of privations and sufferings.
9. Discipline and strict observance.
10. Dangers of Suspicion, Gossip, False Rumours and Alarmist Reports.

DO'S AND DON'TS

FOR THE OFFICERS and MEN of The INDIAN NATIONAL ARMY

Carry it in Your Pocket Always, Consult it Freely

Published by The Headquarters Director of Military Bureau, Indian Independence League, East Asia, Syonan

Do'S

1. Achievement of Independence of your Motherland should be your sole objective. Devote your heart and soul to it.
2. Administer justice tempered with mercy.
3. Always speak the truth; a liar is never respected.
4. Always encourage the spirit of your men. Remember the spirit is mightier than the sword.
5. Always uphold the honour of the Army.
6. A soldier must exercise initiative and determination in his work.
7. Always respect the honour of those who are under your protection.
8. Always stand up when a superior officer comes in.
9. Always be polite. It costs nothing and yet you can be firm.
10. Always be smart on your parade.
11. All lawful commands must be obeyed.
12. Before moving into a Camp, always take necessary measures to ensure:–
    (i) adequacy of rations and water supply.
    (ii) sufficiency of accommodation.
    (iii) suitable lavatory arrangements.
13. Be an optimist, courageous and self-reliant in life.
14. Be practical. Never be late on your parade.
15. Be tolerant to the opinions of others.
16. Be honest in all your dealings and work, for it is the best policy.
17. Be loyal to your superior officers.
18. Cultivate the spirit of self-help.
19. Cultivate an outlook of universal brotherhood.
20. Conserve energy and resources.

21. Cultivate the spirit of chivalry. Remember that the spirit of Indian chivalry is famous in the history.
22. Discharge your duties faithfully.
23. Ensure always the physical fitness of your men. Remember that only by doing so can you fulfil your bounden duty to put at the disposal of your commander the highest number of rifles at the time of action.
24. Exercise daily.
25. Fight hard for your country.
26. First obey and then you will learn how to command.
27. Give clear and complete orders.
28. Give up your seat for a superior officer or a lady when in gathering or in a conference.
29. Give credit to your commander for any achievement in an action, no matter how much you may have done.
30. Have confidence in yourself.
31. Keep secrets closely guarded.
32. Keep your appointments.
33. Knowledge is power, acquire it.
34. Live a frugal life yourself but be generous to others deserving.
35. Live and let live.
36. Loyalty and co-operation lead to success.
37. Love and respect your men and they will love and respect you.
38. Maintain the strictest discipline. This is Foundation of efficiency of the Army.
39. Make Unity, Faith and Sacrifice your life's motto.
40. Obey orders implicitly and carry them out intelligently. Remember upon this depends the efficiency of the Army.
41. Provide healthy recreation and exercise for the men. These are excellent safeguards against venereal diseases.
42. Respect the honour of a woman like that of your mother.
43. Religion pertains to the individual. It is what you live.
44. Resist temptation manfully. If you are unable to resist, get away from the temptation.

45. Rudeness is a sign of lack of se!f control and low breeding.
46. Recitify a wrong whenever you can, it is never too late to mend.
47. See that orders are carried out.
48. Show the utmost toleration in matters religious.
49. Take precautionary measures always in time. Whether it is against disease, attacks of politics. Remember prevention is always better than cure.
50. Take good care of the lives and welfare of the men. Remember you are responsible for them.
51. Train in peace for fighting in war. Constant training greatly increases the efficiency of the army.
52. Trust in God and do the fight.
53. Trust your brother officers and men until proved to the contrary. Remember trust begets trust.
54. Treat a young recruit kindly.
55. Utilise every opportunity to infuse the National spirit in your officers and men.
56. When faced with a problem think over carefully, making allowances for the other man's point of view, and then come to a definite decision.
57. Work hard and with devotion. Hard work never kills a man.
58. When travelling in a train car or bus, give up your seat for an older men, women and the children. Never rush.
59. When there are large number of people to get something say tickets in the railway station or cinema, stand in a queue.
60. You and your men should feel proud that you are Indians.

DON'TS

1. Don't be defeated by failure in a good cause. Try again and again.
2. Don't betray confidence.
3. Don't discuss your superiors. This is bad discipline. Remember, if you do, you too may be discussed by your subordinates.
4. Don't discuss politics unless you are specifically asked by your superior officer. Politics is dangerous for the army; it saps discipline.
5. Don't get drunk and make a fool of yourself. Alcohol is neither a

food nor a necessity.

6. Don't hesitate to take the initiative in a good cause.
7. Don't kill your conscience.
8. Don't lean on others.
9. Don't relax until you have achieved your object and consolidated it.
10. Don't talk losely. The enemy may be listening and you may thus endanger the lives of thousands.
11. Don't brag or boast about your capabilities.
12. Don't hesitate to admit a mistake. It will show up your courage and character.
13. Don't express disagreement in a gathering or conference against your commander or superior officer. If you have divergence of views, settle it up with him first.
14. Don't break up a queue and rush forward.
15. Don't fish for a compliment for a good thing done.
16. Don't dishonour a fallen enemy.
17. Don't use profane language or commit a bad deed. Remember every profane word you speak or a bad deed you do, leaves a track in your brain which predisposes you to repeat it. Be careful.
18. Never belittle the power of your enemy.
19. Never dishonour yourself; death is preferable.
20. Never lose your character. A characterless man is dangerous and is a disgrace.
21. Never betray your Motherland.
22. Never put off till tomorrow what you can do today. Remember a stitch in time saves nine.
23. Never vacillate. Vacillation is the death-knell of an army.
24. Never backbite or carry tales. It demeans you and lowers your self respect. Remember that every time you wish to throw mud on to others, a little of it will stick on to your fingers.

DEPARTMENT OF ENLIGHTENMENT AND CULTURE

D.M.B.—I.I.347L.

PLATOON LECTURE

BRITISH AGGRESSION IN INDIA

British Imperialism—The Cause of Indian Poverty

Freedom is Our Birthright

British Aggression in India (Extract)

My brothers,

Today, I want to talk to you about British aggression in India. As I told you in my previous talk, it was the wealth of our country that attracted all the Western nations to Hindustan. The British came to India in 1608, as a band of adventurers, for purposes of trade only at first. They were called the British East India Company. But very soon, they became very greedy and wanted to establish a British East Company of adventurers wrote to their Agents, in Madras, instructing them to establish a civil and military power, as to create and secure such a large revenue, to maintain the foundation of a large well-grounded, sure, English Division in India, for all time to come.

The battle of Plassey was fought in the year 1757. It was after this battle, the British East India Company agents came into contact with Emperor Shah Alam who was then ruling in Delhi. In the year 1765, the British East India Company agents obtained from Emperor Shah Alam the Diwaney of Bengal, Bihar and Orissa. By this is meant, the British had only the right to collect revenue, and that too, only from these three provinces. This gave a foothold for the British not only to contact the Moghul Court, but also gradually to convert the right of revenue collection into one of acquisition of territory. The Moghul Empire had become disrupted; and the local rulers had become weak and corrupt. The East India Company's English servant adventurers plundered our country, both individually and jointly. They used all the means in their power, both fair and foul, to suit their purpose. The British Agents of the Company set the ruler or chief of one State against the ruler of his adjoining State and produced wars between them; the British themselves took the side of either the one or the other, till they finally swallowed up, either both the states together or one after the other. They plundered and looted all the States, they thus annexed systematically. They accepted bribes from several princes and chiefs and tried to keep them all under their control.

In the annexed areas the British East India Company extorted revenue by severest taxation of land and goods. They untilized all those collections for developing their own trade and also for their own wars and compaigns in India in order to acquire more territory. That is how the British got money for territorial expasion in India.

It is not that the British acquired territory in India without any trouble or difficulty. It took them one hundred years, from 1757 to 1857, to conquer the whole of India. Every inch of territory was contested by every Maharajah, Rajah , Nawab or Chief. But the odds were very much against them. Our Chiefs did not possess them advantage of modern scientific weapons which the British Agents had; but much more than that, was the evil and treacherous infiuence of the British over their own adjoining rulers. Their own friends were converted into their enemy.

In spite of all these disadvantages, our ancient rulers actually defeated the British in several open battles. In the famous battle of Calcutta, Siraj-up Daulah defeated the British. But he was so well-mannered as not ill-treat even his defeated enemy. What did the British do in return? They got Sirajud-Daulah assassinated by foul intrigue so that they could annex his kingdom. This is how the British East India Company annexed nearly the whole of the so-called British India, and kept the rest of the Indian States under their complete control.

Once a map of India was shown to Maharaja Ranjit Singh. He asked what was the meaning of the red blotches in the map. The Maharaja was told that the red colour showed the extent of territory annexed by the British. Then the Maharaja shouted "Jaldi, Sab lal ho jaega" and his prophecy came true very soon. So much for territorial aggression of the British in India.

During the time of East India Company, the British established monopolies for several articles required for food and other essential use, such as rice, salt, tobacco, betal nut, etc. Nobody else but the British could trade in these aritcles and they made all the profits on these articles, absolutely necessary for the use of Indians. When the British ships came to India, they came empty; and when they returned to England , they went back loaded with raw products from our country. In order to prevent the empty ships from rolling, a certain amount of weights had to be put in their hold. The British put Cheshire salt in it and brought this salt from England to India and sold it in India. In order to be able to sell this salt the British in India reduced the production of salt in India and also levied a tax on Indian-made salt. That is the origin of the Indian Salt Tax. The people of India protested many times, but to no purpose.

The British, after establishing themselves in India, started a policy of exploiting the country to their own advantage.They destroyed all our ancient local industries and handicrafts.They oppressed all the Indian artisans and compelled them to give up their respective trade. They did not want the Indian workmen to do or make any article, because the British wanted to dump their own machine-made articles for sale in India, particulary clothing and other articles required for our everyday use. Our country was producing enough raw goods; but they were all exported to England. All Government rules and laws were made in favour of the British rulers in order to enable them to achieve the above object.

In 1814, cotton piece goods was bought by India from England to the extent of half a lakh of rupees; and now, more than one hundred crores of rupees worth of cotton goods are coming from England to India every year. As you know, cotton is grown to a very large extent in India. Before the British came to Hindustan our ancestors used to make most beautiful cloth in quantity not only sufficient for their own use, but also for exportation to distant countries outside India. Now, why should the British take away the raw cotton from our country, convert them into cloth in their mills in England and bring the cloth back to India for sale? Because the British wanted work for their own people in England, work for their ships, etc., and at the same time make huge profits for themselves. And, we have to pay all these additional expenses. If we manufactured our own cloth, as we used to before the British came to our country, there will be none of these additional expenses to pay, and the profits of the manufacturers will be much less, as the cloth is intended solely for the use of our own people. Thus you see how the British have deprived us from making even cloth such an essential article required for our daily use. You will also note how costly it is for us to be under British domination.

That it why Mahatma Gandhi very strongly advocated the use of Khaddar by all Indians without hesitation. There are several lakhs of our people, working as active volunteers, as members of the All-India Spinners' Association. That is how Mahatmaji wanted to stop the drain of one hundred crores of rupees every year to England from India for the purchase of cloth alone.

The present position, in so far as industries are concerned, is that we have to buy most of our requirements from foreign countries, particularly England. Our own industries are still undeveloped. Our people have therefore no employement but agriculture. As the number of people thrown on the land for work is very great, the extent of land available for each individual in India becomes naturally very small. Owing to lack of irrigation facilities, agriculture is dependent on weather conditions; if there is rain our people can cultivate the land. If there is no rain they cannot do so. So, the amount of food material produced in India is very small. It cannot be increased owing to lack of proper facilities. In other countries, the people are not dependent on weather solely for their agriculture; and they have dams, reservoirs and canals, etc. They use also modern machines in agriculture.

The final result is that our brothers and sisters in Hindustan have become extremely poor with famine conditions, starvation, poor nutrition and disease. So much for the economic aggression of the British in India.

The British Military Aggression of India is well worth our study. The Army in India, both British and Indian, is costing more than one fourth of the total income of our country, i.e., 60 crores. The Army in India is maintained for three different purposes. First of all, Indian soldiers could be sent to any country outside India for their own imperialistic purposes. That is why we are all here. When this War broke out, the British declared India as being belligerent, because India is only a tail to Britain in all respects. So, the Government of India were able to send us all to Malaya, Burma, etc., without consulting our Assemblies. Secondly, the Army in India is intended to help in putting down internal disturbances in Hindustan. So , it is really an army of occupation in India. Last of all, the Army in India may be useful for the defence of India against foreign invasion. This is what is happening today on the Indo-Burma border.

The extravagance of the British Army in India cannot be described., Most of the officers were of British nationality. Lord Curzon said that one of the most important units in the scheme of British imperial defence was to provide the British Government with an efficient striking force, ready to attack any one at a moment's notice. The Army in India has been used outside India for British imperial purposes several times.

The strength of the internal security troops, for internal peace, is nearly 70,000. There are more British troops in this than in the Field Army in India. In 1857, during the first War of Indian Independence, the whole of Bengal Army formed one common brotherhood, and acted fatally against the British. In order to prevent a recurrence, the British have provided a very large number of British officers in all the units of the Army. Further they have formed in India Army Battalions, down even to companies, groups based on tribal, sectarian, religious and communal basis.

These groups will fight against the interest of one another and can never unite against the British. So, it is the British idea that the Indians in the Army could never combine against them.

Further, Indians in the Army are never admitted to positions of power and responsibility in the Army, nor do they ever get a chance of commanding or leading branches of the Army, requiring technical skill and knowledge. Without the British officers there is no chance for Indians to assume leadership.

The Auxillary Force of India includes only British and Anglo-Indian residents of India. The Army is not allowed to mix with civilians, which is quite unlike that of Japan or any other modern country. Military efficiency demands close co-operation and contact between the army and the civilians. In India the gulf between the two is very wide. Also, in the Indian Army, the difference between the British Army Officer and the Indian soldier is very wide. There is no camaraderie or espirit de corps.

Thus the British made Indian Army in India could never be patriotic. It is only an Army of occupation in India, meant mainly for suppressing internal revolutions, strikes, hartals, etc. It is not what it should be, as in other independent countries. So much for the British Military Aggression in India.

Politically, the British made such rules and laws in the Government of India, from time to time, as to keep us completely under their power. They wanted the Indians to fight among ourselves and to work for their benefit. From the time the British rule started in India; the policy of the British rulers in India has been one of 'Divide and Rule'. In 1905 Lord Curzon passed the notorious Act for the partition of Bengal into Hindu and Mohammedan areas. This was first opposed by Hindus and Muslims of Bengal, and later by the whole of India. On account of this partition, the policy of Boycott of English goods. Swadeshi and formation of National Schools was adopted throughout the country. Six years later, during the Delhi Durbar, the partition of Bengal was repealed as a result of popular agitation. In 1909, the British Government of India passed the Morley, Minto Reforms. According to this separate councils came into existence, based on religious and sectional differences. Several protests were made by our leaders, but to no effect.

From 1914 to 1918, our people worked wholeheartedly for the benefit of the British in all the theatres of War, in the hope that India would get Self Government under British rule. India contributed over fifteen lakhs of men, besides a very large amount of war materials and donations of large sums of money.As soon as War broke out, the flower of our Army was marched off to Flanders in France and the world knows that it was owing to the bravery and courage of our men, the first advance of the Germans into Mons was stopped; and the tide of battle turned in favour of the Allies against the Germans. What was the result of all this help we rendered to the British? The British passed the notorious Rowlatt Bills in 1919 by which the British could arrest any Indian without charge, on mere suspicion, and punish the Indian people without trial. The dastardly massacre of 2,000 of our men, women and children at Jallianwalla Bagh in Amritsar by rifle and machine gun fire by the British troops and the massacre of innocent. unarmed people by dropping of bombs from aeroplanes from a height of 200 feet in several villages of the Punjab, were the result of the Rowlatt Bills.

In 1920, the British tried to give soothing syrup in the shape of Montague-Chelmsford Reforms which again adopted the policy of 'Divide and Rule'. The Indians shouted for milk, but the British rulers of India gave them rice water instead. Being dissatisfied thoroughly Mahatama Gandhi started the scheme of non-violent non-co-operation against all British institutions and British methods. Mahatmaji wanted to arouse the national consciousness of our people and at the same time, to produce a parallel Indian State within the British Government of India.

Index

P

Q

R